*Encounters with Islam*

T0372714

Too often, Western encounters with the Islamic world commence with stereotypes and end with a renewed distance. Drawing from decades of experience studying the Muslim world, Lawrence Rosen challenges these narrow understandings. Adopting an interdisciplinary approach, Rosen shows the wide-ranging significance of Muslim art, culture, and law around the world. Exploring political, economic, and social encounters within and with the Muslim world across the eras, he considers a wide range of contexts – from fifteenth-century mosaics in Central Asia that reveal a complex understanding of mathematics to the political choices available to the youth of modern-day Morocco and Cairo. With in-depth analyses of art, law, and religion, and how they inform one another, Rosen develops a vibrant, nuanced portrait of the Islamic world. Drawing linkages across time, regions, and cultures, this is a significant anthropological study of the Islamic world from a seasoned scholar.

LAWRENCE ROSEN is the William Nelson Cromwell Professor Emeritus of Anthropology at Princeton University. As both an anthropologist and a law scholar, he has worked for over forty years in the Arab world. Rosen was named to the first group of MacArthur Award Fellows and has been a visiting fellow at Oxford and Cambridge. He has written prolifically, and his previous publications include *Law as Culture* (2008) and *Islam and the Rule of Justice* (2018).

# Encounters with Islam

Studies in the Anthropology
of Muslim Cultures

LAWRENCE ROSEN
*Princeton University*

CAMBRIDGE
UNIVERSITY PRESS

Shaftesbury Road, Cambridge CB2 8EA, United Kingdom

One Liberty Plaza, 20th Floor, New York, NY 10006, USA

477 Williamstown Road, Port Melbourne, VIC 3207, Australia

314–321, 3rd Floor, Plot 3, Splendor Forum, Jasola District Centre,
New Delhi – 110025, India

103 Penang Road, #05–06/07, Visioncrest Commercial, Singapore 238467

Cambridge University Press is part of Cambridge University Press & Assessment,
a department of the University of Cambridge.

We share the University's mission to contribute to society through the pursuit of
education, learning and research at the highest international levels of excellence.

www.cambridge.org
Information on this title: www.cambridge.org/9781009389037

DOI: 10.1017/9781009389013

© Lawrence Rosen 2023

This publication is in copyright. Subject to statutory exception and to the provisions
of relevant collective licensing agreements, no reproduction of any part may take
place without the written permission of Cambridge University Press & Assessment.

First published 2023

Printed in the United Kingdom by TJ Books Limited, Padstow Cornwall

*A catalogue record for this publication is available from the British Library*

*A Cataloging-in-Publication data record for this book is available from the
Library of Congress*

ISBN 978-1-009-38903-7 Hardback
ISBN 978-1-009-38898-6 Paperback

Cambridge University Press & Assessment has no responsibility for the persistence
or accuracy of URLs for external or third-party internet websites referred to in this
publication and does not guarantee that any content on such websites is, or will
remain, accurate or appropriate.

*For Judith*

# Contents

*Color plates can be found between pages 84 and 85.*

# Plates and Figures

**Plates**

# Acknowledgments

The present book has grown out of many of its own encounters. Though too numerous to thank individually, special gratitude must be expressed to Harvard Law School for appointing me as a Senior Fellow in the Islamic Law Program; to Edmund Burke, III, and Abdellah Hammoudi for their enduring guidance through Muslim history and culture; and to my students at Princeton University and Columbia Law School for keeping me alert to alternative interpretations. The essay on Islamic mosaics benefited enormously from my conversations with Peter Lu and Paul J. Steinhardt, and I am also grateful to the Royal Anthropological Institute for granting an earlier version of that chapter the J. B. Donne Prize Essay Award. My editors at Cambridge, Maria Marsh and Rachel Imrie, were enormously helpful in bringing the project to fruition, and I am deeply grateful for their guidance and professionalism. Portions of the book appeared previously in several venues and are used here by agreement with the following publishers: Oxford University Press, *Anthropology Now*, *Bustan*, *The Guardian*, *Anthropological Quarterly*, Cambridge University Press, *Journal of North African Studies*, *Boston Review*, and *Hesperis-Tamuda*.

The book is dedicated to Judith Blank, anthropologist and artisan, whose insight and sense of wonder are as contagious as they are endearing.

# *Note on Transcription*

Arabic spellings, with allowance for Moroccan dialect where appropriate, broadly follow the system used by Hans Wehr in *A Dictionary of Modern Arabic*, with some significant modifications. For example, ' ḍ ā ḥī ṭ sh kh ṣ will be used where a word first appears but not necessarily thereafter. Terms that have gained currency in English, such as Quran, shari'a, and qadi will be presented in recognizable spellings rather than with full diacritics.

# Introduction
## Theme and Variation in the Encounter of Cultures

I don't believe in accidents.
There are only encounters in history.
There are no accidents.

Pablo Picasso

Picasso may overstate the case – or he may be right. Hindsight prediction may make things that happened seem inevitable and certainly we are all prone to such explanations. But the artist had a larger point, namely that relationships, whether human-directed or governed by natural forces, invariably include an encounter, whether probable or fortuitive, that profoundly affects the course of events. Indeed, each element of an encounter impacts others such that a form of Heisenberg effect – in which it may be nearly impossible to spot the mutual effects and the process of the encounter simultaneously – may be at work. Yet if we are to comprehend how such engagements proceed we must first be open to the possibility of their ever-presence – that is, that human interactions may meet accidentally but thereafter the entanglement is such that, except for purposes of analysis, unscrambling repercussions would be both impossible and inappropriate. To study historical and sociological encounters, then, does not have to mean uncovering universal laws or regarding all occurrences as incommensurable. Rather, as we turn the kaleidoscope of social encounters our awareness of what to take into consideration may be indispensably heightened.

In the chapters that follow we will turn the kaleidoscope a number of times, but the common factor in each revolution is a core of features that characterize the cultures of the Arab Middle East. To say that, however, is to be rather easily misunderstood. For it would seem that "characterization" might be equated with essentialization and the reference to "cultures" in the plural would seem to deny shared identification. But neither proposition should be taken so uncritically. Essentializing is abhorrent when it becomes stereotyping; it is appropriate when both nonjudgmental and captures the capacity of any society for self-identity and modification. So, too, speaking of a plurality of Arab cultures does not mean there are no shared elements, theme and variation being vital to an understanding of what is distinctive in any cluster. The result, properly understood, is a recognition that there are features of the Arabo-Berber world that are discernible and that variation is the opposite of reductionism. Consider, in this regard, some of the features to which the present set of essays invites attention.

The starting point may seem rather strange – a Quranic school in Central Asia – where the discovery of a style of mosaic patterns may appear an even stranger place to begin. But here, on the walls of this most unusual building, artisans achieved a design whose underlying mathematics, thought only to have been solved in recent years in the West, were almost certainly understood centuries ago in order for the mosaics to have been possible. These patterns, with their nonreplicating tessellations, must, however, have been more than a mathematical puzzle to be solved: Like the great cathedrals of Christendom, with their vaulted ceilings and their stained glass windows, these tiles bespeak a representation of the God-given world, a world of ever-shapeshifting relationships that is of the essence of a cosmological view brought to the attention of mankind by an illiterate Prophet transmitting the unaltered word of God. And in that extraordinary artistic accomplishment, we can see a deep pattern of human reason and divinely ordained order that constitutes the baseline of many encounters – political and economic no less than social and expressive – that take place within the Muslim world and beyond.

Law, too, may constitute a vital point of entry to an understanding of how Muslim societies cope with the encounters of their own people and outsiders. When the invading forces of the new religion entered lands beyond the Arabian center, they met peoples whose customary practices needed to be accounted for if they were to be enfolded within the expanding House of Islam. Paving the way, however, may have been the accommodation already made in the heartland between the revealed law and the varied practices of the tribes of the region. Law, no less than military power and economic advantage, no doubt played a key role in Islam's advancement, but it did so not by replacing all that went before but by incorporating *as Islam* many local practices. When, therefore, we look at the enfoldment of Berber law within mainstream Islamic law, we may not only be observing a process that has deep historic roots but a vantage point through which we can understand law as a vehicle for meshing the encounter of the local and the normative that has resonance in many other domains of Muslim encounters as well.

One such example is in the meaning of a gift. Islam places great stress on contractual relationships, whether in the Quran as well as in the reported actions and statements of the businessman-turned-prophet at the exemplary center of the faith. But gifts are not mere freewill offerings any more than they are only strategic vehicles for personal enrichment. In their complex pattern, distinctive to each culture and deeply entwined with multiple domains of meaning, the critical point of contact with the other comes more sharply into focus, and with it a more refined sense of just how the concept of the gift makes such encounters both possible and integral to the entire culture. Such gifts may shade into political obligations or press the limits of a bribe, but in each case, an understanding of the categorization of the gift within Muslim cultures is vital to understanding the baseline of civic and personal engagement.

Islamic law, the *shariᶜa*, may be integral to Islam but can we really speak of the rule of law in countries where corruption is rife, where constitutions and codes are manipulated by those in power, and where the judiciary may be cowed into quiescence? Where ordinary people meet the law – where the law meets ordinary people – has received insufficient attention by Western scholars of the sacred law owing to their concentration on textual sources, but it is in the courts and the courtyards where the law lives and it is here that such encounters must be understood. By considering in what ways there is indeed a rule of law basis in the cultures of the Arab world, we will not only move past stereotypes without entering the realm of the overly idealized but will have the opportunity to consider how an alternative mode of fabricating a legal order may be discerned within and among the cultures of the region.

War and politics are, by their very nature, fraught with problematic encounters that reveal as much about each antagonist as their shared modes of engagement. When the United States entered the wars of the Middle East it did so with the professed aim of securing its own territory against future attacks formulated in the region. Since outright colonial appropriation was not on the table the struggle for hearts and minds was thought to grow not from the barrel of a gun alone but from a measured encounter with the people of the region. Toward this end, various programs were tried, most notably the Human Terrain effort employing anthropologists and anthropological techniques. It was a disaster. In the fifth chapter of this book, we will explore how anthropology was used in the war in Afghanistan and why that form of encounter was such a failure.

As we move more into the political realm the events of 2011 in Tahrir Square, Cairo – and even more so the aftermath of those events – show just how much the encounter with power reveals about underlying social and cultural conventions throughout the Arab world. Touted as a youth revolution – when, in fact, it was more broadly based – and said to be facilitated by social media – when, in fact, it was revelatory of how much credibility depends on face-to-face assessment of the speaker – the Arab Spring failed almost everywhere to bring about fundamental change. But in its failure much of how people in the region encounter the powerful, how they appraise their connections to one another in the face of power, and how they cope with the aftermath of their failure come more sharply to the fore.

Insight may come from the margin, whether it is in the mosaics of an obscure religious structure or the encounter with the rare Christian missionary. For in the latter example, we can see that, while the Protestant missionaries who came to Morocco in the late nineteenth century and remained through the first half of the twentieth never succeeded in making significant converts, their encounter with the local Muslim population was by no means trivial. Indeed, their appraisal of the local circumstances and their offer of medical and scientific knowledge was not without impact, even as their assault on the faith of the people was a total failure. The fact that the missionaries are still spoken of with respect is intriguing; that the encounter showed up many features about both groups is revealing. From the margins may come change, but from the margins may, for the social scientist, come a clearer sense of how each party accommodates to change itself.

The final section of the book is denominated critical in a double sense. It addresses two key observers of Islam – Clifford Geertz and Edward Said – both for their critical approaches to the comprehension of Arab societies and political culture and as a vehicle for sharpening our own critical faculties on the insights they offered. Geertz, it will be suggested, went well beyond describing the economic life of the marketplace in his study of the souk of Sefrou, Morocco, while Said did not go far enough – or at least in the most useful direction – in his critique of Western scholarship on the region. By attending to what each actually presented we can see that the encounters they describe – to say nothing of their own encounters with understanding the region – continue to challenge our approaches to the lives of people and politics of the Arab Middle East.

"Do we change every time we have a new encounter?" asks author William Boyd: "Are we endlessly mutable?" The answer remains unclear. What is more certain is that each encounter – whether from within a single culture or across multiple cultures – leaves its mark on both sides of the equation, and if we are to fully comprehend what that equation entails only an array of deeply studied instances will reveal the ways in which this mutual effect works. The cultures of the Arab world are not reducible to single features any more than they are so similar to any other set of cultures as to lose all distinctiveness. It is the encounter that sets the game afoot and we must follow where it may.

# PART I

# Expressive

# 1 | Choice and Chaos
## The Social Meaning of an Islamic Art Form

*How would you represent your faith artistically? You could fashion a statue or an icon that serves as a reminder or actual embodiment of the entity you worship; you could employ a building or a site, separated from the everyday world, that serves to epitomize your belief. You could make your representations totally explicit – recognizable portraiture, life-like sculptures, light-and-shadow evocations – or you could reduce all to such a bare level as to conjure the desired sense of the infinite or the need of the worshipper to bring the requisite spiritual state to the place rather than acquire it there. You could even split the difference, seeking in the representations associated with the place of worship a path between the evident and the visionary.*

*The Quran describes Islam and its adherents as following a middle course, and while it may seem that when it comes to religious representations Islam has opted for the extreme of the non-iconic that may not be the whole story. True, in the years following the Prophet's death his followers avoided overt use of human figuration – even though it was present during his lifetime and the Quran contains no explicit ban – and it is also true that in parts of Muslim southwest Asia stylized human forms continued to be painted. But representation may also be coded or veiled, so mimicking the envisioned cosmos as to be consonant with it. Islamic religious art may accomplish this end when it graces the place of worship with phrases from the Quran – itself understood as the exact and unaltered word of Allah – whose calligraphic style conveys the sense of infinity and sublime reality by its internalized sound no less than its labyrinthian shape. Yet, even that may not be enough: The Word made manifest may evoke ultimate truth but it may not quite give material representation to those aspects of the God-given world that remain much more abstract. How, for example, does one portray relationships, the unseen forces that hold the world together and chaos at bay; how does one show that human nature and the cosmological order are of a piece, that they partake*

9

*of the same forces, the same precepts that organize our ties to one another and to the universe at large? It may, however, have been just such a comprehensive form of representation that, for decades and centuries, was hidden in plain sight on the walls of a building in the heart of central Asia.*

*

Art is the imposing of a pattern on experience, and our aesthetic enjoyment is recognition of the pattern.[1]

Alfred North Whitehead

In 2005, a doctoral student in physics at Harvard, Peter J. Lu, was traveling in Uzbekistan. Looking up at the mosaic tiles on the wall of an Islamic academy (*madrasa*), he was struck by the possibility that, long before mathematicians in the West had worked it out, Muslim designers had determined the means by which a series of geometric forms could, without any gaps, be articulated indefinitely in such a way that clusters of individual elements constantly differ in their relation to one another (see Plates 1.1–1.4). The resultant pattern appears regular but is not actually repetitive. "I discovered this in the evening on Christmas Eve," he recalled. "I then stayed up all night to start mapping the tilings." Having been drawn to the problem of periodic patterns by the work of Oxford's Roger Penrose on quasicrystals, Lu, together with Princeton physicist Paul J. Steinhardt, then began to survey mosaics in a number of Middle Eastern and Central Asian countries.[2] After an

---

[1] Alfred North Whitehead, *Dialogues of Alfred North Whitehead* (New York: Mentor Books, 1956).

[2] For a brief introduction in layman's terms to Penrose's work, see Philip Ball, "Fearful Symmetry: Roger Penrose's Tiling," *Prospect*, September 19, 2013. For nontechnical articles about the mosaics, see Paul J. Steinhardt, "Medieval Islamic Mosaics and Modern Maths," *Islamic Arts and Architecture*, March 25, 2011, http://islamic-arts.org/2011/medieval-islamic-mosaics-and-modern-maths/; and Heather Whipps, "Medieval Islamic Mosaics Used Modern Math," *Live Science*, February 22, 2007, www.livescience.com/4402-medieval-islamic-mosaics-modern-math.html. See also, Paul J. Steinhardt, *The Second Kind of Impossible: The Extraordinary Quest for a New Kind of Matter* (New York: Simon & Schuster, 2019), 46–49. On the relation of math and the occult in Iranian art, see Matthew Melvin-Koushki, "Powers of One: The

exhaustive survey, they concluded that the Muslim artisans had indeed determined how to construct nearly perfect quasicrystalline patterns, possibly as early as the mid-fifteenth century.

Complex mosaic patterns are, of course, found in many parts of the Muslim world (see Plate 1.1). At places like the Alhambra, for example, the artists rendered ever more complicated periodic patterns but never developed the most complex quasicrystalline form (see Plate 1.4). Since the mathematics of quasicrystals had, until just a few decades ago, stumped Western scholars for centuries and (in Steinhardt's opinion) no ordinary artisan could have created these patterns by chance, the question the scientists naturally asked was whether the Muslim architects and craftsmen actually understood the underlying mathematics of these patterns.[3]

To the art historian and social scientist, however, quite a different set of questions arises: Why did it matter to those who fashioned and viewed these mosaics to represent their vision in accord with this mathematical blueprint? What is it they sought to represent and how does that choice of figurations connect with the larger culture in which it is embedded? Indeed, what resonances are discernable in the structure of social relations and those other forms of expression – poetry, architecture, music, and narrative – that reinforce the meaning this style of geometric representation embodies? To suggest some answers to these questions we must first understand in somewhat greater detail what exactly these Muslim artisans accomplished.

\*\*

Until very recently, mathematicians were convinced that this type of never-ending, nonreplicated, yet symmetrical tiling pattern had not

Mathematization of the Occult in the High Persianate Tradition," *Intellectual History of the Islamicate World*, 8 (2017): 127–99.

[3] How designers communicated to the artisans is not entirely clear, although the existence of some manuals suggests that knowledge may not always have been kept secret or only transmitted orally. See W. K. Chorbachi, "In the Tower of Babel: Beyond Symmetry in Islamic Design," *Computers and Mathematics with Applications* 17 (1989): 751–89. The ninety-seven-foot Topkapi Scroll (c. 1500 CE), though lacking instructions, conveys many geometric forms artisans could have used. See Gülru Necipoglu, *The Topkapi Scroll* (Santa Monica: Getty Center, 1995).

been achieved because the mathematics needed to compose such patterning remained unknown. Indeed, it was assumed that these highly complex forms of symmetry were not only absent from artistic representations but also did not exist in nature.[4] So was it possible that these Muslim artisans had actually grasped the technique for producing such forms? The best candidates, dating from as early as the thirteenth century, appeared to come from Iran, Turkey, and Central Asia.[5] However, the majority of mosaics that Lu and Steinhardt studied failed the test of true quasicrystalline patterns. But some clearly succeeded, in particular those at the Darb-i-Imam shrine built in 1453 in Isfahan, Iran.[6] Indeed, a careful analysis of over 3,700 tiles at that structure showed that only 11 exhibited small gaps, a factor the scientists believe is attributable to inadequate repairs made over the

---

[4] In 2011, the Nobel Prize in chemistry was awarded to Daniel Shechtman for his discovery of quasicrystals: "[In 1982] he was studying a mix of aluminum and manganese in his microscope when he found a pattern – *similar to Islamic mosaics* – that never repeated itself and appeared contrary to the laws of nature." Associated Press, "Israel's Daniel Shechtman Wins Nobel Prize in Chemistry," *The Washington Post*, October 5, 2011 (emphasis added). See, generally, David R. Nelson, "Quasicrystals," *Scientific American* 225 (1986): 42–51. On the discovery of quasicrystals in nature, see Luca Bindi et al., "Natural Quasicrystal with Decagonal Symmetry," *Scientific Reports*, March 13, 2015, www.nature.com/articles/srep09111. On his own decades-long search for such matter, see Steinhardt, *The Second Kind of Impossible*.

[5] Although there has been some suggestion that these forms may have been carried by artisans of the Timurid Dynasty from Mongolia and China, Peter J. Lu (personal communication) has expressed doubts about this connection. There is, however, some indication that a thirteenth-century Armenian Madonna may be the product of girih math, though whether the artisans involved came from or had contact with those in the Muslim world is unknown.

[6] See, generally, Peter J. Lu and Paul J. Steinhardt, "Decagonal and Quasi-Crystalline Tilings in Medieval Islamic Architecture," Science 315 (2007): 1106–10; and Paul J. Steinhardt, "Quasicrystals: A Brief History of the Impossible," *Rendiconti Fisiche Accademia Lincei*, 2012, wwwphy.princeton.edu/~steinh/Steinhardt_Rendiconti%20Lincei%202012.pdf

For additional illustrations, see http://science.sciencemag.org/content/sci/suppl/2007/02/20/315.5815.1106.DC1/Lu.SOM.pdf. See also Lu's website, which includes a lecture and detailed bibliography on quasicrystals: www.peterlu.org//content/decagonal-and-quasicrystalline-tilings-medieval-islamic-architecture. Steinhardt (personal communication) thinks Darb-i-Imam may be the only clear example we have of quasicrystalline mosaics. Even its dating, he suggests, is uncertain, for while the building is from the fifteenth century, the mosaics could have been done in the eighteenth century.

centuries.[7] Could the artisans have accomplished their goal without understanding the underlying mathematics? Lu believes not. It is, he says, "quite reasonable to believe that its particular designers knew what they were doing mathematically."[8]

Quasicrystal patterns fill all of the space they occupy, leaving no gaps (see Plate 1.6.). Moreover, if you slide the copy of one pattern over another, they never fit exactly, although they may if properly rotated. The highly sophisticated math necessary to accomplish this patterning may have been embodied in a series of standardized tiles decorated with lines that, when properly arranged by the workmen in what Lu has referred to as "a crib sheet of expert tips, [passed] from master to master," could create overlapping patterns of quite different

[7] "'These are not quite perfect quasi-crystals,' he [Lu] told *New Scientist*, because the patterns show a few defects where a single tile was placed incorrectly. He suspects the defects were mistakes by workers putting together the design specified by the designer. 'It's only 11 defects out of 3700 Penrose tiles, and each can be corrected by a simple rotation,' he says." Jeff Hecht, "Medieval Islamic Tiling Reveals Mathematical Savvy," *New Scientist*, February 22, 2007.

[8] "'Our analysis indicates that Islamic designers had all the conceptual elements necessary to produce quasi-crystalline girih patterns using the self-similar transformation method: girih tiles, decagonal symmetry, and subdivision.' Lu also stated: 'We can't say for sure what it [this discovery] means. It could be proof of a major role of mathematics in medieval Islamic art or it could have been just a way for artisans to construct their art more easily. It would be incredible if it were all coincidence, though. At the very least, it shows us a culture that we often don't credit enough was far more advanced than we ever thought before'." David Baron, "Medieval Islamic Architecture Presages 20th-Century Mathematics," *Harvard University Gazette*, February 22, 2007. Lu and Steinhardt acknowledge that the designers' knowledge may have been incomplete: "Although the Dar-i-Imam pattern illustrates that Islamic designers had all the elements needed to construct perfect quasi-crystalline patterns, we nonetheless find indications that the designers had an incomplete understanding of these elements." Lu and Steinhardt, *Decagonal*, 1109. As Wilford reports:

The geometric star-and-polygon girihs, as quasicrystals, can be rotated a certain number of degrees, say one-fifth of a circle, to positions from which other tiles are fitted. As such, this makes possible a pattern that is infinitely big and yet the pattern never repeats itself, unlike the tiles on the typical floor. This was, the scientists wrote, "an important breakthrough in Islamic mathematics and design." Dr. Steinhardt said in an interview that it was not clear how well the Islamic designers understood all the elements they were applying to the construction of these patterns. "I can just say what's on the walls," he said. Mr. Lu said that it would be "incredible if it were all coincidence." "At the very least," he said, "it shows us a culture that we often don't credit enough was far more advanced than we ever thought before."

John Noble Wilford, "In Medieval Architecture, Signs of Advanced Math," *New York Times*, February 27, 2007.

scales.[9] Known by the Persian word *girih*, the patterns involved are explained by Professor Al-Hassani:

Girih designs feature arrays of tessellating polygons of multiple shapes and are often overlaid with a zigzag network of lines. It had been assumed that straightedge rulers and compasses were used to create them – an exceptionally difficult process as each shape must be precisely drawn. From the fifteenth century, however, some of these designs are symmetrical in a way known today as "quasi-crystalline." Such forms have either fivefold or tenfold rotational symmetry – meaning they can be rotated to either five or ten positions that look the same – and their patterns can be infinitely extended without repetition.[10]

Could the artisans of Darb-i-Imam have achieved their result simply by trial and error? Steinhardt (*The Second Kind of Impossible*, 92 and 106) writes of his experiments with tile patterns that might form a Penrose pattern:

So if you were given a pile containing these tile shapes and asked to cover a floor with them using pictures of the complete pattern as a guide, you might wind up with an ordinary crystal pattern because they are so simple to construct. You might also make a random pattern. But the chance that you would be able to make a quasicrystal pattern is very small.... If you started putting the tiles together one by one, chances are that you would run into difficulty after only a dozen or so pieces even if you meticulously followed all of the interlocking rules each time you added a tile.... If you continued adding tiles, you would soon find yourself creating another defect. And then another and another and another.

Steinhardt does acknowledge that Roger Penrose "had managed to construct a quasi-crystal tiling without being aware of its hidden quasiperiodic order" and that with sufficient time perhaps even the "homemade paper puzzle" that he and Lu worked on might yield such a result. And it is even possible that the mathematicians' approach is not the only way to grasp the underlying rules. But at least from these scientists' perspective, and not withstanding how long the early artisans may have struggled to find a working solution, the weight of evidence suggests that no amount of tinkering is likely to produce a quasicrystalline pattern.

Not all analysts, however, are certain that the Muslim artists had solved the necessary mathematics. Physicists Don Levine of the Israel Institute of Technology and Joshua Socolar of Duke University "doubt that the architects truly understood quasi-crystals but say Lu and Steinhardt have generated interesting and testable hypotheses." John Bohannon, "Quasi-crystal Conundrum Opens a Tiling Can of Worms," *Science* 315 (2007): 1066. See also the published responses to the *Science* article by Lu and Steinhardt, *Decagonal*. Lu strongly contests the comments by Levine and Socolar (personal communication).

[9] Lu is quoted in Whipps, *Medieval*.
[10] Salim Al-Hassani, "New Discoveries in the Islamic Complex of Mathematics, Architecture and Art," *Muslim Heritage* (2007), www.muslimheritage.com/article/new-discoveries-in-islamic-complex. Another commenter explains: "A quasicrystal is unique: It shares many properties of normal crystals, but lacks some fundamental properties. A typical crystal has a predictable structure

Sebastian Prange picks up the story:

The tilework on the Bukhara madrasa is an example of the stylized geometric strap-work – typically based on star or polygon shapes – that is emblematic of traditional Islamic ornamentation. This form of design is known as *girih* patterns, from the Persian word for "knot." It is generally believed that such designs were constructed by drafting zigzag outlines with only a straightedge and a compass. But Lu perceived something more: "I saw five-fold and ten-fold stars, which immediately aroused my curiosity about how these tilings had been made." He wondered how Islamic craftsmen had been able to design such elaborately symmetrical patterns centuries before the advent of modern mathematics.

Lu returned to Harvard with this question in mind and, working closely with Professor Steinhardt, set to mapping the abundant pentagonal and decagonal motifs of the Uzbeki madrasa. Sifting through hundreds of additional images of other medieval Islamic buildings, he was able to identify five underlying shapes that account for the geometric complexity of their designs: a decagon, a pentagon, a hexagon, a rhombus, and a "bowtie" (see Plates 1.4 and 1.5). Although these are not immediately visible, they form the basis for the most complex, or "knotty," girih designs. Lu describes these five shapes as "girih tiles" and regards them as the tools that enabled craftsmen to construct highly complex patterns over large surfaces without gaps or disruptions in their symmetry.[11]

with three-, four-, or six-fold symmetry. A quasicrystal can present five-fold symmetry. Five-fold symmetry is unique because it does not have translational symmetry: One portion of a pattern is not identical to other portions. This deviates from one of the fundamental properties of a crystal, making the quasicrystal a 'freak of nature'." Ava Cutler, "Moroccan Mosaics: A Creative Blend of Art, Nature, and Mathematics," *Morocco World News*, April 5, 2020. www.moroccoworldnews.com/2020/04/298478/moroccan-mosaics-a-creative-blend-of-art-nature-and-mathematics/ See, generally, István Harittai, ed., *Fivefold Symmetry* (Singapore: World Scientific Publishing Co., 1992).
    Put somewhat more technically, quasicrystalline structures are nonperiodic; that is, the spacing of the clusters is not equal, that is, they operate by "two different repeating frequencies whose ratio is irrational" [i.e., nonrepeating]. Steinhardt, *The Second Kind of Impossible*, 62. They can only be understood mathematically with the aid of "matching rules ... mysterious interlocks that prevent the tiles from being put together in any kind of periodic pattern." Ibid., 49.

[11] Sebastian R. Prange, "The Tiles of Infinity," *Aramco World* (September–October 2009): 24–31. See also the lecture, with numerous illustrations, by Paul J. Steinhardt at Harvard University, March 3, 2020, at www.youtube.com/watch?v=IZEiaF_-FeA&list=PLEOjXOX2PyGyroEc4U4xVrhoubC1zp1qP&index=2

These complex patterns are, of course, only one of many Islamic art motifs and certainly not the most common. Less complicated tessellations – along with the arabesque, architectural features, pottery designs, and textiles – are only a few of the other artistic productions characteristic of various Muslim cultures.[12] Yet without turning the quasicrystalline patterns into the reified essence or ultimate goal of Islamic design, the Western recognition of these extraordinary achievements affords an opportunity to reconsider the meanings attached to the artists' creations.

Assessing the meaning of any art form is, of course, a matter of interpretation, and knowing what each viewer or artisan may see in a work, especially when they have left no written record of their thoughts, is not possible. But neither is it necessary. Rather, as in any interpretive endeavor, one seeks to relate seemingly diverse elements to which those who entangle their lives with such forms organize their expressions and acts. Seeing an art form in its sociocultural context can reveal the connections through which meaning is engendered. Many Western analysts, however, have approached Islamic art without considering the social meanings brought to such representations, concentrating instead on the recondite texts of Muslim theologians, speculating as to what such designs *must* mean, or simply assuming that the criteria of explanation employed in the art criticism of their own traditions are universally applicable. While wonderful studies have been made of the history and styles of Islamic art, Oliver Leaman has a point when he says that "the wildest generalizations are constantly made about Islamic art."[13] This becomes all the more evident when one reviews some of the Western critics' interpretations of Islamic art.

To a number of Western commenters Islamic art is about pure forms – indeed Platonic forms – by means of which the truth of a cosmic reality is aligned with reason. As one proponent of this viewpoint notes: "Like Plato, the Muslim sees geometry and exact proportion as a direct expression of the divine and takes mathematics to be the key

---

[12] See, generally, Loai M. Dabbour, "Geometric Proportions: The Underlying Structure of Design Process for Islamic Geometric Patterns," *Frontiers of Architectural Research*, 1 (2012): 380–91.

[13] Oliver Leaman, *Islamic Aesthetics: An Introduction* (Notre Dame: Notre Dame University Press, 2004), 15. The disagreements among Islamic art scholars are explored in Laura U. Marks, *Enfoldment and Infinity: An Islamic Genealogy of New Media Art* (Cambridge, MA: The MIT Press, 2010), 28–30.

to understanding the structure of the cosmos.... In a most Platonic manner the Muslim believes the geometric patterns draw attention away from the physical world to one of pure forms, and they point to the purity of essential relationships which lie beneath the visual surface."[14] The abstract nature of the art as a mode of drawing away from the physical world is said to be prompted by the Islamic prohibition on portrayal of animate, especially human, forms, such concretization being "an obstacle to the emptying of the mind" in order to apprehend the divine. Loia M. Dabbour makes comparable assumptions, arguing that "The language of Islamic design springs primarily from the abstract ... [patterns having been] developed as visual tools for contemplating the underlying mathematical nature of the universe."[15] Omar Nasim thus argues that "the best way to represent abstract concepts such as worldview is to use abstract vehicles of representation.... Just as Islam does not clothe its Deity in any mythological/anthropomorphic garb, so was the art of Islam bound not to accept the representational imagery."[16] Similarly, Alexandre Papadopoulo asserts that "the painter had to abandon the tangible appearances of nature," and since "all animate beings are individuals" yet representations of them are forbidden "it is essential for the artist to suppress any hint of their individuality."[17] Even when it is not just elaborate periodic tessellations but full-scale quasicrystalline mosaics like that at Darb-i-Imam, commenters may link an aversion to representational art to a generalized propulsion to human creativity:

[N]on-periodic tilings had been discovered more than 500 years ago... [w]hich makes us wonder why on earth would those Muslim decorators be interested in creating something so complex. My reasoning is as follows. It is known that, in Islam, people are very restricted with what kind of things they

---

[14]  Asli Gocer, "A Hypothesis Concerning the Character of Islamic Art," *Journal of the History of Ideas* 60 (1999): 683–92, at 691. Oleg Grabar also relies on Plato, but his analysis moves in a somewhat different direction, seeing in the ornamentation of Islamic art a mysterious role for mediating between form and emotion. Oleg Grabar, *The Mediation of Ornament* (Princeton: Princeton University Press, 1992).

[15]  Dabbour, *Geometric*, 380.

[16]  Omar W. Nasim, "Toward an Islamic Aesthetic Theory," *The American Journal of Islamic Social Sciences* 15 (1998): 71–90, at 82.

[17]  Alexandre Papadopoulo, *Islam and Muslim Art* (London: Thames and Hudson, 1979), 55.

are allowed to decorate their temples/mosques/shrines. Gods and the like are not allowed. Human forms are not allowed. Animals or plants are not allowed (exception: in Iran, but that is, I am being told, a remnant of the pre-Islamic religion). Any concrete objects are not allowed. This is why Muslims have very few things they can play with: abstract patterns, tilings, geometric figures. But, even within this restricted framework, humans' minds can be quite creative. Humans have an innate need to be free, to explore, to wonder, to create. When authority or religion impose restrictions and rules, humans will try as much as they can to break them, even unconsciously. It seems that this is a prime example of the innate need for freedom of expression.[18]

Many commenters take an equally romanticized view of Islam and its arts, often based on images of the religion's origin in desert spaces. Cyril Glassé, for example, writes:

To counter the natural tendency of desert peoples to "condense" ideas and their figurative representations into psychological "hardenings" … Islamic art has, in addition to not using realistic images, cultivated means which actively produce the opposite effect. That is, Islamic art often seeks to dissolve psychic knots by the rhythmic repetition of design motifs, particularly of geometric designs and arabesques, in order to bring the beholder a taste of infinity, and by abstraction, to restore a sense of space as a means of escape from imprisonment with forms.[19]

Similarly, Soraya Syed claims that Islamic art "seeks to manifest the sacredness of virgin nature whose laws and structures are related to

---

[18] Takis Konstantopoulos, "Penrose Tilings in Helsinki," http://randomprocessed .blogspot.com/2014/11/penrose-tiling-in-helsinki.html (November 15, 2014).
[19] Cyril Glassé, "Images," *The New Encyclopedia of Islam*, 4th ed. (Lanham, MD: Rowman & Littlefield, 2013), 213. Some commenters make a similar attribution to Islamic law: "Floating above Muslim society as a disembodied soul, freed from the currents and vicissitudes of time, it represents the eternally valid ideal towards which society must aspire." Noel Coulson, *A History of Islamic Law* (Edinburgh: Edinburgh University Press, 1965), 2. By contrast, in a fashion much more consistent with the argument here, Malise Ruthven states that: "the Shariʿa may also be compared to the interlaced pattern characteristic of Islamic design which can be extended indefinitely, like wallpaper patterns." Malise Ruthven, *Islam in the World*, 2nd ed. (New York: Penguin, 1984). On the relation of Islamic law to society, see also Lawrence Rosen, *The Anthropology of Justice: Law as Culture in Islamic Society* (Cambridge: Cambridge University Press, 1989); and Lawrence Rosen, *The Justice of Islam: Comparative Perspectives on Islamic Law and Society* (Oxford: Oxford University Press, 2000).

the mathematical world," while Thomas Arnold argued that Muslim artists had to replace genuine displays of emotion with conventional signs, such that "[e]ven moments of ecstatic delight leave the actors in the scene with unimpassioned faces, as though they did not know that they were attaining the zenith of delight in the sphere of human experience."[20] Richard Ettinghausen asserted that by the use of soft materials like clay, brick, plaster, and wool Islamic art shows itself as portraying "a sense of unreality and impermanence ... an indication of the consciousness that everything in this world, and certainly the artistic creation by the human hand, are of transitory character."[21] This same etherealized approach to Islamic art is expressed by Titus Burckhardt when he says that Islamic art is simply "the exteriorization of a contemplative state [that does] not reflect particular ideas." He too calls forth the image of nomadic origins:

[T]he function of Islamic art is analogous to that of virgin nature, of the desert especially, which likewise favours contemplation, although from another point of view the order created by art is opposed to the chaos inherent in the nature of the desert.... [Islam] maintains in a certain fashion, and on a higher and spiritual plane, the position of the nomad who is not involved in the turbulent evolution of a world composed of the mental projections of man and of his reactions towards these projections.[22]

To other Western scholars Islamic art is almost entirely about religion, indeed often the mystical aspects of religion. Ernst Grube, commenting on the infinity of Islamic patterns, sees in them "a disregard for temporary existence.... One of the most fundamental principles of the Islamic style is the dissolution of matter."[23] In the same vein, Sebastian Prange contends:

Geometric patterns in Islamic architecture and ornamentation were used as much for spiritual as for artistic reasons. As Robert Irwin writes in his study of Islamic art, such patterns may have been viewed "as exteriorized

[20] Soraya Syed, "Unity and Diversity: Lessons from Sacred Islamic Art," *Q-News: The Muslim Magazine*, 337 (November 2001): 37; and Thomas Arnold, *Painting in Islam* (Oxford: Clarendon Press, 1928), 134.

[21] Richard Ettinghausen, "The Character of Islamic Art," in *The Arab Heritage*, ed. Nabih Amin Faris (Princeton: Princeton University Press, 1946), 251–67, at 262.

[22] Titus Burckhardt, "The Void in Islamic Art," *Studies in Comparative Religion* 4 (1970): 96–99, at 97 and 99.

[23] Ernst J. Grube, *The World of Islam* (New York: McGraw-Hill, 1967), 11.

representations of abstract, even mystical, thought" – aiming to inspire contemplation or to make a statement about the imponderable harmonies of a
divinely ordered universe. Sufism in particular is closely linked to the practice of geometry, above all in the form of symmetries, as a way of giving
physical expression to mystical thought.[24]

In each of these approaches to Islamic art what is often slighted is a
grounded consideration of how the artistic representation makes sense
within the larger social and cultural context of the native viewers.
Vital as such an approach is to the study of any artistic tradition, it has
special importance in the Islamic context precisely because of the tendency to assume that since many of the forms are reasonably similar to
those in the West they must of necessity be approached by people from
the region in a similar fashion. Indeed, because many other features
of Muslim societies also have resonance in the West – marketplace
bargaining, monotheistic belief, scientific achievements, sophisticated
literary traditions – and many Islamic advances were actually adopted
by the West over the centuries, the assumption that similar representations must be seen similarly is inviting. But it is precisely because of
this perceived similarity of representational form and assumed meaning that it is important to challenge such assumptions by attending
more precisely to the distinctiveness within the Muslim world of "the
natives' point of view."

If we take as our entry point, the complex quasicrystalline designs
several features of these forms will be of particular importance to an
interpretation of their social and cultural connections: that while the
edges along which the tiles are laid are replicated the clusters of individual elements are nevertheless highly distinctive in their arrangement
toward one another; that even though it is crucial that no gaps exist
between or among the individual elements, the interconnecting zigzag
lines that orient the tiles are conceived as "knots" that tie individual
pieces together while also suggesting larger and smaller enclosures of
space; that the resultant pattern can go on infinitely yet retains variation throughout; that individuation arises from any one element's relation to those in its surround rather than from some essential quality;
that symmetry – as Nobel Laureate Steven Weinberg notes – exists

[24] Prange, *Tiles*. On Sufism, geometry, and architecture, see Samer Akkach,
*Cosmology and Architecture in Premodern Islam* (Albany: State University of
New York Press, 2005).

when the rule being applied remains the same notwithstanding one's point of view and, furthermore, that symmetry consists in the laws that govern the interplay of elements rather than in features that inhere in them individually, for without such underlying principles the arrangement of the constituent elements would be utterly chaotic.[25]

When we turn to the sociocultural context of the moșaics, the question a student of the social history of art would pose may be phrased in the following way: Why did it matter to the creators of these quasicrystal designs to figure out how to display their subject in this fashion? A quite different example may help frame the issue. Why, we may ask, does it matter to us to know that objects fall at the rate of thirty-two feet per second square? Why is it not enough to know they fall at roughly that rate, or not to know the rate at all? At some point answering the question must matter. Perhaps in this case it began to be of concern not when an apple dropped on Newton's head but when people were trying to make a cannonball drop on the enemy's head. Similarly, when we ask why it was important for the creators of the tile patterns to know how to create their work according to a quasicrystalline pattern, the reason may be that to do so was to represent the world as they understood it and thus to make their art both graspable and reaffirming. Taking this tack we can begin to interpret the meaning of this art form in the light of the ways it summarizes and connects a multiplicity of domains in the cultural life of the Muslims involved.

Before suggesting an interpretation of the sociocultural context of Islamic art a note of caution is, however, necessary. The very idea of speaking about "Islamic art" is understandably problematic. Obviously, when dealing with cultures that span the globe, claiming a common set of local interpretations simply because of a shared religious base may seem imprudent. While the cultural interpretation offered here is based on extensive interviews and a far greater review of sources than can be cited, the analysis offered must be couched in rather broad terms.[26] Clearly, local and individual variants are

---

[25] Steven Weinberg, "Symmetry: A 'Key to Nature's Secrets'," *The New York Review of Books*, October 27, 2011.

[26] These points are further developed in Lawrence Rosen, *Bargaining for Reality: The Construction of Social Relations in a Muslim Community* (Chicago: University of Chicago Press, 1984); Lawrence Rosen, *The Culture of Islam: Changing Aspects of Contemporary Muslim Life* (Chicago, University of

crucial and there is a risk of being anachronistic and replicating in the interpretive style of social analysis the criticisms raised above about some Islamic art scholarship. Since the aim here is not to analyze all of Islamic art in every place or time but to see, much more precisely, why the quasicrystalline pattern might have been sought out by its progenitors, the present inquiry is somewhat more circumscribed. Moreover, if the reader approaches the argument by asking whether variations in related places and times resonate with this account we may be able to consider more carefully both localized examples and the process of cultural resonance more generally.

\* \* \*

Without a profound simplification the world around us would be an infinite, undefined tangle that would defy our ability to orient ourselves and decide upon our actions.... We are compelled to reduce the knowable to a schema.[27]

Primo Levi

The image of the marketplace, the bazaar, is a fitting place to begin. There, where hawking and haggling are the order of the day and potential chaos is ameliorated by patron–client relationships and mutual indebtedness, negotiating one's way is a personal act requiring the ability to concentrate on what is knowable and realistic. This orientation carries over into social relationships generally, where the content of one's attachments are essentially negotiable rather than strictly determined by kinship, residence, or affinity. As Levi suggests generally, each person must, therefore, construct a web of interpersonal ties that are carefully and constantly watched over and nurtured. Indeed, when everything from a price in the bazaar to the nature of a given relationship is subject to negotiation, the facility to weave together a set of interpersonal obligations is not only vital to garnering a measure of security but also the indispensable indicator of personal identity. In the process of forming such networks, some individuals are obviously more

Chicago Press, 2002); and Lawrence Rosen *Varieties of Muslim Experience: Encounters with Arab Cultural and Political Life* (Chicago: University of Chicago Press, 2008).
[27] Primo Levi, *The Drowned and the Saved* (New York: Vintage, 1989).

successful than others. But regardless of their scale, the mechanisms through which such networks are formed are shared. Thus, one can speak of larger and smaller constellations of obligation that spread out across time and space as each individual seeks to move to effect in a world that is ordered by the repertoire of relational possibilities, the regularized modes of fashioning such relationships, and the sheer force of one's ability to create bonds of indebtedness in a fearful and uncertain world.

Clifford Geertz's summary of this interpretation is worth quoting at length:

> This promiscuous tumbling in the public realm of varieties of men kept carefully partitioned in the private one, cosmopolitanism in the streets and communalism in the home, is, of course, a general feature of Middle Eastern civilization. Often called a mosaic pattern of social organization – differently shaped and colored chips jammed in irregularly together to generate an overall design within which their distinctiveness remains nonetheless intact – it is made possible by a number of characteristic ideas: that religious truth is so little subject to argument and so little responsive to temporal concerns that it ought not to hinder practical activities; that non-Muslim groups are not outside Muslim society but have a scripturally allocated place within it; that law is personal and determined by who one is, not territorial and determined by where one is; and that, though usually cruel and always capricious, the state is a machine less for the governing of men, who are anyway more or less ungovernable, than for the amassment and consumption of the material rewards of power. Nothing if not diverse, Middle Eastern society ... does not cope with diversity by sealing it into castes, isolating it into tribes, or covering it over with some common denominator concept of nationality – though, fitfully, all have occasionally been tried. It copes with diversity by distinguishing with elaborate precision the contexts (marriage, diet, worship, education) within which men are separated by their dissimilitudes and those (work, friendship, politics, trade) where, however warily and however conditionally, men are connected by their differences.[28]

Reinforcement for such an orientation comes from numerous cultural domains. There is the perspective supplied by the Quran, where

---

[28] Clifford Geertz, "Suq: The Bazaar Economy in Sefrou," in Clifford Geertz, Hildred Geertz, and Lawrence Rosen, *Meaning and Order in Moroccan Society* (New York: Cambridge University Press, 1979), 141; reprinted as *Sūq: Geertz on the Market* (Chicago: University of Chicago Press, 2022).

the word for "knowledge" is second in frequency only to the name of God, and where even the name of the sacred text, which means "recitation," reinforces the idea that awareness requires enactment. As Marshall Hodgson noted, the Quran is not a treatise, a statement of facts and norms, but an event, an act.[29] Envisioning the world as a terrain within which the knowledgeable person maneuvers to his own advantage and those of his dependents is further underscored by ideas of time. For time is seen not as a directional pathway or the unfolding of ultimate truths by means of duration but, in Louis Massignon's words, "a Milky Way of instants," a series of highly context-dependent associations and relationships the totality of which define a person.[30] An example may help here. I have often shown to Arab and Berber informants a set of pictures taken at different times in the life of a man who is not known to them and asked them to tell me about this person. Most Westerners looking over my shoulder would probably begin to order the pictures chronologically. But that is not what my informants do. Instead, they comment on how one sees this person with one group of people and then with another set, the narrative not relying on chronology. Clearly, as they emphasize, time does not reveal the truth of persons; nested sets of negotiated relationships do.

This image of time as relational is underscored by the organization of the Quran simply from longest to shortest chapter, and by the revelation of its truths not through chronology but seeing the Prophet and mankind in a variety of situated contexts. Similarly, in Muslim courts judges want to know with whom the parties are connected in order to determine the repercussions of any ruling for those networks. When asked if similar cases ought not to be decided similarly the common response is that no two cases are ever the same – even for the same people or situation – since at each instant, the web of interconnected ties will have varied, however slightly. Knowing the systemic implications of each person's ties, judges insist, will lead to a greater chance of achieving the goal of placing the litigants back into negotiating their own relations with one another. If time and space are identified by the

---

[29] Marshall G. S. Hodgson, *The Venture of Islam*, Vol. I (Chicago: University of Chicago Press, 1974), 367.

[30] Louis Massignon, "Le Temps dans la pensée islamique," *Eranos-Jahrbuch, 1951*, 20 (Zurich: Rhein-Verlag, 1952): 141–48, at 141.

people who occupy them rather than by natural or inevitable forces, then one might extend Franz Rosenthal's formula that in the Muslim Middle East history is biography by arguing that biography, in turn, is relational.[31]

In many cultures, individuals are viewed as a concatenation of roles that can be separated from one another. So, for example, a public official may be expected to set aside personal beliefs when carrying out a given duty – indeed, be capable of completely compartmentalizing the different parts of his or her personhood. In the Arab world, however, the idea of segregating diverse aspects of one's self is largely inconceivable, for the self is imagined as a knotted unity and any compartmentalization would ring false. When, for example, I mention that several US Supreme Court justices have said that they personally oppose the death penalty but as judges they must nevertheless apply it informants invariably suggest that if I knew the judges well enough – their relations with others, their characteristic ways of forging negotiated bonds, the full range of contexts within which they have had to operate – I would find no inconsistency in their assertions. Just as Islam is seen as a unity of belief in which any admixture would undermine the coherence of the sacred and the community of believers, so, too, the unfractionated self can be responsive to varying contexts while still maintaining an indissoluble integrity.

Space, too, is conceptualized as the grounds upon which the ties between persons is enacted, such that no piece of land is without its name, no territory devoid of a history of those whose connections to one another are its defining feature, no gaps left indifferent to or unbounded by ever-varying clusters of human activity. Accordingly, ownership is less about someone's relation to a given thing than their relationship to others as it concerns that thing. Even appropriate games buttress this relational orientation. In the early years of Islam, for example, there was a debate about the appropriate game for Muslims to play. Proponents of a game of dice called *nar* said that since humankind are like dice in the hands of Allah and only He can know a person's fate *nar* was the proper game for believers to play. No, no, said the supporters of chess: People have been endowed by their Creator with reason to better their situations and those of their

---

[31] See, generally, Franz Rosenthal, *A History of Muslim Historiography* (Leiden: Brill, 1952).

(a)                                        (b)

**Figure 1.1** (a) Prophet Muhammad riding his steed Buraq, eighteenth century, artist unknown. Wikimedia Commons: public domain. (b) Fatima receiving cloak from angel Gabriel before Prophet Muhammad (on right), sixteenth-century version of fourteenth-century original. Chester Beatty Library, Dublin. Wikimedia Commons: public domain.

dependents, so chess is the more appropriate pastime. In the end, *nar* was declared heretical and chess an apt Muslim game.

Such orientations thus pervade numerous domains, not the least of them the representational. Indeed, the emphasis on the negotiating individual who draws on the repertoire of relational possibilities to respond to changing contexts forms the vital backdrop to artistic comprehension. Consider, first, the presumed ban on human representations. The only passage cited from the Quran (Surah 5:110) regarding such figures is actually about Jesus: It says that he alone was able to fashion the likeness of a bird from clay and infuse it with life, but only by the grace of God. In the early years of Islam, not only was the human form frequently represented but so was the image of the Prophet himself (Figure 1.1a). Sometimes the full face of the Prophet was shown, sometimes his visage was partially, sometimes fully, veiled or erased (Figure 1.1b). While later

**Figure 1.2** Prophet Muhammad as a young man. Photo by Lehnert and Landrock, 1910. Universal History Archive/Universal Images Group/Getty Images.

theologians, fearful that such figures might be approached like idols, argued against any use of portraiture, pictures even of the Prophet Muhammad – including in the early years of Islam on prayer rugs[32] – can be seen in political rallies in Iran through to the present day (Figure 1.2).[33] At the same time, portraiture is not favored by most Muslims (particularly Arabs and Persians) not solely for religious

[32] See Priscilla P. Soucek, "The Life of the Prophet: Illustrated Versions," in *Content and Context of Visual Arts in the Islamic World*, ed. Priscilla P. Soucek (University Park, PA: Pennsylvania State University Press, 1988), 193–218; and Richard Ettinghausen, "The Early History, Use and Iconography of the Prayer Rug," in *Islamic Art and Archaeology: Collected Papers*, ed. Richard Ettinghausen (Berlin: Gebr. Mann Verlag, 1984), 282–97.

[33] See, generally, Oleg Grabar, "Seeing and Believing: The Image of the Prophet in Islam: The Real Story," *The New Republic*, no. 4871 (November 2009),

reasons but because a portrait tells the viewer almost nothing he or she would need to know about the person represented. For while Westerners imagine that they can tell something about a person's character from that individual's depiction, Middle Eastern Muslims consistently state that a picture tells you almost nothing you need to know to assess another: Only seeing their interaction with others can supply the information needed to understand individuals' situated ties and how they form such bonds.[34] Thus moving pictures are meaningful, but static portraits are not. And the few paintings that do show people are usually ones in which the person is interacting, directly or symbolically, with others. Just as the story of a man, as in the responses to the photos shown informants, is told not chronologically but through the situations of his dealings with others so, too, the absence of portraiture is consistent with – indeed vital to – the choice of forms of representation in the plastic arts.

In a sense, then, a portrait is not a God-like claim to potential animation but is viewed as its very antithesis: It dissolves animation, rendering the figure motionless and thus unable to relate to the viewer through imaginable interaction. From the comments of numerous informants one comes away with the impression that for many contemporary viewers (consistent with sacred and historical texts), it is not that a portrait fails to show a figure's inner state, but that one can only determine another's intention (*niya*) and believability from his or her actions – the very thing, in their reading, a picture cannot convey.[35] Where faces have been portrayed they usually indicate some interaction with others, often through a stylized set of conventions. But just as people regard as "lies" (*kdub*) films that portray people acting in ways in which they do not, in fact, engage others, so, too, they argue that if you know a person's connections

---

433–37. On the Iranian pictures of the Prophet as a young man, see Pierre Centlivres and Micheline Centlivres-Demont, "The Story of a Picture: Shiite Depictions of Muhammad," *ISIM* [International Institute for the Study of Islam in the Modern World (Leiden)] *Review* 17 (2006): 18–19.

[34] On the changing interpretation of portraiture in the West, see Laurie Fendrich, "The Lie of the Portrait," *The Chronicle Review: The Chronicle of Higher Education*, November 11, 2005: B10-11. On the absence of portraiture in Islamic art, see Rosen, *Varieties*, 93–104.

[35] On intentionality, see Rosen, *The Culture of Islam*, 108–29; on portraiture in Islam, see Rosen, *Varieties of Muslim Experience*, 93–104.

you will know the individual's inner state because the two are indissolubly attached. Commenters like Thomas W. Arnold thus often miss this point when they say:

There is one characteristic of the figure painting of the Muhammadan period which is deserving of special attention, viz. the infrequency of any attempt to give emotive expression to the faces of living persons represented in these pictures.... The painter ... was apparently willing to spend hours of work upon the delicate veining of the leaves of a plane-tree or the shades of colour on the petals of an iris, but it does not seem to have occurred to him to devote the same pains and effort upon the countenances of his human figures and make them show by their expressions their mental attitude towards the scene in which they are playing a part.... Even moments of ecstatic delight leave the actors in the scene with unimpassioned faces, as though they did not know that they were attaining the zenith of delight in the sphere of human experience.[36]

To the contrary, from the viewpoint of many Muslims, no portrait can convey what really matters, namely modes of relationship. Indeed, even in the West, one only has to ask what it is one thinks is seen in a portrait about another's character, or understand the effect various psychological theories have had on the course of portraiture, to appreciate that for people in the Middle East a picture may be iconic, but it does not indicate what is essential to know about another – the ways one might relate to him.

Seen from this sociological perspective, the quest for nonrepresentational forms like the quasicrystalline pattern of the mosaics is consistent with the cultural emphasis on human interaction. For what is true of human relationships is true of these patterns – namely, that the world is one in which human beings, endowed by their Creator with the capacity to negotiate their own attachments, form highly personalistic relationships which, like the clustered pieces in the mosaic, are contextual, nonreplicating, and extend outward as far as the individual is able to carry them. In such individualistic relationships, as in the mosaic patterns, each edge – each point of potential contact – is of the same initial orientation and dimension, angular distortions being minimized even as each unit contributes to a complex symmetry while simultaneously exhibiting a diversity of scale and

[36] Arnold, *Painting*, 133–34.

frequency.[37] Gaps, whether in Allah's creation or within the Community of Believers (*umma*), poses the risk that other matter cannot be stopped from filling in, thus resulting in that admixture with fundamentals that Islam rejects as strongly as nature does a vacuum. Indeed, quasicrystals and the created universe share the fact that there is only one way each can be constructed. So, too, the fact that no two star-shaped clusters at the heart of a girih design "have exactly the same surroundings if one continues far enough from the center of the star" is replicated in the sense that context is at the core each individual's identity.[38] And just as the social and political worlds are seen as encompassing larger and smaller constellations of personally fabricated networks, so too, as Lu and Steinhardt note, "the most striking innovation arising from the application of girih tiles" is that one can generate larger and smaller representations out of the same shapes and modes of interrelationship.[39]

To the viewing Muslim, such patterns may be regarded as representational of the world within which each person must maneuver and

---

[37] The technical explanation offered by Lu and Steinhardt states: "Quasiperiodic order means that distinct tile shapes repeat with frequencies that are incommensurable, that is, the ratio of the frequencies cannot be expressed as a ratio of integers. By having quasi-periodicity, the symmetry constraints of conventional crystallography can be violated, and it is possible to have pentagonal motifs that join together in a pattern with overall pentagonal and decagonal symmetry." Lu and Steinhardt, *Decagonal*, 1008.

[38] The internal quote is from Steinhardt, *The Second Kind of Impossible*, 46; on the concept of *homo contextus* in the Arabo-Berber world, see Rosen, *Bargaining for Reality*, 165–79.

[39] In more technical terms: "[T]he most striking innovation arising from the application of girih tiles was the use of self-similarity transformation (the subdivision of large girih tiles into smaller ones) to create overlapping patterns at two different length scales, in which each pattern is generated by the same girih tile shapes." Lu and Steinhardt, *Decagonal*, 1008.

One may also speculate that the architects and master craftsmen, like the theologians of the period, were influenced by Aristotle's idea that the number of items in an array may stretch to infinity but the infinite number of sets into which they could be grouped might be at least as vast, just as the mosaics represent individual units that are innumerable yet replicable, while the sets of relationships into which they can be arranged can be infinitely variable and extensive. See, generally, A. W. Moore, "Infinity and Beyond," *Aeon*, March 8, 2017, https://aeon.co/essays/why-some-infinities-are-bigger-than-others. On the mathematics of infinity and Islamic art, see Marks, *Enfoldment*; and Micky Piller, *Escher Meets Islamic Art* (Bussum, Netherlands: Uitgeverij Thoth, 2013).

within which the most essential truth of persons is configured, namely the highly variable negotiation of those interdependencies that are central to anyone's identity. Like chess and the telling of a man's life, action shows individualization, not mere replication, and underscores the constant need to seek information about others' connections if one is to know how best to maneuver in the world. For Muslims, the link between knowledge and action is neatly articulated in a phrasing from Wall Street that Muslim informants readily enjoy: "To know but not to act is not to know." Form follows function, then, as surely in the social as in the architectural realm. Action can be seen through motion pictures or marionettes, but not in immobile portraits, hence the ready acceptance of the one and the rejection as relatively meaningless of the other. Time, too, is consonant with a vision of man as by nature and divine command an active being, a quality represented by the use of nonrepetitive patterns, the elimination of gaps in a *girih* pattern, literary styles that do not depend on an absolute beginning and end, and in the avoidance of empty spaces mankind is meant to bind up with his relationships.

Human sociality is further consistent with the patterning that the Muslim designers utilize. To many Westerners, the arabesque, for example, appears as a design that is constantly repeated. But it is (to borrow Paul Bowles' characterization of Moroccan ritual music) "deceptive repetition."[40] For to many Muslim viewers, a very different interpretation is often articulated, namely that a choice is being made at each juncture in the design. That the result appears as recurrent is not the point. What counts are two things: that in the replication of a design, whether of art or of life, choices are constantly being made even if the result of any series appears identical, and that when choices are aligned with the regularizing precepts of a God-given order, they stand as the sole counter to chaos.

Indeed, in Islamic thought chaos (*fitna*) is a key concept. Chaos invokes both danger and opportunity, for the root of the Arabic term not only translates as "disorder" but also generates such additional meanings as "allure," "entice," "captivate," and "tempt."[41] The premonitory fear

---

[40] Quoted in Adam Shatz, "The Hypnotic Clamor of Morocco," *New York Review of Books*, March 30, 2016.
[41] See, generally, Louis Gardet, *Dieu et la destinée de l'homme* (Paris: Librairie Philosophique J. Vrin, 1967).

that the community of believers will descend into chaos is countered, then, by representations that transmit a sense of order that can be realized only if the application of reason to relationship accords with the foundational principles that create such order. And the mosque or religious school building is a particularly apt location for the display and reassurance of such principles. For the religious venue is a site of ritual reversal, a place where five times daily one departs from the constant negotiation of relationships with all their potential for disorder and temptation to re-envision the steady, the predictable, and the enduring in a world that tests these precepts at every step. Representations of apparent duplication, like the use of prayer beads or stylized calligraphy, underscore this conjoiner of choice and orderliness. Replicated patterns are thus essential to the abatement and harnessing of chaos, in the full recognition that, as novelist Ward Just once put it: "the answer to chaos is repetition."[42] However, in the Muslim context, such patterns are not seen as merely repetitious. The attitude of Muslim viewers may be like that wished for by Paul Valéry when he said that it is desirable "to substitute for the illusion of a unique scheme which imitates reality that of the *possible-at-each-moment*, which I think more truthful."[43] Indeed, because the artistic pattern is more analogous to a wallpaper design than a single geometric figure, large parts of the pattern can be lost yet the design survive to be renewed. So, too, in social life, the web of relationships can be decimated by war, disease, ill luck, or incompetence yet belief in the design and one's ability to recapitulate it remain ever possible and alluring.

Moreover, the quasicrystalline pattern reinforces in many Middle Eastern cultures the immanent nature of what has been called the "frame tradition."[44] The idea here is that rather than an overall design that governs where each element must be placed within a bounded domain the frame tradition allows constant additions that are not predetermined yet fit with the purpose and composition of the whole. So, in architecture – whether sacred, domestic, or political – rooms

[42] Ward Just, *The Weather in Berlin* (New York: Houghton Mifflin Company, 2002).
[43] Paul Valéry, *The Collected Works of Paul Valéry: The Art of Poetry* (New York: Vintage Books, 1961), 104 (original emphasis).
[44] See Katherine S. Gittes, *Framing the Canterbury Tales: Chaucer and the Medieval Frame Narrative Tradition* (New York: Praeger, 1991); and Rosen, *Bargaining For Reality*, 179.

may be added at any time rather than being limited in advance by the architect's design. In music, passages can be attached at will, rather than being governed by the original score, and are not constructed with a definite ending prescribed. Such classical poetry as the *qasida* exhibits the same agglutinative capacity. Yet all of this takes place within a frame, even if it is one that is not rigidly bounded. Just as the quasicrystalline pattern can go on to infinity, just as the edge of each cluster may exhibit the possibilities of variation and choice by meeting at a distinctive angle yet the entirety be cabined within a bounded domain, so, too, are the relations among men at once discontinuous and infinitely variable, yet shaped by the regularized ways in which attachments may be formed. To look up at a pattern that replicates and reinforces this God-given design in a space where the quotidian is temporarily suspended and reversed only to be set upright again is to attach the mundane world of reality to the cosmic through a readily comprehended representation of their natural unity.

It is in the same vein that the social meaning of space recurs in the tile patterns. It will be recalled that the Persian word *girih* means "knot." In Arabic, the root for "knot" (*a-r-b*) generates such words as "desire," "need," "resourceful," "clever," and "goal," thus conjoining the sense of enabling surround and intelligent direction. Indeed, the image of the knot often serves not only as a metaphor for irrigation systems and bodily humors but for the construction of social relationships, not just in the sense of tying people together or being linked to a guiding teacher or source of nurturance but in the subtler notion of enclosure as a form of freeing through opposition. A Moroccan informant, referring to the setting up of a loom as the "knotting" (*sdyia*), notes that the term:

evokes the capturing of the rūḥ, the alive breath of the loom ... A society is like a loom, it must be articulated. If you make the threads go simply straight, there can be no rūḥ, the textile opens up and everything unravels. Society is born from disagreement! If I disagree with you, if there is a discrepancy between us, a gap is open and the textile, the society, holds us together. It is like a knot ... if you want to tie something using the whole leaf, it breaks; if instead you split the leaf and knot the two halves by way of a third, it'll never break.[45]

---

[45] Stephania Pandolfo, *Impasse of the Angels: Scenes from a Moroccan Space of Memory* (Chicago: University of Chicago Press, 1998), 119 and 125.

In a more general sense, as mathematician Gregory Buck notes for a broad range of Arab decorative arts:

The designers evidently understand the fundamental facets of mathematical knot theory (which we now apply to DNA). They comprehend the symmetry properties some knots have (and others lack), and they clearly have command of the concept of alternating knots – if you trace any strand you will find that it travels under one crossing strand then over the next, and so on.... [H]ow does one even get started? The designs are so complex, the symmetries so demanding, that a novice could easily be flummoxed from the start.[46]

Such images, then, bespeak the expectations and uncertainties of everyday social life for the attentive Muslim – the difficulties of establishing an interwoven web of indebtedness, the knotty joinder of social relations, and the definition of the substantive by the spaces created among the strands. Moreover, these defined spaces resonate with the apprehension of social space in other key respects. One of the defining features of the cultures of the Middle East, for example, is a deep-seated ambivalence to power in all its manifestations. We see this not only in the political realm, where cartoons and joking serve to cut the powerful down to size, but in rituals and remarks about religious and legal figures who are thus reminded of their dependence on the choice a client may make of a patron upon whom he should depend. Spaces are often represented, therefore, as interstitial, as risking the danger of mixed categories, as the seedbeds of both chaos and choice. Images of interstitial space and facilitating knots pervade other conceptions as well. In the political realm, it is often the enemy's acknowledgement that is indispensable to the choice of leaders for one's own group, legitimacy arising not from inherited office but from stitching together a personalistic web of alliances. Even before being assigned to heaven or hell one may be placed in the betwixt-and-between realm of *barzakh*, a purgatory-like place set between categories where one awaits the final judgment.[47]

The patterns on the wall are the patterns of life and as such they are further replicated in and reinforced by other cultural artifacts. Take the example of poetry. It is one of the more striking features of the Quran,

46 Gregory Buck, "Algorithms of Boundless Beauty, a Review of Jean-Marc Caséra, 'Arabesques: Decorative Art in Morocco'," *Science* 292, no. 5516 (2001): 445–46, at 445.
47 See, generally, Christian Lange, *Paradise and Hell in Islamic Traditions* (Cambridge: Cambridge University Press, 2015).

as well as the sayings of the Prophet, that poets are unequivocally vilified.[48] The reason, though, is not far to seek. In these cultures, command of language is one of the most important tools one can possess for creating and servicing one's network of indebtedness. To control language is to control the definition of a situation; to be a man who is good at such endeavors is, in the Arabic vernacular, to be a man "of word." Yet the poet is dangerous. For he may capture the situation in terms that are antithetical to the revealed word, he may undermine the unity of the believers by splitting them into groups with competing visions of reality, and he may lead people to mix elements that adulterate the purity of The Message and thus propel the community into unbelief and chaos. The poet is simultaneously a threat to the community of believers and an indispensable creator of possible relationships, the resourceful embodiment of a rage for chaos and the one whose choices may bespeak a heartfelt rage for order. Far from being freed from the real world, the poet, as M. G. Carter suggests, constitutes the world.[49] Like the *girih* patterns, the poet does not merely repeat what has gone before; indeed, the danger he poses by capturing the categories of experience must be kept in check by the algorithm of an orderly, infinite, and renewable cosmos just as his designs, like those on the wall of a mosque, render visible the motion that describes a man who is free.

\* \* \*

[48] "In pre-Islamic Arabian society poetry played a leading role in political life. Poets were the propagandists of their tribes and it was thought they were inspired by jinns [genies; invisible creatures of the netherworld]. The Prophet knew, therefore, that he had to harness the power of poetry to the cause of Islam." Stephen Vernoit, "Artistic Expressions of Muslim Societies," in *The Cambridge Illustrated History of the Islamic World*, ed. Francis Robinson (Cambridge: Cambridge University Press, 1996), 250–90.

An alternative interpretation would suggest that the Prophet sought to eliminate poetry, rather than co-opt it, not because the poets were diabolically inspired but because they were socially dangerous: He had to reduce the threat that poets pose by their capacity to capture the terms of any issue – political, social, or religious – particularly since they might challenge the Prophet's own message. The poet's threat, along with doubt, is, of course, a central theme in Salman Rushdie's *Satanic Verses*. See Rosen, *The Culture of Islam*, 158–73.

[49] M. G. Carter, "Infinity and Lies in Medieval Islam," in *Philosophy and Arts in the Islamic World*, eds. U. Vermeulen and D. De Smet (Leuven: Uitgeveru Peeters, 1998), 233–42. For an ethnographic example of the role played by a Moroccan poet, see Clifford Geertz, "Art as a Cultural System," *Modern Language Notes* 91 (1976): 1473–99.

The real is as imagined as the imaginary.[50]

Clifford Geertz

That the quasicrystalline patterns have deep social significance should no longer come as a surprise to even the most ardent proponent of art as an expression only of emotional and aesthetic appeal. Indeed, as Geertz indicates generally, one must always go well beyond the confines of art to understand the meaning of art, just as one must for any cultural product. So, for example, the argument that Islamic art does not allow for the representation of humans may be misplaced. For the essence of mankind, in this worldview, is his need to maneuver in a world of uncertainty, forging the relationships that alone can fend off chaos. If, like quasicrystals, the world of reality is envisioned as knotty, edgy, cornucopian, infinitely extended, and ambivalent, then the interstitial enclosures that shape that world and the framework that, as the Quran repeatedly asserts, distinguishes between "the limits of God" and "the free domain of man," are also the shape of the human situation. One does not need a portrait or photographic representation to apprehend that essence when it is possible to capture it in a highly individualistic yet frame-bound pattern. Seen in that light the Muslim artist *is* rendering humans, and in a manner that is no less realistic for being abstract. So, too, other Muslim artistic themes – notably the arabesque – coalesce and radiate their social import by underscoring the relation of choice and chaos, infinite variation, and the equivalence of constituent parts that are central to the human condition.[51] As others have noted, the need such artistic representations address is for an object rich enough that society may see itself in it, and by that act deepen the relation one has to the broad array of implications that design entails.[52]

In their quest for understanding how such meanings inform a given society social scientists have taken a wide range of approaches.

[50] Clifford Geertz, *The Interpretation of Cultures* (New York: Basic Books, 1977).
[51] Hodgson argues that the arabesque crystallizes, through its possibility of infinite repetition and equality of component parts, a distinctively Islamic social "style," one that can, for example, be found as much in the way historical tales are told as in artistic forms. Marshall G. S. Hodgson, *The Venture of Islam*, Vol. II (Chicago: University of Chicago Press, 1974), 345.
[52] Paraphrasing Geertz, "Art as a Cultural System," 1483, who is paraphrasing Michael Baxendall, *Painting and Experience in Fifteenth Century Italy* (Oxford: Clarendon Press, 1972).

Clifford Geertz, for example, maintains "that works of art are elaborate mechanisms for defining social relationships, sustaining social rules, and strengthening social values.... [Artists] materialize a way of experiencing, bring a particular cast of mind out into the world of objects, where men can look at it."[53] To this one might simply add that "looking" may also be described as "recognizing," such that what is portrayed fits, makes sense, and is seen as the way things are. Andrew Gell makes a somewhat different point, arguing that artistic objects provoke attachments – that far from being passive, art is instrumental in influencing the actions of others.[54] He agrees with Marilyn Strathern's suggestion that relations are substantially between persons and things, with the latter being substituted for the former in a number of instances. It is, she suggests, often the partible person, subject to the power of art to mediate the relations individuals form with reference to it, who is irresistibly embroiled in the artist's work.[55]

In the Middle Eastern context, each of these perspectives casts a useful light on the social implications of the mosaic patterns. But Gell's notion of art provoking relations may be less applicable to this region than to societies without a tradition of literacy and in which the representations are seen as possessing the power to affect the world more than reflect it. So, too, Strathern's point about the partible person's approach to art may be less true for the Middle East than among the people of New Guinea, where she has worked. In Middle Eastern cultures, things are not substitutes for persons in any fungible sense, personhood is not fractionable, and emphasis is placed not on role-playing but on maintaining the unity and totality of one's identity through negotiated ties to others. Indeed, given that inapposite relationships risk admixture (*shirk*) and hence chaos (*fitna*), it is the vision of nonreplicating, infinitely variable, choice-determined maneuvering that is made evident in the mosaics mounted in the one place where individuals take a break from the market-like fray to recall the principles that give the world order. It is not an attitude of simply contemplating the divinity, as Burckhardt

---

[53] Clifford Geertz, *Local Knowledge* (New York: Basic Books, 1983), 99.
[54] Andrew Gell, *Art and Agency: An Anthropological Theory* (Oxford: Oxford University Press, 1998).
[55] Marilyn Strathern, *The Gender of the Gift: Problems with Women and Problems with Society in Melanesian Anthropology* (Berkeley: University of California Press, 1986).

and others claim[56]; it is one of seeing the world as it has been created for mankind and recognizing how one must sustain one's expectations within it. Ever attentive to their surround, Middle Easterners see themselves in a world of active relationships, not one in which mere gazing will create and settle the image of oneself and one's dependents.

We may never know exactly what prompted the Muslim artists to plumb the depths of symmetry. Did they see that in the quasicrystalline there is a hierarchy of clusters – "layer by layer and hierarchical growth" – that seems to accord, through its "mysterious interlocks," with the world Allah has given us? If the Western scientists sought in the formulae a way to conjoin theory and the material, did these artisans seek to represent the unity of the material and the incorporeal, where no gap could adulterate the coherence of the worldly and the spiritual? What is very likely is that what could be represented on the wall of a sacred place in these societies constitutes a template for that world of reasoned relationships it is incumbent upon humans to realize and sustain. It is both "a model of and a model for" a construct of the imagination. We may never know the full array of intentions that went into discovering how this world could be accessed through a complex mathematical device nor every way in which those viewing such designs imputed meaning to them. There is no doubt some truth in the proposition that Islamic patterns may serve their viewers as "a source of contemplation that allows our minds to wander and contemplate the infinite."[57] But one must be cautious about projecting our own aesthetic sensibilities, for whatever else may be true these representations are deeply embedded in a world of common-sense relationships, and it is very possible that the desire to show this bargained-for reality may have prompted the search for the formula by which such a cosmos could be made manifest. And it is, perhaps, in the quest for that underlying order and in the apprehension of the visual as a guide to it that the Muslim viewers can simultaneously recognize and pursue the kind of world into which Allah has so astonishingly implanted them.

---

[56] Burckhardt, "The Void in Islamic Art." This is no less true for Sufi orders and other mystical sects of Islam. For the belief is common to these groupings, as to the attributes of a holy "madman," that one is responding to an order that is not visible to inhabitants of our everyday world but – rather like the djinns, those Quranically validated creatures of the parallel netherworld – such individuals are adhering to a coherent order that is similar in many respects to our own.
[57] Dabbour, *Geometric*, 391.

# PART II

# *Legal*

# 2 | *Tribal Law as Islamic Law*
## *The Berber Case*

*There is no Islamic law. Not in the singular. Rather, there is a wide range of practices that fit comfortably under that broad rubric. Unlike the Hebrew Bible, for example, the Quran is not filled with layer upon layer of specific legal directives: Inheritance rules and a constant yet generalized emphasis on contractual relations are certainly included, but much is left uncodified and, given such Prophetic Traditions as the proposition that "my community will not agree in error," ample room is left for local practice. It is true that the diverse schools of law that developed after the Prophet's death set forth detailed rules, and though many features are shared in common, there remain significant differences among them. But for the most part, Islamic law as it is actually enacted is perhaps best seen not as a unified entity but in a theme and variation sense.*

*And surely those variations can be substantial, from the matrilineal Muslims of Malaysia whose inheritance practices vary from those of Wahhabi Arabia to the uncharacteristic power of women to divorce men among some Muslims of northwest Africa. Law and custom thus intersect, resulting not in the victory of one pure form over another but in a broad array of localized amalgams. Legal hybrids, simultaneous alternatives, and situational applications thus result from the action of one form of law in the presence of another. To look closely, whether in the case of Islamic law or other world-spanning regimes, at any one variant is insufficient to appreciate the full extent of diversity, but it does afford an entrée to the processes that underlie the capacity for variation itself. To choose the example of the Berbers of North Africa is, therefore, to explore the relation of culture, law, and custom in ways that may help us to understand how Islam and its approach to law have spread throughout so much of the world while still giving considerable scope and legitimacy to the local.*

\* \* \*

This essay was first delivered at Harvard Law School's Islamic Law Program while the author was serving as a Senior Fellow. I am grateful for the comments of the participants in the discussion.

41

The Berbers of North Africa occupy an intriguing position in the Muslim world. Having accepted Islam in the early years of the Arab expansion – yet to this day regarded by some of the Arabic-speakers as only lightly Islamized – the Berbers, like other converts in history, have retained some of their earlier, pre-Islamic practices. More importantly, Berbers envision those practices not as separable from Islam but *as* Islamic. In doing so they partake of several propositions that continue to facilitate Islam's absorption of diverse peoples.

First, there is the widely recognized idea that whatever does not clearly contradict a central tenet of Islam is not to be regarded as incompatible with the faith. Obviously a belief in one God and Muhammad as the last in the line of prophets is not to be adulterated. Beyond that, however, Islam, as many commenters have noted, is what Muslims believe and do. And in the case of the Berbers, certain practices that may not seem to accord with orthodox Islam are supported by the recognized importance of local custom. For example, Berbers commonly allow less inheritance for women than the Quran and Maliki school of Islamic law permit, they have (particularly in the past) made greater use of collective oaths, and (when not overborn by warlords and states) employed fines and compensation somewhat more than physical punishment or imprisonment.

Second, there is the central importance of custom in Islamic law. The standard view among Western scholars of Islam is that the sources of Islamic law are limited to the Quran, the authoritative acts and utterances of the Prophet, and the teachings of the schools of law that developed in the years after Muhammad's death. Drawing implicitly on their background in the civil law systems of Europe (rather than the common law systems stemming from Great Britain), these scholars have approached custom as something that stands apart from law and ceases to have a separate identity once incorporated within the law. Islamic law, however, takes no such approach. It is true that scholars and legists often opposed the use of custom, arguing strenuously that only the revealed sources should constitute the basis for the shari'a. But the use of legal fictions (*hiyal*) and actual deference to local customs was common in the everyday practice of the law. So, for example, the right of preemption in the purchase of a neighbor's property, though not recognized in the canon, was available. So, too, were various ways of getting around the ban on usury. It would be more accurate, therefore, to say that Islamic law sees custom as distinctive yet integral to the law, even though Muslim scholars disagree as to its status as an actual source of law.

Indeed, when custom is at issue, the assumption, found in text and practice in every age and part of the Islamic world, is clear: Custom *is* Islamic and may even take precedence over the formal religious law. Thus we find the common saying in North Africa that "custom governs over the shari'a" (*'urf kat- ḥakem 'al shr'a*) or that "a contractual stipulation (*shert*) takes precedence over the shari'a." Such assertions are seen not as contradictions of the Sacred Law but as fulfillments of its deeper purpose (*maqāṣid*), namely, to allow scope for humans, endowed by God with reason, to forge the relationships through which a Community of Believers (*umma*) can alone hope to do good, avoid evil, and sustain itself against chaos (*fitna*).

Given its amalgamative quality, Islamic law can be incorporated in local practice without the local populace feeling that they have lost their own distinctive legal schema. Moreover, many local practices – both substantive and procedural – fit rather well with the structures of Islamic law developed by clerics and governmental agents. It is true that many of the Muslim scholars looked down on local law-ways. Yet, the 'high' normative versions of Islamic law clearly partake of such similarities with many local variants as to render their interdigitation all the more viable. This is particularly the case in the relation of Berber law to 'formal' Islamic law. And the point of connection that will be suggested here is that both partake of many aspects of what might be called a broader 'tribal ethos' that pervades the law of the jurisconsults and the law of the local alike. It is, therefore, helpful, to consider first certain aspects of tribal culture and its extension as an informing ethos.

Tribes have usually been analyzed in one of two ways – either as a stage in the cultural evolution of human societies (the famous: band → tribe → chiefdom → state progression) or as structural forms based on language, kinship, and territory. However, neither of these formulations could be sustained as more examples were added to our knowledge, leading many anthropologists to give up on the concept of tribe altogether. But if we switch our metaphors from the crystalline and evolutionary to images of the malleable and cultural a more useful approach may perhaps be suggested.

Consider the amoeba. If you ask, "what is the shape of an amoeba?" you have already missed the point, for what is crucial to amoebas is not their momentary form but their capacity for shape-shifting. Similarly, tribes have a series of informing cultural orientations that can produce different structural outcomes. Among these features are the following:

1. Tribes do not like too much power in too few hands for too long a period of time. They have multiple devices for dividing and indeed undermining power, from the use of such levelling devices as ritual reversals, structured joking patterns, and rotation of purpose-specific leadership, to forms of redistribution that ensure wealth cannot be converted into enduring power. Indeed, such mechanisms of social control have as a predominant aim the goal of placing people back into working relationships with one another, bonds of mutual indebtedness being more likely to prevent social chaos (*fitna*) than insisting on uniform rights unmodified by case-by-case considerations.

2. Reciprocity is vital. Relationships demand measured, though often strategic, return. Surplus is subject to redistribution, particularly to fend off starvation by the weakest.

3. Kinship is emphasized but not rigidly fixed. Genealogical manipulation, adoption of outsiders, and recasting history are adaptive devices for coping with changing circumstances.

4. Far from being characterized by a loss of individuality, tribal peoples are intensely personalistic. Individuals' character and relationships define them rather than inherited position or kin connections alone.

5. Individuals are on the same moral plane. Tribes are not primitive democracies, but no one person can claim moral superiority over another as a matter of birth or momentary position.

6. Ambivalence is played up, both in the highly contextual application of norms and as a mechanism for avoiding violence by acknowledging each individual's sense of legitimate injury.

7. When it comes to legal disputes, a broad range of information is relevant to each inquire and any resolution must be fashioned to the case rather than being resolved by a mechanical appraisal of decontextualized acts.

If we set these features alongside a number of aspects of Berber customary law (*'urf, izerf*) and Islamic law (*sharī'a*), we can see a wide range of common factors. First, the bounds of relevance are cast quite widely, it being vital to understand who each person is in relation to others and hence what the full range of their dispute may entail. For example, a marital dispute may involve interfamilial property quarrels or a fight over land may harken back to unresolved inheritance issues. In such a system, it is only by seeing all precipitating factors in context that one can achieve a resolution that is more-or-less acceptable to all parties. Indeed, second, the goal is not so much to ascertain rights and obligations as it is to place the contending parties in a situation where they can return to negotiating their own relationship. Third, in order to determine facts the primary emphasis falls on establishing the veracity of those presenting them. Whether one uses a system of certifying reliable witnesses for future disputes based on an individual's connections and reputation in the community or by assigning oath-taking based on who is regarded as most likely to know the truth, the embedded nature of the individual within a network of social relations is taken as an indicator of both credibility and consequence. Collective oaths bring a fuller set of factors into the case, informal song duels bring out public opinion, and even the payment of blood money (*diya*) – which is still relevant in Iran, Pakistan, the UAE, Saudi Arabia, parts of Iraq, and the Horn of Africa – emphasizes the familial and per-sonalistic nature of the resolution that is sought. Custom, in particular, comes into play, whether in organized courtroom proceedings or in resolution through intermediaries, even if it displaces mainstream Islamic law precepts.

If, then, we take a number of such features as they are manifested in normative Maliki Islamic law in North Africa and set them alongside comparable features of Berber customary law-ways the parallels are quite striking:

| Berber 'urf/izerf | Shari'a |
|:---:|:---:|
| Emphasis on contractual relations | Same |
| Use of individual and collective oaths | Same |
| Mediation by 'big men' and descendants of the Prophet (*shurafa'*) | Go-between (*wasīta*), *shurafa'*, judge (*qadi*) as mediators |
| Property as beneficial use and relational | Same |
| Focus on the individual's personal network | Reliable witness certification |
| Oral testimony | Writing as the reduction of the oral |
| Focus on consequences for other relationships | Same |

| | |
|---|---|
| Mechanisms for sharing | Poor can sue for support by rich |
| Goal is to reconstitute working relationships | Same |
| "Adoption" occurs through kinship fictions | No formal adoption, but ways around |
| Blood payments to limit violence | Only informally in North Africa |
| Confiscation, limited but possible | "If you're away your right is away" |
| "Not unduly concerned with rules" | More rules, but context is crucial |
| Ease of divorce, women have property | Women win majority of cases; habus |
| Custom as a source of law | Same |
| Use of equity and public interest | Same |
| Women win cases frequently | Women win most family law cases |

There are a number of points worth elaborating from this brief comparison. Note, for example, that in both instances, procedure is vital – in many cases more so than substantive rules. The use of oaths as a fact-finding mechanism, the employment of intermediaries where possible, the constant exploration of the parties' broader relationship – these and many other features that could be listed indicate that the mechanisms by which matters are addressed is integral to the goal of reconciliation and the avoidance of further social chaos. Moreover, an emphasis on procedures of the sort used by these two variants also underscores the flexibility of the system, for not only are the rules of procedure rather open-textured but granting them priority channels judicial discretion toward a middle course of neither too much variation nor too restrictive a consideration of the relevant.

A second feature shared by both is the stress on oral testimony. Notwithstanding the penchant of Muslim courts for keeping records, it is, as I have argued elsewhere, best to see written forms of evidence as the reduction to writing of oral testimony.[1] That is, the question is

---

[1] See the discussion of evidence in Lawrence Rosen, *The Anthropology of Justice: Law as Culture in Islamic Society* (Cambridge: Cambridge University Press, 1989).

not necessarily whether something was correctly inscribed but who it is that is speaking through this piece of paper. In this sense, it is not the text that makes the person believable but the person who makes any text believable. By inspecting the document as one would a present witness – asking about the party's background, knowledge, connections, etc. – focus is placed on credibility through interconnected relationships, the underlying presumption being that a person of known embeddedness is less likely to risk adversely affecting a carefully negotiated network by lying. Here, too, one can see (as in any legal system) a particular range of cultural assumptions about persons, relations, and consequences that deeply inform both procedural and substantive law.

The comparison also highlights the pragmatism of both systems. The concept of beneficial use, whether in irrigation or 'abandoned' land, underscores the tribal ethos of resources less as matters of dominion than of placement in the service of relationships. So, too, custom often serves not as a set of stultifying norms but as mechanisms for personalizing results, tempering strict rules, and focusing attention on goals and not just rules. So, to cite but one example, cases show that often a formal element of a contract may not have been met yet those deciding the dispute emphasize that the broader purpose of placing something in productive use has been achieved and therefore some aspect of the contract should be preserved. Similarly, in a child custody dispute, where Islamic or state law are quite clear, the decision may be made to award control to the party who is better educated, employed, or admired in the community notwithstanding the statute or scholars' opinions awarding custody by age and kinship. The Islamic law concepts of *istislah* and *istihsan* – of deciding what is equitable and in the public interest even when 'the law' commends otherwise – is yet another instance of the pragmatism and personalism of both systems and of a shared orientation toward using custom as a waypoint in reaching such conclusions.

In a sense, this similarity between shari'a and Berber law should not come as a surprise. Undoubtedly, there was some interchange over the centuries between Berbers and Arabs in terms of Islamic law, but well into the colonial period there is no question that Berber legal regimes were quite distinct. The similarities between the two may be attributable not to the interchange or imposition of the one on the other but to a common orientation that not only facilitated interchange but the broader socio-religious influences shared by both. Islam and its law

**Figure 2.1** French officer oversees Berber law court. Public domain. Credit: Michael Peyron.

were forged in the context of the tribal ethos previously described, one that displays many similar features in the culture and legal regimes of both Arabs and Berbers. Thus even if one were not a member of an actual tribe, the features that are characteristic of tribes reach over into the broader society, urban no less than rural, and suffuse multiple domains, the legal among them. Indeed, many dichotomies posed by Western observers – urban vs. rural, nomad vs. settled – do not constitute sharp cleavages in the Arabo-Berber world. Colonial encounters and national independence have, of course, dramatically affected both Berber law and the application of the shari'a. Particularly in Algeria, but also in Tunisia and Morocco, the French carefully studied Berber customary law and set about including it within their control (Figure 2.1). Whereas the British in India, for example, sought to redact Muslim and Hindu law, the French exercised their power mainly through bureaucratic oversight. When the French Protectorate over Morocco began in 1912 – the northern strip of the country being under Spanish control – the colonizers were quite prepared to leave the Berbers to handle most of their own legal affairs, including for a short time even criminal matters. Then, in 1930, as nationalism began to fluoresce, the French issued the famous Berber Dahir (edict) that sought to place the Arabs under Islamic law and the Berbers under their own customary law. The effect, however, was the exact opposite of what the French expected. Instead of separating them the edict brought Berbers and Arabs together, the former being incensed that people did not understand that they regarded their customary law *as* Islamic law, not separate from it, the latter being alienated by further French interference in the extension of normative Islam and Moroccan unity. Throughout the remaining quarter century before Morocco achieved independence there were some 145 Berber law courts and six *'urf* appellate courts that continued to operate in the country, but they all ceased operation with Moroccan independence in 1956.

Juxtaposing Berber and Islamic law not only adds to understanding how a shared tribal ethos may suffuse multiple domains and institutions: It might also suggest a wider reading of Muslim history in general. Islam arose in a tribal context and spread rather quickly to a wide range of tribes and communities infused with a tribal ethos, a spread that tends to be attributed to the role of warfare, trade, and religious proselytizing. But it is possible that law played no less important a role. For if local practice that did not contradict one of the relatively few legal precepts in the Quran – and if the Quran itself (Sura 7:199) validates custom – then newly converted groups could not only maintain their customs but could also regard them *as* Islamic. And if we see the Prophet as having a sociological jurisprudence – with an emphasis on contract, procedure, personal credibility, etc. – then perhaps we might look more closely at the role of law in the spread of Islam for its amalgamative capacity rather than as a strict set of imposed legal doctrines and attendant personnel.[2]

Whether Berber law has a future remains very uncertain. The Amazigh (Berber) revival – of literature, music, and language – is a matter that each of the North African nations has sought to control through co-opting. While there have been numerous displays of the Berber flag and pan-national conferences have been held to promote Berber culture, government programs have been half-hearted if not stultifying (Figure 2.2). Where once Berber children were forbidden to speak a Berber dialect at school now there are programs for its

---

[2] See Lawrence Rosen, "Muhammad's Sociological Jurisprudence," in Lawrence Rosen, *The Justice of Islam* (Oxford: Oxford University Press, 2000), 176–86.

**Figure 2.2** Protester raises Berber flag. Credit: Jalal Morchidi/Anadolu Agency/Getty Images.

teaching; where once there were radio stations that studiously avoided any use of Berber, now there are news programs in the different variants. But the school programs are limited and the newscasts are said to be elementary and linguistically impoverished. Morocco's parliament subsequently put an end to the Royal Institute set up to promote Berber culture (Figure 2.3). Other North African governments have expressed concern about Berber populism. For the most part Berber protests in Morocco have tended to be more about gaining access to the system than separation from it. It is, of course, possible that Berber identity is lying dormant. To recapture an earlier analogy: Just as an amoeba can go into a cyst form when needed, only to emerge from seeming death at a later time, so it might be possible for further expressions of Berber

**Figure 2.3** Moroccan Berber Institute cartoon. The figure in the jar, the Berber symbol for a free man, is seen here as confined by government policies. Courtesy: Rachid Raha, Le Monde Amazigh.

culture to be hunkered down awaiting more favorable circumstances. As Berber cultural identity fluoresces throughout North Africa, the question thus arises whether even Berber law may re-emerge to some extent, in some locales, alongside the elaboration of Berber dialects, rituals, and other cultural identifiers. But, given its long hiatus and that so many relationships (marital, land titling, etc.) have been constructed through national and mainstream Islamic law, the revival of Berber law in any direct form is unlikely. Nevertheless, for scholars and participants alike the Berber law example remains a telling instance of how a highly elaborated pan-national system of law may map rather easily onto local practice to yield neither a simple hybrid nor a situationally specific choice of laws but a system in which the local may be envisioned as a variation on the dominant law thereby gaining legitimacy through (and for) both sources. It is in that form, rather than as a falling away from some primordial ideal or bastardized amalgam unworthy of respect, that Berber law may long remain at once alive in the local imaginary and enfolded within the larger framework of the Sacred Law.

# 3 | The Meaning of the Gift

*What should an anthropologist do when he or she encounters people for the first time in the field? My initial teacher in anthropology told me to sit down and eat with them. Others have suggested presenting a gift, a form of exchange that has long been at the heart of the anthropologist's personal and observational experience as well as in the construction of theories based on that experience. In the Muslim world, gift-giving is crucial to social relations, legal rule-making, religious validation, and personal maneuvering. It also forms an important part of the political backdrop, whether in the hands of a monarch or the ingratiation by a supplicant. As such, the gift constitutes a test of how a web of socioeconomic connections serves to vitalize interpersonal encounters and support a society's characteristic design. Any account of how Muslims in the Middle East encounter one another would, therefore, be incomplete without understanding the life-engendering nature of gifts.*

*

To take to give is all, return what is hungrily given.

*Dylan Thomas*

A gift is just a loan.

*Rachel Persky*

Objects possessed, objects bestowed: As Dylan Thomas indicates, the meaning of each goes well beyond the material nature of the thing or having it within one's grasp. After all, an object from one's youth or a keepsake from the departed carries meaning beyond the tactile, and a Proustian madeleine is more than a "'tween-meals snack." So, too, a gift – whether to a particular person or as a charitable contribution – is not just the parting with an object, nor is fixing its worth simply a matter of the market price. Whatever the personal import of one's offering more

52

is often at stake: the relationship formed through the prestation, the role of the state in controlling its disposition, and the balancing of interests and intentions in law, religion, and expressive symbols. It would, therefore, be misleading to reduce the meaning of a gift to a single consequence, but it would be equally misleading to fail to note the cultural factors that permeate such actions in the time, place, and culture of which they are so vital a part. To consider the meaning of gifts in the context of the Arabo-Berber world is, as in any anthropological venture, to unpack the publicly shared symbols by which the participants themselves conceive of their experiences, and to do so by seeing the connections among multiple domains that so seemingly simple a matter as a gift can reveal.

But let's start closer to home. Suppose you give your roommate a present on her birthday. On your birthday she gives you – nothing. Next year on her birthday you give her another present. On your birthday she gives you – nothing. How do you feel about that? If resentful or just disappointed, why? After all, isn't a gift just a freewill offering, a grant of something with no claim or even expectation of return? And yet, to say you feel no sense of injury by your roommate's inaction sounds disingenuous at best: Surely you do feel hurt. So the question remains, why? For social scientists, the starting point in addressing this seeming contradiction brings us to the work of Marcel Mauss.

In *The Gift*, Mauss argued that gifts actually stitch a society together by some form of elaborate reciprocation that, reinforced by concepts of honor, status, and supernatural sanction, vitalize the shared representations that characterize the society. Though grounded in Durkheimian theory, Mauss parts from his mentor by emphasizing that in small-scale societies solidarity is not merely the mechanical repetition of identical acts among all members but that, in Adam Smith's sense of the concept, gifting operates as a kind of invisible hand of which people are nevertheless quite aware and which, within bounds, they both replicate and manipulate. Moreover, Mauss saw gifts as integral to all other domains of social engagement so that, for example, a wedding gift was also a bond between separate groups, validated often by divine invocation, and generating a series of subsidiary activities that energize a wide range of socioeconomic ties. Positioned against both utilitarianism and Marxism, Mauss' vision firmly links multiple domains into a coherent pattern even though his theory ignored the gift's role in levelling

differences – and hence the accumulation of power – in many of the
societies he chose as his exemplars.

If we turn, then, to gift-giving in the portions of the Arabo-Berber
world with which I am most familiar we need to consider three things
in particular: how gifts have been articulated in the Islamic law and
custom of the region, how gifts facilitate or obscure everyday relationships, and how – as a vehicle for creating relations among strangers –
they succeed or fail to create relations of trust in a society wary of
social chaos.[1]

The offer and acceptance of a gift takes place against a backdrop of
religious and legal considerations.[2] Transfers of property during the
lifetime of the donor are commended by both prophetic tradition and
the customs of most Muslim cultures: "Send presents to each other
to increase your mutual love," said the Prophet – though the premier
redactor of the Traditions of the Prophet (*ḥadīth*), Muhammad ibn
Isma'il al-Bukhari, renders the last clause as, "gifts take away ran-
cor." The Arabic term for a gift, *hadīya*, comes from a root meaning
"to guide someone on the right way," and in related derivatives indicates "moving forward," "exchanging," and "conferring something
on another." Despite the fact that gifts may create bonds of mutual
indebtedness and thus reduce the fear of social chaos (*fitna*), Islamic
law treats ordinary gifts as straightforward donations that should
entail no legal obligations. Thus the donor must surrender possession
of the property (either actually or, in some variants, constructively),
the recipient must accept it (the declaration of the gift being made
either orally or in writing by anyone otherwise capable of entering
into a contract), and the recipient must be a living person. Certain
restrictions apply: The gift may not be made with the intention of
avoiding the donor's debts, the property must presently exist, a gift

---

[1] On the concept of trust, see my chapter, "Whom Do You Trust? Structuring
Confidence in Arab Society and Law," in Lawrence Rosen, *The Justice of Islam*
(Oxford: Oxford University Press, 2000), 133–50.

[2] Among the most accessible background sources on the Islamic law of gifts
are: Yvon Linant de Bellefonds, *Des donations en droit musulman* (Cairo: D.
Photiadis, 1935), and his "Hiba," in *Encyclopedia of Islam*, 2d ed., Vol. 3, ed.
Bernard Lewis, et al. (Leiden, Netherlands: E. J. Brill, 1971), 350–51; Franz
Rosenthal, "Gifts and Bribes," *Proceedings of the American Philosophical
Society*, 108 (1964), 135–44, and his "Hiba," In *Encyclopedia of Islam*, 2d
ed., Vol. 3, Bernard Lewis, et al., eds. (Leiden, Netherlands: E. J. Brill, 1971),
342–50.

made in one's final illness may not exceed the one-third that could be transferred by testament, and while a gift is valid that carries a condition (so long as there is no actual exchange) a gift that depends on a condition first being met is not valid.

Additionally, a gift must not be separable from other items (e.g., one cannot give land exclusive of the crops on it), the object must generally be owned privately rather than communally, and the property must be of known value and itself be lawful (hence a forbidden substance, like liquor, may not be the subject of a gift).[3] There is variation among the schools of Islamic law on certain aspects of gift-giving. The Maliki school (which is dominant in North Africa) permits the donor to retain a life interest in the property, while the Hanafi permits a gift used as support, payment of another's debts, or as part of an exchange that services the recipient's needs or obligations. Once the prerequisites of a lawful gift have been met, it cannot generally be revoked – except, in some schools of Islamic law, by the donor's father or a male ascendant – especially if it is a gift to a close relative or spouse.

There is also the intriguing Tradition of the Prophet in which he said: "Accept invitations, do not refuse gifts, and do not beat the Muslims." Why these three propositions are linked is unclear. The first and second suggest that it is the relationship that is the vital aspect of the gift; the third seems out of place. If there is a logic to the triad, however, it may still be the importance of the relational, for beating a person will make another more resentful, less likely to be an ally in another context, and much less likely to engage in the reciprocity that the invitation and the gift affirm. Similarly, Islamic commenters usually indicate that one may, in fact, refuse a gift but only if accepting it is likely to lead one into sin. What is left unsaid is how one ought to gauge the return prestation. Often the trick is to give back more than was offered in order to create precisely that relationship of debt that is crucial to social relations. Indeed, in debt there is relationship: Calling things equal is

---

[3] The overwhelming majority of Muslim scholars and nations permit the donation (but not the sale) of a body organ after death or during one's lifetime (provided it does not harm the donor). See, generally, Abdulaziz Sachedina, *Islamic Biomedical Ethics* (Oxford: Oxford University Press, 2009). A sacrifice may also be seen as a form of gift: For the background case of the Prophet's sacrifice of camels and the gift of his hair shortly before he died, see Brannon Wheeler, "Gift of the Body in Islam: The Prophet Muhammad's Camel Sacrifice and Distribution of Hair and Nails at His Farewell Pilgrimage," *Numen*, 57 (2010), 341–88.

tantamount to calling off a relationship since it is the running imbalance of obligation that keeps the "game" of forging social bonds alive. Indeed, such an interpretation is not incompatible with another Hadith of the Prophet which says, "Whoever does you a favor, respond in kind, and if you cannot find the means of doing so, then keep praying for him until you think that you have responded in kind."

Certain themes thus unite the disparate elements of Islamic gift laws and practices. As in prayer, the gift lies in its intention (*niya*), an intention that is largely regarded as manifested by one's acts. Just as in contract and criminal law – to say nothing of everyday attributions of another's state of mind – people are presumed to possess the necessary inner state or they would not engage in the actions they do.[4] Deception is, of course, not unimaginable, but the cultural logic – the cultural fiction, if one prefers – is, like legal fictions, both a way of remaining true to the proposition that intent matters and a practical way to imagine that one is accessing it. Indeed, as Bourdieu notes, particularly when the gift is a charitable contribution (but not necessarily in that situation alone), a double fiction is operative, namely that the donor is giving without expectation of return and that the recipient is not accepting the gift with the condition of reciprocation.[5] In fact, both may expect the transaction to involve a return, whether (in the case of charity) by the divinity making the return or by the donée effectively acknowledging the superior position of the donor. In this sense, the religious and social sanctions and expectations may serve to preserve the social status quo as well as, in the case of charity to the poor, keeping the less fortunate both peaceful and grateful.

Gifts may, therefore, have the purpose of avoiding conflict and creating or reaffirming social bonds. Thus a father may still maintain control of his offspring by being permitted to revoke a gift, whereas the stress on the irrevocable nature of gifts to other relatives may help to cut off intrafamilial disputes.[6] So important are gifts to the construction of

[4] See Lawrence Rosen, *The Culture of Islam* (Chicago: University of Chicago Press, 2002), 108–29.
[5] On the development of the concept of gift in Bourdieu's work, see Ilana F. Silber, "Bourdieu's Gift to Gift Theory: An Unacknowledged Trajectory," *Sociological Theory*, 27, 2 (June 2009), 173–190.
[6] For background and comparative examples, see Noor Liza Mohamed Said, et al., "Revocation of Gift (Hibah) According to Islamic Law and Its Practice under Syria Civil Law 1949," *International Business Management*, 7, 1 (2013), 1–7.

the bonds of obligation that hold relationships and society as a whole together that one Tradition of the Prophet, as collected by Bukhari, holds that: "It is unlawful for a person to give a gift then later take it back, except for a father (to his son), and whoever does so is like a dog that eats, then vomits, and returns to eat its vomit."

Though it may not be formally denominated as such, a gift is seen in Islamic thought as a form of contract, and thus partakes not only of the Prophet's admonition to engage in gift-giving but the Qur'anic emphasis on keeping to one's contracts (e.g., Sura 2:282, 5:1). In and of themselves, gifts do not nominally create a situation of mutual obligation or underscore a bond between social equals. To the contrary, they may constitute the expectation of exchange between those who are superior and those who are actually or potentially dependent. On one occasion, for example, I saw a Moroccan present an overflowing gift of his garden produce to a man whose forebearer had served as a patron to the donor's family on past occasions – a benefactor whose help might be sought again in the future. Thus the term *hiba*, normally applied to any grant or donation, also refers to those "gifts" that demonstrate the expected remuneration of client to patron, or ruled to ruler.[7] The same term is found in early Islamic documents indicating a gift to one's future father-in-law (which might be added to the bride's dowry), while Berber informants have indicated that a bride's brother may be given a payment by her intended as a way of easing any tension between the two.[8] The term used for this payment, however, is that for a bribe, *rishwa*. Indeed, judges or military commanders were, at certain moments and places, regarded as "entitled" to the "gifts" that confirmed their positions and relations. Since the mid-twentieth century, many Muslim countries have codified the laws of gift giving, commonly assimilating them to the law of obligations and contracts generally, while "gifts" to officials exist outside of formal law.

Note, too, that many rules of gift-giving are couched in the present tense. The same is true in Islamic contract law, where (notwithstanding

[7] On the exchange of gifts of art among rulers and those close to them, see Linda Komaroff, *The Gift Tradition in Islamic Art* (New Haven: Yale University Press, 2012).
[8] On practices in the early Islamic period, including gifts to a future father-in-law, see, e.g., Youssef Rapoport, "Matrimonial Gifts in Early Islamic Egypt," *Islamic Law and Society*, 7, 1 (2000), 1–36.

various legal fictions and extralegal maneuvers to the contrary) trans-
actions are not oriented toward specific future exchanges but relationships forged at the moment of agreement. Indeed, many commenters
refer to gift-giving as a form of contract. Like contracts a gift estab-
lishes and ratifies an actual tie between the parties which, in turn,
becomes a key aspect of one's social identity. For to know another
is to know with whom he has bonds of indebtedness, who his network of potential allies embraces, and hence how any action of one's
own toward this individual might affect or be affected by a much
wider range of persons. Gifts, then, are part of the weft and warp of
the web of obligations any man must establish in order to be a man
whose actions have consequences – indeed, quite simply, to be a man.
This emphasis appears quite markedly, for example, in the course of
arranging a marriage.

The raising of the bridewealth payment (*ṣdāq, mahr*) is what makes
a marriage valid, rather than any religious ceremony. While the bridewealth is often regarded as a gift to secure the bride against widow-
hood or divorce, the contracted sum is commonly accompanied by
additional gifts which may or may not be regarded, customarily and
by law, as part of the bridewealth itself. More to the point, since it is
marriage that significantly defines a man and raising the bridewealth
usually requires that a man rely on his relatives and associates, the
process of collecting the sums necessary creates and demonstrates
that he possesses a network of allies, the defining feature of manhood. Moreover, transfer of the bridewealth, like contracts and gifts,
is couched in terms of present relationships, a network created by
and around an individual exercising his God-given rational capacities
to forge a set of relations that collectively constitute the orderly and
peaceful community of believers (*umma*). Thus, the entire marriage
process, with its gifts and contractual transfers, must be seen as a key
vehicle for a man proving his connectedness to a world of obligations
and hence to being a man who moves to effect in the world.

Gifts also replicate other principles that are central to both law and
custom. We saw, for example, that a gift of property must include the
fruits that may be derived from that property. In refusing to separate
the two elements, the law of gifts partakes of the broader principle
that one ought to make beneficial use of any property and that, under
certain circumstances (adverse possession, absence for a specified time,
the needs of others), one may lose property to someone who can make

full use of it.[9] The gift may, then, replicate some aspects of the broader concept that, whatever the source of one's dominion, use of productive items is expected and may even constitute an unwritten condition of its attribution.

Gifts, like contracts, vary in meaning with their overall contexts. A gift to charity is not the same as one in a ceremonial situation, nor are any of the forms of conducing reciprocation without their own variations or implications. A gift may, for example, imply a compulsory return, whether in kind, equivalence, or increased value. Thus a sacrifice at a saintly shrine as a vehicle for compelling the saint to return life in some form – as pregnancy for a barren woman, health for a dying child, or cure for a mortal ailment – is a gift only in the sense that it seeks to right an imbalance. Indeed, in the North African context, it is seen as a burden the saint is not free to deny. In that regard – and employing the same term – it replicates in the spiritual domain the conditional curse (*'ar*) that may be used toward another human being or group to compel a life-supporting response, such as sanctuary from an enemy or support in an important election.[10]

Gifts across religious/ethnic lines pose their own considerations. It was very common in North Africa, when significant numbers of Jews were interspersed among the Muslims, for exchanges of a very personal nature to take place between individuals from the two confessional groups. On each other's holidays, presents were often exchanged, while it was not unusual for a Muslim and a Jew who

---

[9] For example, the grant to another of one's surplus water may, in the view of some jurisconsults, be revoked if the donor has need of the water, while others hold that even if the benefactor has such a need, provided that the donation has been made public it may not be revoked. Whether need is identical to beneficial use (the term I prefer) is debatable. What is clear is (a) publicity means that people rely on the representation and order their own relationships as a result, such that revocation could then disrupt a wide array of resultant relationships; and (b) the concept of need or beneficial use underscores how much possession turns on parties making use of what Allah has provided them. For a case of water use as a potentially revocable gift in the 14th–16th c., see David Powers, *Law, Society, and Culture in the Maghrib, 1300–1500* (Cambridge: Cambridge University Press, 2002), 95–140, especially 111, 125–31.

[10] The classic study of the *'ar* in Morocco is Edward Alexander Westermarck, *Ritual and Belief in Morocco*, Vol. 1 (Hyde Park, NY: University Books, 1968 [1926]), chapter X. For further examples, see Lawrence Rosen, *Bargaining For Reality: The Construction of Social Relations in a Muslim Community* (Chicago: University of Chicago Press, 1984), 66–68, 122–24, and passim.

shared an interest in a piece of property to regard the "gifts" that were exchanged as part of their overall relationship. There are even instances in which a dispute would be settled with a visit by both parties to the site of a Jewish saint, followed by the sharing of a meal and the further exchange of presents. Such contacts across the margin thus underscore the central place of the gift as a form of contract.

Clearly, then, in actual practice and in the legal framework that surrounds it, gifts in this part of the world have conditions attached to them. Gifts can be given to publicly announce a relationship, to humiliate an opponent, to convert substance into status, or – when pressured by society to engage in the distribution or conspicuous consumption of some of one's wealth – to level the accumulation of too much power in one person's hands. All of these features are present in the North African variant of gifting, and all are countered at times with generosity and attentiveness, emotional valence and localized taste, acquisitive impulses and alliance building. Given the strong emphasis on contractual relations in the Quran and a social system grounded on interpersonally negotiated ties, it is hardly surprising that gifts should meld into this pattern as an additional vehicle for the formation of those bonds of indebtedness that, like an electrical system held together by negative and positive, runs through the whole of the culture. What stands out in the North African context – though it is hardly unique to them – is the multifaceted employment of the gift as a vital conduit in the interplay of constructing and dispersing power in a social system where the bonds of indebtedness hold society together and curb the omnipresent fear of chaos. Perhaps in this arrangement, the true gift of the gift is its place in fabricating a world that imparts a sense of the orderliness of experience and hope for peace in a universe of disquieting uncertainty.

# 4 | Islamic Conceptions of the Rule of Law

To speak of "the rule of law" in a number of present-day Muslim countries may seem, not only to Westerners but also to many citizens of the Islamic world, at best hypocritical and at worst a cruel joke. How, after all, can one speak of the rule of law when a woman may be killed for a marriage not approved by her father or brother, when a constitution can be changed at the whim of a ruler, or when corruption is so pervasive as to leave much of the citizenry feeling dirtied and disaffected? And yet the rule of law remains more than an ideal, more than a vague concept, and more than a useless analytic concept employed only by academic lawyers. For if we try to understand the rule of law not as a universal concept but for what it means in the context of any particular culture and its system of law, it may be possible to discern features that are not incompatible with the sense in which this phrase is commonly employed.

*

## The Rule of Law as a Concept

"The rule of law" (to soften a more salacious analogue) is a veritable courtesan among concepts: It shamelessly associates with whatever seems most profitable and basks in whatever plaudits can cover its more questionable associations. To many it simply lacks any real substance. Justice Rosalie Silberman Abella of the Canadian Supreme Court has said that "Rule of Law is a euphemism no one understands," and one dictionary can only offer the tautology that the rule of law is "a state of order in which events conform to the law."

The meaning of the phrase has long been contested, as we can see, for example, in the debate among the contributors to the 1994 Nomos

volume entitled *The Rule of Law*.[1] Thus, some of the authors argue
that scope for differing points of view (even arising to the level of
civil disobedience) is vital to any rule of law, while others suggest that
what is required are measures that resolve the contradiction between
majority rule and majoritarian dominance. Several others, continuing
the debate between H. L. A. Hart and Ronald Dworkin, disagree over
whether specific tests or only general principles can determine when
and how moral versus legal precepts should govern. Still others ask:
Does the rule of law require that rules be the result of rational choice,
or does it demand the careful incorporation of – or studied distance
from – binding institutions?

Such characterizations of the rule of law in the literature have long
been central to Western discussions. Medieval thinkers resorted to
law when they began to question unlimited monarchic power, while
those of the early modern era (Montesquieu, Locke, and Paine among
them) boldly proclaimed that the law is king, rather than the other
way around. So, too, the American Founders modified the ancient
Greek emphasis on the rule of law as rule by the best of men when
they employed the concept of virtue (at least as embodied in those
who shared common constraints for being white, male, free, and land-
owning) as a necessary adjunct to any formal distribution of powers.
Definitions have sometimes closed in on certain features. The *Oxford
English Dictionary*, for example, speaks of the rule of law as a gov-
ernor on individual behavior, all persons being "equally subject to
publicly disclosed legal codes and processes." But the universal attributes noted by philosophers and lexicographers may themselves beg
precision, especially when they are really attached to a specific concept
of human nature and public tranquility, and when they cannot always
be reconciled with the concept of justice that may be found in different
cultural traditions.

What is true in Western jurisprudence and philosophy is no less true
in the Islamic world. For while one could list any number of works in
which religiously inflected ideas of the rule of law have been the source
for endless debate among the literati, those debates may, as in the

---

[1] Ian Shapiro, ed., *The Rule of Law: Nomos XXXVI* (New York: New York
University Press, 1994). The issues are briefly outlined in Lawrence Rosen,
*Islam and the Rule of Justice* (Chicago: University of Chicago Press, 2018),
78–80. See also Geoffrey Cupit, *Justice as Fittingness* (Oxford: Clarendon
Press, 1996).

West, have as much to do with power struggles as with philosophical rigor. And yet, as in the history of any religious or political argument, the terms of discourse may have a characteristic quality however much the internal variation and reconfiguration may have been the source of great debate, if not indeed great crimes, among those favoring one view over another. Thus, in turning to the specifics of the idea of the rule of law (or its functional equivalents) in countries where Islam is the predominant religion, one must necessarily speak in terms of themes and variations rather than pretend to a singular voice informing every nuance or alternative that may have been put forth over so vast a timeframe and distance as the Muslim world embraces.

Put somewhat differently, can we discern some common denominators in what may be thought of as the range of precepts that may be covered under the rubric of the rule of law? Indeed, are there indigenous equivalents to this concept in Islam and if so what are their constituent features? If, as students of social history and not just the history of legal scholars, we also look to popular conceptualizations of persons, time, and conduct, can we triangulate in on something like a sense of the rule of law that is deeply embedded in Muslim cultures more generally? In doing so, we will want to have recourse initially to the ideas of those Muslim scholars who have addressed the issue, as well as to propositions that appear to inform the daily lives of ordinary believers.

## Principles of Islamic Law

Looking at some of the key writers who have thought about and debated the place of the law in a society and polity informed by Islamic principles, several themes stand out: that no worldly leader may stand above the Sacred Law (*shari'a*) yet may be responsible for determining its applicability, that as a matter of cultural common sense one cannot (and for that reason, should not) assume that the law can be applied without recourse to the wisdom and credibility of those who bespeak it, that justice requires assessing the claims made upon power by an individual who is himself taken as a whole social person, that equivalence rather than uniform equality or abstract rights is the measure of fairness, that no entitlement exists when one fails constantly to service one's claims, and that the law is not solely a body of positive rules but of situated appraisals of social repercussions applied through procedures that are consistent with what is known about human nature and what holds a society together. While these "cultural postulates" will have to be unpacked in their everyday manifestations, we can see how they also suffuse – again, in a theme-and-variation sense – many of the formal commentaries, judgements, and debates that have characterized Islamic jurisprudence over the centuries.[2]

To most Islamic legal thinkers, the preservation of a community of believers (*umma*) free from social chaos (*fitna*) is a foremost consideration, and toward that end, the founders of the four main schools of Islamic law were quite prepared to defer to political authority and to rely for substantive guidance on analogies drawn from provisions in the Quran and the accepted collections of the Prophet's sayings and acts (*hadith*, *sunna*). Personal reasoning (*ijtihād*) – whether of the majority or a particularly well-regarded scholar articulating a minority position – is recognized as a valuable addendum to the Quran and the Traditions of the Prophet by many scholars, provided it sounds in the practices of the people, the broad aims of the sacred law, or the public good. Some, like the tenth-century writers al-Farabi and al-Razi, influenced by Greek ideas, rely on the "first chief" to guide the community, the constraints of personal virtue being paramount in avoiding the injustice that follows upon the failure to balance contending interests. Avicenna (Ibn Sina, 980–1037) is only one among many who, in his approach to legal constraints, stresses the importance of reciprocity in actual or partner-like relationships. Other commenters of the same era (including the shafi'i jurist al-Mawardi) pick up on the Prophetic saying that "my community will not agree in error" to emphasize the role of consensus and consultation both as a restraint on leadership and as a form of social bonding. Like many of his predecessors, al-Ghazzali (1058–1111) does not focus on institutional ways to constrain misguided leaders noting, as does Averroes (Ibn Rushd, 1126–1198), that necessity commands obedience either to a ruler or learned man, while the more autocratic Ibn Taymiyya (1263–1328) vests almost unlimited power in a leader if he strives to hold people strictly to the tenets of the faith. Later thinkers, such as Nasir ad-Din Tusi (1201–1274), like their forbearers, resort to the concept of balance as equivalence without specifying precisely how this accounting

---

[2] See, generally, Wael Hallaq, *A History of Islamic Legal Theories* (Cambridge: Cambridge University Press, 1999).

should proceed other than as an emanation from a just ruler. And while Ibn Khaldun (1332–1406), notwithstanding his role as judge and political adviser, is not usually thought of mainly as a legal philosopher, his approach is consistent with that of many jurisprudential scholars in its emphasis on social solidarity, the need of men to be dominated by superior leaders, and the belief that religious law does not censure the role of the authoritative figure as such, only the evils that a particular tyrant may perpetrate.

It does no violence to the distinctive nature of these and many other Islamic commenters on the role of the law to suggest some common cultural themes that transcend their individual approaches and the times within which they were set. Preeminent among these features is the dependence on the ruler as a person rather than as the depersonalized occupant of an institutional role. Perhaps the absence of a clear line of succession to the Prophet himself – indeed perhaps owing in part to the murder of several early caliphs and the schism of the community into the Sunni and Shiite branches – reinforced the focus on the personality of whoever has taken hold of a given office. But it would be a mistake to think that this represents either some inherent taste for absolutism, the incompatibility of Islam and the rule of law, or that there was not, in fact, a broad array of limitations placed on the power of the ruling figure. Admittedly, some of the constraints may have been more in the nature of idealized practices than actual behavior. Islam distinguishes between those tasks (like prayer) that each individual must perform for him or herself (*ferd al-'ain*) and those that must be done by someone on behalf of the community of believers as a whole (*ferd al-kifāya*). This has led some Muslims to refuse service, say, as a prayer leader or religious judge (*qadi*) lest they mislead the community by even inadvertently failing to perform that role properly. Others, like an Egyptian qadi in the ninth century CE, argued that new court officials should be appointed every six months to avoid tempting corruption.[3] Notwithstanding such ideals, the concept of independent judges and scholars, as we shall see, is not without some reality. That many commenters have stressed the ideal qualities that a judge should possess and that institutional constraints should receive less consideration than personal virtues is consistent, therefore,

---

[3] See Ghulam Murtaza Azad, "Conduct and Qualities of a Qadi," *Islamic Studies*, 24 (1985), 51–61.

with a cultural ethos that situates the main source of confidence in the pursuit of justly enacted powers in identifiable persons rather than impersonal structures.

Two possibilities, then, exist: that the rule of law depends on virtuous persons applying it, or that the rule of law requires counterbalancing mechanisms that limit the power of those who apply it. While most of the writings of classical Islamic law scholars would, as we have seen, suggest that reliance on the virtuous law-enforcer is by far the dominant orientation, a more accurate picture emerges when both possibilities are considered. For while the religious scholars – whether Sunni or Shiite, Arab or Persian, Asian or Middle Eastern – almost always emphasize the just ruler who is faithful to the letter and spirit of the shari'a, there have almost always been countervailing forces that need to be considered. Primary among them are the other players in the marketplace, the procedures and presumptions employed by the judiciary, the legal consults ('ulamā) whose opinions on particular cases may be solicited by contending litigants, and the alternative dispute resolution mechanisms to which disputants may have recourse.

## The Role of the Marketplace

The Prophet was a merchant, as was his wife. And, as in the marketplace, Islam places great stress on the principles of contractual relationships and reciprocity. Provided that none of the relatively few propositions of a law-like nature contained in the Quran is violated, Allah has designated as one of the rights of mankind (ḥaqq al-insān) the ability to arrange their own agreements. This does not mean that all such relationships will go smoothly; indeed, there is a saying that "God placed contentiousness among men that they may know one another," for it is in just such dealings that one must attend to the distinctiveness of the other, his cultural ways, and his own network of social attachments. Moreover, while scholars – both Muslim and Western – tend to cite as the sources of Islamic law only the Quran, the Traditions of the Prophet, and the approaches of the four main schools of law, the fact is that custom ('urf, adat) is the unmarked category and, quite often, the prevailing source of law. In every age and every part of the Muslim world, one thus finds some version of the proposition that a contractual stipulation takes precedence even

over the shari'a and that local custom *is* shari'a, not something separate from it. Whether it is matrilineal Malays from Sumatra or the
Berbers of North Africa who regard their distinctive inheritance practices *as* Islamic, custom is popularly seen not as something separate
from shari'a law but as an integral aspect of it. As such, custom serves
as a check on the strict application of textbook shari'a and, in many
instances, as a factor that an autocratic ruler ignores at his peril.

We tend to think of religion as lodged in the place of worship, the law
as housed in the courts, and the seat of philosophy as exclusive to the
academy. But not only do ordinary people lead intellectual lives, they
live their religion, their law, and their philosophy in the public sphere.
Thus, to view the marketplace, for example, as solely the realm of the
economic is to possess a highly truncated view of how Islamic law and
its inbuilt constraints may operate in everyday life. For the market is
not only the natural environ of every Muslim from the Prophet on but
a domain in which the rule of law is also given expression. Consider,
for example, the nature of contractual agreements. Contracts must be
expressed in the present tense, not as something that has yet to achieve
performance. This means that such an agreement is really the validation of an existing and negotiated arrangement, evidence not only of
the terms of a deal but also of a relationship – indeed a relationship
that has consequences for the networks of indebtedness possessed by
others, the totality of which both define and order society. By creating
and sustaining, in a highly publicized manner, the connections one has
forged with others a man demonstrates that he is fulfilling his God-
given capacity to arrange his ties to others through the employment
of his reasoning powers and that he is contributing to keeping the
community of believers whole by applying these precepts in his most
ordinary of daily activities.

At the same time that one bargains in the marketplace, one is also
putting certain constraints on the centralization of power. For while
it is true that most regimes have controlled the marketplace through
inspectors, taxation, and regulatory schemes, it is also true that the
application of custom, the arrangement of interpersonal obligations,
and the system by which agreements are formed constitute ways in
which power is dispersed, the regularization of relationships is given
substantive form, and a key aspect of the rule of law – the more-or-less
even application of principles both widely recognized and informally
sanctioned – is given actual effect.

## Judges and Jurists

The same may be said of the role of the judiciary. Here, one could speak of the formal elements of power distribution and, perhaps more importantly in the Muslim context, the mechanisms that may not seem to be overtly oriented toward the limitation of power yet have, directly or indirectly, that effect. Traditionally, Muslim judges were appointed by the powers that be. Yet there are numerous reports of local people rejecting someone sent from the capital or simply finding ways of avoiding his disposition of cases. In theory, the ruler's own decisions were separate from those reached by a qadi, though it would be naïve to claim that the influence of the former on the latter was not, in most instances, profound. Still, litigants sometimes had a choice of venues where they could be heard. Moreover, scholarly opinions (sing. *fatwā*) were frequently sought and presented to the court. Because a judge's reputation and personal following were essential to his overall credibility, both his own judgments and his use of the proffered fatwas was at once a hedge on his own decisions and yet another vehicle through which the dispersal of power reinforced local conceptualizations of a rule of law.

Judicial decisions, though usually brief and unpublished, did not really set precedents. Nevertheless, it is not inaccurate to think of Islamic law as a variant on common law systems of law.[4] Here the key ingredients of a common law approach are that facts are adduced from the bottom up by local witnesses and experts, and a system of variable categories is developed by reference to a range of specific cases. The result, intentional or not, is to once again distribute power in such a way that it is difficult for any one person or institution permanently to cumulate power to the exclusion of other avenues and challengers to its implementation.

Traditionally, no formal system of appeals existed in Muslim court structures. The purported theory was that no human could decide a matter with absolute certainty, hence an array of approaches by localized qadis, rather than a definitive statement of the law by a high court, was consistent with the belief that if similar processes of attending to cases was applied diverse results were acceptable. Indeed, because

---

[4] This argument is elaborated in Lawrence Rosen, *The Justice of Islam* (Oxford: Oxford University Press, 2000), 38–68.

many Muslim judges to this day argue that cases are never identical, the proposition that similar cases should be decided similarly is not consistent with their emphasis on the unique relationships and personalities each case involves. From this perspective, a rule of law that treats things as if they were identical would violate common sense and the belief that justice demands a focus on the defining features of each case. If, however, a similar style of considering evidence and a shared sense of the criteria by which the sound judgment of a virtuous judge is applied, then justice – and what Westerners might call the rule of law – will have been honored.

Islamic law is often regarded as containing a body of positive law and to the extent that scholars published manuals and treatises in support of particular approaches to particular types of situations that characterization is not inaccurate. But it is, at best, only part of the story. For the proposition that, as Noel Coulson argued, in Islam the chair (of the scholar) is more important than the bench (of the jurist) can be misleading.[5] Unlike continental systems of law, from which most Western scholars have projected their image of Islamic law, neither codes nor scholarly treatises were the predominant, much less the sole, basis for judgments. As we have seen, custom has always played a key role – particularly since it is popularly regarded as not incompatible with the shari'a but part of it. Even more important has been the role of legal procedures.

Judicial procedures – including the rules of evidence, legal presumptions, and the role of witnesses and expert testimony – are important for their capacity to resonate with commonsense assumptions within a given culture and because procedural regularities may also reflect the role of the state and the limits of its power.[6] In Islamic law, the emphasis on personalism over institutions comes through quite clearly in the

---

[5] See Noel Coulson, *A History of Islamic Law* (Edinburgh: Edinburgh University Press, 1965). See, generally, Nathan J. Brown, *The Rule of Law in the Arab World: Courts in Egypt and the Gulf* (Cambridge: Cambridge University Press, 1997); David A. Funk, "Traditional Islamic Jurisprudence: Justifying Islamic Law and Government," *Southern University Law Review*, 20 (1993), 213–94; and Baber Johansen, "Sacred and Religious Element in Hanafite Law – Function and Limits of the Absolute Character of Government Authority," in Ernest Gellner, et al., *Islam et Politique au Maghreb* (Paris: Editions du CNRS, 1981), 281–303.
[6] See the chapters in Baudoin Dupret, ed., *Standing Trial: Law and the Person in the Modern Middle East* (London, I. B. Tauris, 2004).

rules of procedure. Thus, tremendous emphasis is placed on witnesses who themselves have been recognized as reliable by virtue of their overall reputation in the community, which itself is a function of how well embedded they are in a set of kinship, local, and negotiated ties to others. Experts are witnesses whose special knowledge – whether of the marketplace, irrigation, medicine, or the likely ways people of different locales arrange their contractual relations – are vital to judicial decision-making. But note, too, that in the emphasis on these personal qualities, the state is also being limited by knowledgeable persons. Just as the jury in the Anglo-American world gets the state off the hook for deciding against individuals, so too in most Islamic legal regimes the use of local people bringing information to the court takes some of the responsibility – as well as some of the power – away from the ruler and distributes it more widely.

Similarly, rules of procedure not only aid in determining what actually happened in a given dispute but reflect views of human nature that are integral to the distribution of powers through law. Thus, if, for example, it is assumed that the person to whom certain items are usually attached (e.g., the household goods to a wife, tools to a husband), the law is underscoring (a) that justice requires an accounting of an individual's status and a judgment based on seeing persons in their proper category as well as for whatever additional attributes they may have taken on, and (b) that the state may not punish people for what may be in their minds if their actions, visible to all and retrievable by judicial process, do not bear out that interpretation. So, too, if an oath is to be used to settle the facts in a case the person entitled to take that oath first and thus cut off the other's claim is being allowed to step outside of presumptions the state could have enforced through the law by applying to a higher power than a human official. And when the distribution of oath-taking is based on a cultural assumption of who is most likely to know where the truth actually lies, it is through such views of humankind that individuals are both empowered against an arbitrary state and the values of the collective are reinforced.

## Justice as Equivalence

That a person's status and overall set of connections should weigh significantly in most Islamic legal proceedings might seem antithetical to the rule of law as treating all persons equally. But consider this: Is it a violation of equality if women who are deeply committed to Catholicism believe that only men should serve as priests, or that similar views should inform the approaches of Orthodox Jewish women to being called up for the reading of the Torah, or Muslim women to serving as prayer leaders? Or, from their perspective, do these women believe that the religiously informed tasks they per-form, whether in the home or through segregated rituals, are of equivalent importance to those undertaken by men? If they do, then what may be at work is a concept of justice not as equality or identi-cal treatment of men and women but that the distinctive nature of each demands that they be treated true to their category and thus equivalently. If rights are the keynote of many Western conceptions of the rule of law, justice (*'adl*) is clearly the concept that is central for many Muslims, and that concept does not imply absolutely iden-tical treatment of persons in every situation but a clear assessment of the whole person, including his or her distinctive nature. And when equivalence – however assessed – is the focus of judgment, and when that process is pursued according to precepts broadly shared within the culture, it is impossible to characterize the results as failing to abide by some sense of a rule of law even if it is not the one that is put forth in other societies and religions. Here, too, then, cultural assumptions, alongside formal structures, can serve as a check on the power of the state.

## Informal Arbiters

However centralized power has been in Islamic states – whether in the person of a sultan or a big man who has employed pseudo-democratic means to gain office – not all legal power is at every moment under the ruler's control. Legal scholars (*'ulama*) may vary in their impact, whether they serve alongside the head of a regime or as consults in individual cases. But they do possess an alternate source of legitimacy which – depending almost entirely (as in all other aspects of these cultures) on their personal forcefulness, their individual capacity to build networks of dependence, and their ability to capture through language the terms by which a matter may be addressed – can at times be interposed against the powers of the central authority. And since their intervention may itself partake of characteristic features for establishing their legitimacy, one can properly speak of their contribution as part of the rule of law.

The ulama are, however, by no means the only players who may generate a dispersal of power regularized by social convention and hence contribute to the rule of law as seen through local eyes. Often, disputants will go to people outside of the formal legal structure to have their differences addressed. The go-between (*wasīṭa*) is more than an informal arbiter: This individual – whether a kinsman, neighbor, or other respected figure – at once intercedes (even usurps) the power of the state to decide issues but does so in such a way as to reinforce local conventions and customary practices. Moreover, their approach actually resonates with that taken by formal courts in many parts of the Muslim world. For if one asks what the goal is that such forums seek to achieve the answer is often not that of Western courts – to assess facts and determine rights – but to put the parties into a position where they are most likely to negotiate their own differences. Once again, the ability to use social values – seen as Islamic values – and local people to achieve a degree of peaceful resolution of a dispute is not just a matter of legal pluralism in some abstract sense but of limiting state power and establishing regularity through local personnel and local conceptualizations. That, too, is partaking of a rule of law.

Consider in addition the fact that, contrary to Western stereotypes, if they pursue their family law cases to judicial decision women throughout the Muslim world win all or much of their lawsuits anywhere from 65 to 95 percent of the time.[7] The reasons appear to include that the cases they pursue tend to be clearly favorable to them, that Islamic law has long favored the poor, that the rules of evidence do not uniformly disadvantage women, and that pressures are often brought to bear on men to settle their wives' lawsuits. Once again, legal presumptions and the role of court experts do not simply work against the interests of women. And the image of women as reluctant to argue their own interests is seriously problematized by viewing such documentaries as Ziba Mir Hossein's *Divorce Iranian Style* or *Justice at Agadez*, which follows a Muslim judge in Niger.[8]

---

[7] The data supporting this assertion is detailed in Rosen, *Islam and the Rule of Justice*, 28–62.
[8] See also Mark Fathi Massoud, *Shari'a, Inshallah: Finding God in Somali Politics* (Cambridge: Cambridge University Press, 2021).

Westerners, too, have often characterized Islamic legal decision-making as largely dependent on the unbounded discretion of the qadi. Max Weber, who spoke of *kadijustiz* in these terms, is often cited here even though Weber was careful to state that his was an ideal type construct and that he knew actual Islamic legal adjudication was not simply arbitrary. In fact, careful studies of such discretion suggest that while judgment is indeed connected with the range of inquiry to which any judge may subject litigants there are clear precepts and limits to which judges commonly adhere. Foremost, as we have suggested, are the procedural rules for adducing and weighing evidence, the presumptions that allot burdens of proof, and the preferred aim of creating some sort of workable continuity to an existing relationship. Though less apparent, perhaps, than a formal structure of divided powers, these features are crucial to the local variant of an Islamic rule of law.

## Corruption

It would, however, be naïve to ignore the threat of corruption in any legal system. Assessing its role in Muslim adjudication is difficult to quantify and still more difficult to separate from other aspects of the political and social forces at work. What we do know with reasonable certainty is that the separation of the judiciary from governmental influence (if not direction) is far from perfect.

In the 2020 report by Transparency International, most of the Muslim countries of the Middle East ranked near the bottom of those scored as least corrupt: Egypt ranked 117 out of 180 countries, Algeria 104, Iraq 160, Syria 178, and Iran 149. Across the region, one in three people say they have paid bribes in court or for social services and one in four that they paid off police, these rates rising to one-half in parts of North Africa and up to 75 percent in Jordan, 84 percent in Yemen, and 92 percent in Lebanon.[9] Judges may be pressured by those exercising political power: Thus, in June of 2015, President Abdel Fattah el-Sisi publicly browbeat the Egyptian judges who he said were failing to move against the Muslim Brothers he accused of assassinating a public prosecutor. In many other instances, the lack

[9] www.transparency.org/en/cpi/2020/index/irn

of funding and modernization of courts, the poor training of judges, and the oversupply of law graduates who are ill equipped for practice create an environment in which corruption can flourish.[10] Setting the standards for judicial independence often remains unclear. For example, a court in the state of Texas was called upon to decide the claim of an American oil company that a decision reached against them in a Moroccan court was improperly influenced by the palace and should therefore not be enforced by the American court.[11] At the trial level, the court did indeed find that there was such influence and that the Moroccan judiciary was insufficiently independent for its rulings to be given effect. However, the court of appeals found to the contrary and ruled in favor of granting comity to the foreign judgment, thus creating an interesting question as to what kind of influence goes beyond the bounds of a rule of law.

Elsewhere, I have argued that corruption for many people in the Arab world means failing to share with those in one's network of allies whatever largesse comes one's way.[12] That does not, however, mean that people regard all means for effecting that end as equally moral or desirable. Indeed, it is the feeling of having to engage in almost daily corruption that makes people feel both sullied and complicit. To have to bribe a teacher for a child's grade, an orderly for access to one's hospitalized kinsman, or a clerk to prepare files for a court hearing were all instances of what led many to participate in the events of the Arab Spring. On a number of occasions, too, lawyers and judges have taken courageous actions in their quest for judicial independence, and there is little doubt that most lawyers would love to be able to exercise their professional capabilities free from corruption. As standards of ethics are articulated and as organizations of legal personnel are more widely created, the quest for a

---

[10] See, e.g., Abdulmajeed Alshalan, *Corrupt Practices in Saudi Arabia*, S.J.D. Thesis, University of Indiana School of Law, June 2017; www,repository .law.indiana.edu/etd/45; Bouzou Daragahi, "Middle East: Against the Law," *Financial Times*, October 31, 2013. As for legal training, while Egypt produces 15,000 new law graduates each year, the lawyer of a major Cairo firm estimates that only thirty might be sufficiently well trained for employment in his organization.

[11] See the discussion of the case at Karka Dieseldorff, "US Court Says Morocco's Justice is 'Fundamentally Fair'," *Morocco World News*, October 7, 2015.

[12] Lawrence Rosen, "The Culture of Corruption in the Arab World," in Lawrence Rosen, *Islam and the Rule of Justice*, 99–107.

meaningful concept of the rule of law will first have to pass through the maelstrom of institutionalized corruption.[13]

## Constitutions and Human Rights Conventions

At various times, many Muslim countries have addressed the balance of powers and the rule of law through the adoption of national constitutions and codes, a number of which have followed European models. What gets incorporated in any nation's foundational charter or codified laws, of course, reflects both the circumstances that have led up to their adoption and the broader concept of power that they embrace. In India, the British effectively created a body of substantive Islamic law that had not previously existed, while the French in North Africa redacted case law and treated it like a code. Following independence, many of these codes persisted, especially in criminal and commercial law, sometimes alongside modified codes of personal status that ranged from those remaining very close to traditional Islamic law in the countries of the Arabian Peninsula to the highly Westernized laws of Tunisia. Certainly, revisions in some codes do seek to equalize the status of men and women. Notwithstanding massive protest marches in 2000 for and against its adoption, the Moroccan Code of Personal Status (*Moudawwana*), for example, now provides that marriage is "under the direction of both spouses," that both parties can seek a divorce on equal grounds, that a woman does not lose child custody upon remarriage, and that a woman does not require the permission of a marital guardian to wed.

Most Muslim countries have not only centralized their law codes but the organization of their judiciary as well. Where once any respected scholar might be able to certify another as sufficiently learned that the latter might apply the shari'a, now government-controlled educational programs predominate; where once a qadi might be somewhat independent of the ruler, now the Ministry of Justice assigns posts and controls advancement, thus potentially jeopardizing judicial independence. However, on occasion judges have

---

[13] See Frédéric Volpi, "Pseudo-democracy in the Muslim World," *Third World Quarterly*, 25 (2004), 1061–78. See, generally, Richard H. Fallon, Jr., "'The Rule of Law' as a Concept in Constitutional Discourse," *Columbia Law Review*, 97 (1997), 1–56.

protested against governmental interference, and lawyers in Egypt, Tunisia, and Morocco have taken to the streets to make their views known. At its best, lawyers and judges wish to be able to practice their professions independently; at its worst, they are badgered, coopted, or threatened into following direction from above.

More recently, international human rights conventions pose the question whether the standards of Western nations can be said to command worldwide adherence or whether these resolutions run counter to Islamic law. When, for example, the United Nations Universal Declaration of Human Rights was offered for adoption in 1947 Saudi Arabia refrained from acceptance – but then even the American Anthropological Association opposed it as an imposition of Western values. Bilateral treaties on the laws governing migrants from Muslim countries to Europe serve to regularize the status of those who live and work outside of their home countries. And although religious law courts have remained a voluntary option for religious adherents in a number of instances in North America and Europe, the aftereffects of the Salman Rushdie affair, 9/11, and various terrorist attacks have led to a backlash against Islamic law in the West. Thus, the Archbishop of Canterbury was roundly criticized for suggesting that some personal status matters might best be handled by Muslims in their own religious law courts, while various jurisdictions in the United States and Canada attempted to pass laws forbidding the application of shari'a within their territories. The result is, to some degree, to deprive religious Muslims of the rule of law they understand and to replace it with one whose substance and methods may run counter to their perceived sense of order and justice.

## Conclusions

Ultimately, we are confronted with a series of concepts about how and in what manner one can speak of a rule of law when cultures and religions vary quite widely. Where many Muslims may see the identical treatment of persons as a failure to recognize legitimate differences or place their confidence in those persons whose relationships they believe serve as a more credible basis for constraint than impersonal institutions, Westerners may see systems that violate their idea of the rule of law as one that should be blind to just such features. At one level, there is great overlap between Muslim and many non-Muslim visions of the rule of law – that fairness demands attending to all the facts, that no one individual should have unchallenged and unlimited power over another, that truth does not lie within the ambit of the powerful but with sources that transcend any one momentary possessor of control – while at the same time, they exhibit quite different approaches to the distribution of power and the criteria by which authority should be acknowledged. One need not, therefore, be an unrepentant relativist or a claimant of universal values to nevertheless respect the organizing principles by which others place limits on power and treat one another with that degree of consideration to which they would expect any valid system of law to treat them as well.

# PART III

# Political

# 5 | *Anthropological Assumptions and the Afghan War*

*The war in Afghanistan entwined a series of questionable anthropological assumptions. Quite aside from the direct involvement of anthropologists in the war's "human terrain" project, American policymakers continued a mistaken view of the tribes of the region, the reasons why there had been no attacks on the American homeland from the Afghan-Pakistan border region, the nature of suicide bombing, and the reasons why a singular model for all counterinsurgency plans may fail. By carefully analyzing these assumptions, anthropologists may offer a more refined critique of their own work, the factors that contributed to the loss of the Afghan war, and the questionable aspects of the broader war on terror.*

\*

These are the times that try anthropologists' souls. Legal cases may force one to choose among contending ideas; public policies may test one's concepts against reality. But no greater challenge to one's theories exists than when they are applied in war.[1]

The involvement of anthropologists in warfare is hardly new. Ruth Benedict's study-at-a-distance of the Japanese in *The Chrysanthemum and the Sword* may be the most famous instance, but it is hardly unique: Anthropologists have participated in war-related work from at least the time of World War I. It is not, however, the merits of

---

[1] Portions of this chapter were delivered as the Lt. Jones-Huffman Memorial Lecture at the United States Naval Academy, Annapolis, MD. The author is grateful for comments on earlier drafts of this chapter by numerous military officers, State Department officials, and NGO workers who have served in the region. Because none was interviewed for attribution, they are not identified here. This chapter was prepared during my tenure as a Mellon Fellow of the Stanford University Center for Advanced Study in the Behavioral Sciences, and I am grateful to the Center and its fellows for comments on earlier drafts.

anthropology's involvement in war that is at issue here but the assumptions, whether muted or explicit, that have continued to affect the political and military decisions of several administrations in pursuit of the Afghan war. The problems become more visible when a number of those assumptions are considered for the anthropological issues they incorporate, issues that include the nature of tribes in the region, whether the Afghan-Pakistan border has indeed been the launching site for attacks on the US homeland, the sociological underpinnings of suicide bombings, the meaning of social differentiation in the cultures of the area, and the extent to which similarities at a professedly global level mask the realities of the local.[2]

## Why Do Tribes Matter?

Early in his presidency, during a three-month review of the war in Afghanistan, Barack Obama reportedly told his advisors: "I just want to say right now, I want to take off the table that we're leaving Afghanistan ... What I'm looking for is a surge. This has to be a surge."[3] Notwithstanding the enormous cultural differences posed by the Afghan situation – differences of which the administration was well aware – this policy remained quite close to the military strategy applied in Iraq. However, even though it is a matter of disputed interpretation, many military and civilian figures now agree that whatever momentary diminution in violence may have occurred in Iraq during the so-called "surge" was not simply due to the insertion of additional troops.[4] Not only was violence tailing off in urban areas already

---

[2] For a comparison of the issues analyzed in this essay with a series of myths about our involvement in Afghanistan, as enumerated by a blue-ribbon panel, see Afghanistan Study Group, *A New Way Forward: Rethinking U.S. Strategy in Afghanistan* (2010). www.afghanistanstudygroup.com.

[3] Peter Baker, "How Obama Came to Plan for 'Surge' in Afghanistan," *New York Times*, December 6, 2009. See also Bob Woodward, *Obama's War* (New York: Simon & Schuster, 2010).

[4] Andrew Bacevich – a West Point graduate, veteran of the Gulf War, and professor of history – thus wrote: "The surge ... functions chiefly as a smoke-screen, obscuring a vast panorama of recklessness, miscalculation and waste that politician, generals, and sundry warmongers are keen to forget." Quoted in Frank Rich, "Freedom's Just Another Word," *New York Times*, September 5, 2010, WK5. See also David Kilcullen, *The Accidental Guerrilla* (New York: Oxford University Press, 2009), and David Kilcullen, *Counterinsurgency* (New York: Oxford University Press, 2010). The prestigious Afghanistan

"cleansed" of competing religious groupings when additional troops were sent into those cities but the more significant change came with the involvement of the nation's tribes.[5]

For years the United States ignored the region's tribes, even though three-quarters of Iraqis identify with some 150 different tribes, most of the 40 percent of Afghans who are Pashtun identify with two major tribal groups, and those living along the Pakistani border are divided among 60 major tribes and an additional 77 in the region of Baluchistan.[6] For years American soldiers referred to the tribes as part of "Indian country," while officers were ordered by Washington to stay out of tribal politics.[7] Military and state department officials, who saw tribes at best as a premodern form of organization, neither

Study Group, in its list of "Myths and Realities in the Afghan Debate," states categorically that the surge failed in most respects. A member of Congress who serves on two intelligence committees also told me in a private phone conversation: "The surge was not what turned things around."

[5] It should be noted, for example, that ethnic killing continued after the surge and actually heightened the flight abroad of some two million Iraqis, including most of the country's middle class, Deborah Amos, *Eclipse of the Sunnis* (Washington: Public Affairs, 2010), 26–29.

The United Nations refugee office reports that, as of late 2010, of the 100,000 refugees who have returned to Baghdad, 61 percent said they regretted coming back and 87 percent said they could not support their families upon returning. See John Leland, "Iraq's Ills Lead Former Exiles to Flee Again," *New York Times*, November 27, 2010.

[6] A listing and map of the tribes of Iraq, translated from Arabic sources, are most accessible for English readers at http://en.wikipedia.org/wiki/Arab_tribes_in_Iraq; a listing of the Pashtun tribes of the Afghan-Pakistan region, also based on original sources, can be found at http://en.wikipedia.org/wiki/Pashtun_tribes.

[7] On the "Indian country" metaphor, see Steven W. Silliman, "The 'Old West' in the Middle East: U.S. Military Metaphors in Real and Imagined Indian Country," *American Anthropologist*, 110, 2 (2008): 237–47. See, generally, The Economist, "Iraq's Tribes May Hold the Balance of Power." *The Economist*, May 22, 2010, and Elizabeth Bumiller, "Unlikely Tutor Giving Military Afghan Advice," *New York Times*, July 17, 2010. The controversial anthropologist/defense analyst Montgomery McFate was, whatever her other faults, accurate when she wrote in 2004: "Once the Sunni Ba'thists lost their prestigious jobs, were humiliated in the conflict, and got frozen out through de-Ba'thification, the tribal network became the backbone of the insurgency. The tribal insurgency is a direct result of our misunderstanding of Iraqi culture." Montgomery McFate, "The Military Utility of Understanding Adversary Culture," *Joint Force Quarterly*, 38 (July, 2005): 42–48. See also Montgomery McFate and Janice H. Laurence, eds., *Social Science Goes to War: The Human Terrain System in Iraq and Afghanistan* (Oxford: Oxford University Press, 2015).

understood the nature of tribes as a class of political forms nor why they mattered.[8] It was in large part when the tribes came to the Western forces – not the other way around – that things began to change. This "Awakening Movement," which began in Anbar Province in the winter of 2005–6, involved tribal leaders who decided to cooperate with American forces to end the violence against them and other Sunnis that was being perpetrated mainly by foreign al-Qaeda militants – and then only after the Sunnis had lost what was effectively a civil war in the big cities. As American casualties declined, the program (which involved significant payments to the tribesmen) was expanded to include remunerations to Shiite militia as well.[9] Thus, as a number of military officers have acknowledged, it was the desperate straits of the urban Sunnis and the connection made to the Western forces by the tribes – not the later surge – that accounted for the decline in killings even in the Sunni heartland of Adhamiya Province.[10]

---

[8]  See Greg Jaffe, "To Understand Sheiks in Iraq, Marines Ask 'Mac'," *The Wall Street Journal*, September 10, 2007; Art Keller, "Exclusive: al Qaeda Bomb-Factory Video," *Foreign Policy*, May 14, 2010.

[9]  See Erica Goode, "Worrisome Signs of Tension Beset Sunni-Led Awakening Groups in Iraq," *New York Times*, September 22, 2008. To appreciate the full complexities of the Awakening, see the interviews in Timothy S. McWilliams and Kurtis P. Wheeler, eds., *Al-Anbar Awakening: American Perspectives, Vol. I* (Berkshire, UK: Books Express Publishing, 2009), and Gary W. Montgomery and Timothy S. McWilliams, eds., *Al-Anbar Awakening: American Perspectives, Vol. II* (Berkshire, UK: Books Express Publishing, 2009). Having failed to form a unified winning coalition in the elections of March 2010, the Awakening Movement itself began to fractionate and come under increasing attack from insurgent forces. See Tim Arango, "Dozens Killed in Iraq Suicide Attack," *New York Times*, July 18, 2010.

[10]  As an army colonel with a Ph.D. from Stanford who teaches at West Point has said: "To think the reduction of violence [in Iraq] was primarily the result of American military action is hubris run amuck [sic]." Gian Gentile, "A Strategy of Tactics: Population-centric COIN and the Army," *Parameters: US War College Quarterly*, 39 (2009): 5–17, at 10–11. See also Steven Simon, "The Price of the Surge: How US Strategy Is Hastening Iraq's Demise," *Foreign Affairs*, 87 (2008): 57–76. Interviews with former insurgents support this claim, as do published statements by British commanders and the American soldier who stated that "it was the Awakening, not the surge, that was 'the game changer'." Sam Collyns and James Jones, "'America Used to Be Our Enemy No. 1. But Now It's al-Qaida,' say Former Insurgents," *The Independent* [London], September 29, 2010. Whether it is true that without the surge, other assertedly successful operations by General Petraeus would not have been possible is, of course, impossible to demonstrate, as one can

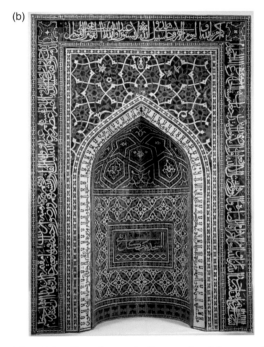

Plate 1.1a Complex periodic mosaics. Mosque of Hassan Modarres, Kashmar.
Credit: Sonia Sevilla, CC0, via Wikimedia Commons.
1.1b Mihrab (Prayer Niche), 1354–1355 CE Credit: Harris Brisbane Dick
Fund, 1939. Metropolitan Museum of Art, CC0, via Wikimedia Commons.

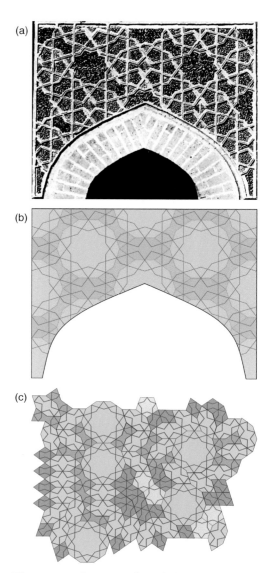

**Plate 1.2a** Elements of underlying gridwork. Spandrel from the Abbasid Al-Mustansiriyya Madrasa, Baghdad, Iraq, 1227–1234 CE; Girih tile underlying pattern drawn by and courtesy of Peter J. Lu.
**1.2b** Girih tiles. Drawing by Peter J. Lu.
**1.2c** Girih tiles. Cronholm144, CC BY-SA 3.0, via Wikimedia Commons.

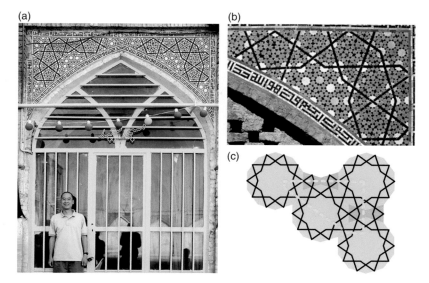

Plate 1.3a Peter Lu at Darb-i-Imam, Isfahan, Iran, 1453 CE, discovers quasi-crystalline patterns. Courtesy of Peter Lu.
1.3b Girih-tile subdivision found in the decagonal girih pattern on a spandrel from the Darb-i-Imam shrine, Isfahan, Iran (1453 CE). Courtesy of Peter Lu, United States public domain. www.sciencemag.org/content/315/5815/1106.full.
1.3c Underlying quasicrystal pattern. Credit: İnfoCan, CC BY-SA 3.0, via Wikimedia Commons.

Plate 1.4a Quasicrystalline elements not fully aligned. Credit: Cronholm144, CC BY-SA 3.0, via Wikimedia Commons.
1.4b Topkapi scroll. Gülru Necipoğlu. Drawing courtesy of Peter Lu and Paul Steinhardt.

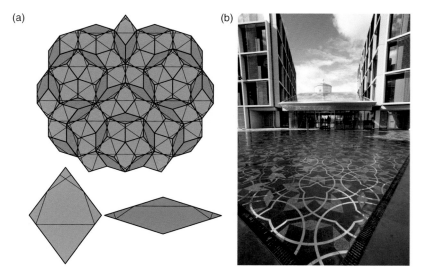

**Plate 1.5a** Penrose pattern correctly aligned. Credit: Geometry guy, CC BY-SA 3.0, via Wikimedia Commons.
**1.5b** Perfect Penrose pattern, Oxford University Mathematical Institute. Credit: Alain Goriely, CC BY-SA 3.0, via Wikimedia Commons.

**Plate 1.6a** Penrose pattern on tiled floor, Helsinki, Finland. Courtesy of Anna Amnell.
**1.6b** Penrose pattern on tiled floor, Helsinki, Finland. Courtesy of Anna Amnell.
**1.6c** Sir Roger Penrose. Credit: Solarflare100, CC BY 3.0, via Wikimedia Commons.

Tribes have, of course, been the classic subject for the anthropological study of kinship and political organization, as well as the test site for theories ranging from the evolutionary to the functional to the structuralist. A careful comparative study, however, suggests that, for all their variation, tribes possess a family resemblance that, when the insights of earlier studies are combined, reveals especially salient features that have affected the impact of those who have sought to insert themselves into tribal affairs. Thus Marshall Sahlins showed that reciprocity is central to the "sectoral morality" that produces "a pattern of alliances and enmities, its design shaped by tactical considerations,"[11] Robert Lowie that tribes are internally variable because they "sample alternate social forms" from other tribes,[12] Morton Fried that tribes often emerge and recede in response to the rise and effects of state structures,[13] Paul Dresch that the moral structure utilizes leveling mechanisms that yield "an avoidance of any absolute judgment,"[14] and (in the view of many scholars who have studied the Middle East in particular) that tribes are not simply organized around "balanced opposition" or segmentary structure but are capable of reconfiguring their histories and genealogies to suit changing ecological and political needs.[15] Thus, notwithstanding significant differences between and

never prove a negative. Compare, Farid Zakaria, "In Iraq, an Opening for Successful Diplomacy," *The Washington Post*, December 21, 2009, A19, for the claim that: "The surge in Iraq was a success in military terms."

[11] Marshall Sahlins, *Tribesmen* (Englewood Cliffs, NJ: Prentice-Hall, 1968), 17.

[12] Quoted in James Boon, *Other Tribes, Other Scribes* (Cambridge: Cambridge University Press, 1982), 102.

[13] Morton Fried, *The Evolution of Political Society* (New York: Random House, 1967). For comparative updates and applications of this thesis, see Cynthia Chou and Geoffrey Benjamin, eds., *Tribal Communities in the Malay World: Historical, Cultural and Social Perspectives* (Singapore: Institute of Southeast Asian Studies, 2003), and James C. Scott, *The Art of Not Being Governed: An Anarchist History of Upland South-East Asia* (New Haven: Yale University Press, 2010).

[14] Paul Dresch, "Imams and Tribes: The Writing and Acting of History in Upper Yemen," In Philip S. Khoury and Joseph Kostiner, eds., *Tribes and State Formation in the Middle East* (Berkeley: University of California Press, 1991), 252–87, at 255.

[15] See Fredrik Barth, *Nomads of South Persia: The Basseri Tribe of the Khamseh Confederacy* (Oslo: University of Oslo Publications, 1961); Clifford Geertz, *Islam Observed* (New Haven: Yale University Press, 1968); and John Waterbury, "Legitimacy without Coercion," *Government and Opposition* 5, 2 (1970): 253–60.

among the tribes of Iraq and Afghanistan, a range of variation on common themes is clearly discernible.[16]

Taken together, these insights suggest that tribes are shape-shifters, amoeba-like in their capacity to adapt to the political forms surrounding them. Tribes, most analysts now believe, do not predate states in some evolutionary hierarchy but may, among other manifestations, arise in response to states or fluctuate between settled versus nomadic moments, coalescing and receding as the situation demands. They are not inherent democracies, but there are shared levelling features, including that no one individual can claim moral superiority over any other, that for any authority to attach, tribesmen must usually demonstrate the qualities associated with a given position rather than merely inherit it, and that numerous devices exist for leveling power since it is commonly believed that too much power should not reside in too few hands for too long a period of time. Moreover, looking beyond formal structures based on kinship and descent, some of these features may inform the social and cultural life of the broader nations within which they are embedded: Just as one need not be a Protestant to be imbued with the Protestant Ethic, one need not be part of an actual tribe to identify with these features of a tribal ethos.[17]

Notwithstanding the rejection by most anthropologists of a unilinear progression from band to tribe to chiefdom to state, President Obama, in his Nobel Prize speech, suggested that he thinks tribes do indeed occupy a place in some evolutionary scheme: "War, in one form or another, appeared with the first man. At the dawn of history, its morality was not questioned; it was simply a fact, like drought or disease – the manner in which tribes and then civilizations sought power and settled their differences." And though he may have meant

---

[16] On the tribal structures of the Afghan region, see Thomas Barfield, *Afghanistan: A Cultural and Political History* (Princeton: Princeton University Press, 2010), David B. Edwards, *Heroes of the Age: Moral Fault Lines on the Afghan Frontier* (Berkeley: University of California Press, 1996); David B. Edwards, *Before Taliban: Genealogies of the Afghan Jihad* (Berkeley: University of California Press, 2002), and David M. Hart, *Qabila: Tribal Profiles and Tribal-State Relations in Morocco and on the Afghanistan-Pakistan Frontier* (Amsterdam, Netherlands: Het Spinhuis, 2001).

[17] This analysis of tribal structures, and support for such a view in the literature, is elaborated in Lawrence Rosen, "What Is a Tribe, and Why Does It Matter?" in Lawrence Rosen, *The Culture of Islam* (Chicago: University of Chicago Press, 2002), 39–55.

it partly as a metaphor, he went on to quote – and then reiterate – John F. Kennedy's call for "a more practical, more attainable peace, based not on a sudden revolution in human nature but on a gradual evolution in human institutions."[18] The Obama administration thus continued their predecessor's belief that tribes are archaic entities – at best a step along some evolutionary path – entities that outsiders may try to skip over in attempting to forge democratic institutions or usefully manipulate, given tribes' fissiparous and anarchic structures. It is particularly striking that Obama's administration adhered to this rather static view even after the Iraqi tribes reemerged to make their political and military importance obvious.

While the Obama administration may ultimately have grasped the tribes' centrality, they still operated under the mistaken view that tribes have unvarying forms into which an alien power can insert itself with reasonably predictable consequences. Tribal "leaders," for example, were still described as having institutional authority or only personal followings rather than being envisioned in terms of the means by which networks are assembled and constrained.[19] Caught between a theory of tribal entities as untrustworthy because of shifting alliances and a theory of tribes as calcified anachronisms, tribes tend to be regarded as possessing either some discernible hierarchy or constituting a mere assemblage of competing individuals. Because tribal structures are, however, malleable and may be either latent or manifest, the mistake is often made of focusing almost exclusively on issues of tribal structure or apparent leadership, an error that is compounded by thinking that all an invasive force must do is find the tribe and offer the bribe.[20] It is true that, when he was the commander

---

[18] Barack Obama, "Text: Obama's Nobel Remarks," *New York Times*, December 11, 2009.

[19] U.S. Army, "My Cousin's Enemy Is My Friend: A Study of Pashtun Tribes in Afghanistan," Afghanistan Research Reachback Center White Paper, TRADOC G2 Human Terrain System (Fort Leavenworth, KS, September 2009) (unclassified).

[20] For example, in its approach to the Afghan tribes: "One hallmark of the American agreement with the Shinwari tribe is that $1 million in American development aid will go directly to Shinwari elders. The money will bypass Karzai government officials, whom Shinwari elders dismiss as corrupt and ineffective." Ruhallah Khapalwak and David Rohde, "A Look at America's New Hope: The Afghan Tribes," *New York Times*, January 29, 2010. Just what ever constitutes "development," of course, remains unclear. Moreover,

of forces in the region, General David Petraeus recognized that
Afghanistan was not Iraq – that there was no tradition of a powerful centralized government that even in modern times reached the
entire country. Yet, as the *Wall Street Journal* reported: "Although
he has said many times that Afghanistan isn't Iraq, General Petraeus
on Thursday [September 2, 2010] sketched out an Afghan strategy
that literally took a page from his Iraq approach. Gen. Petraeus's diagram of his Afghan strategy was based on a slide he showed Congress
during the Iraq surge and even uses the same name: 'Anaconda,' a
title meant to evoke a snake encircling the insurgency."[21] It therefore
remained unclear whether a surge in Afghanistan that encompassed
the tribes in a manner analogous to that of the Iraqi experience would,
notwithstanding an appreciation of the differences between the two
countries, prove to be effective: Simply "surging" additional troops
without understanding the tribal ethos that suffuses the broader culture of each country was no more certain to bring about "success" in
Afghanistan than it had in Iraq.

> as another report on the same tribe's decision states: "But no one expects
> to be able to duplicate the scale of the Iraq effort, because in many parts
> of Afghanistan, the Taliban have not only intimidated or killed local tribal
> leaders but insinuated themselves into the very fabric of the hierarchies of
> the tribes." Dexter Filkins, "Afghan Tribe, Vowing to Fight Taliban, to Get
> U.S. Aid in Return," *New York Times*, January 28, 2010. As for the Sunni
> tribes of Iraq, by the fall of 2010, many of those paid to remain part of the
> "Awakening Movement" had begun to drift back to support of al-Qaeda
> elements: See Timothy Williams and Duraid Adnan, "Sunnis in Iraq Allied
> With U.S. Quitting to Rejoin Rebels," *New York Times*, October 16, 2010.
> [21] Julien E. Barnes, "Petraeus: U.S. Lacks Afghan Tribal Knowledge," *The Wall
> Street Journal*, September 2, 2010. See also Petraeus' key statement about
> tribes in "Petraeus: Afghan Tribes Could Fight Militants," *Military Times*,
> November 6, 2008. Petraeus also seemed to contradict claims that he saw
> Afghanistan as fundamentally different from Iraq: "'We have never had
> the granular understanding of local circumstances in Afghanistan that we
> achieved over time in Iraq,' the general said. In Iraq, Petraeus recalled, U.S.
> and coalition military commanders knew who the local tribal power brokers
> were, how the social systems were supposed to work and how they actually
> functioned. 'That enabled us enormously,' he said. 'We are just completing
> the process of getting the inputs right here and now [and] we have to employ
> those inputs'." Jim Garamone, "Afghanistan Now Has Forces, Resources,
> Petraeus Says," *Armed Forces Press Service*, December 23, 2010. www
> .defense.gov/news/newsarticle.aspx?id=60702. Whether Afghan tribes were
> seen as truly different from those in Iraq is elucidated by a careful reading of
> U.S. Army, "My Cousin's Enemy Is My Friend."

## Why Were There No Attacks Directed by al-Qaeda and Similar Organizations on the American Homeland in the Years Following 9/11?

The key statement in the Obama administration's announcement of its Afghan policy came in the president's speech in December 2009 at West Point when the president said: "In the last few months alone, we have apprehended extremists within our borders who were sent here from the border region of Afghanistan and Pakistan to commit new acts of terror."[22] Almost no commenters picked up on this statement because most people continued to assume it was true. But to whom was the President referring? If it was Najibullah Zazi, his father and friends, arrested for allegedly gathering bomb-making materials after a visit to Pakistan, the matter was at best ambiguous. The government acknowledged that the men went to fight in the area and that, even if the two al-Qaeda leaders they encountered there suggested they attack within the United States, the plan to bomb the New York subways was entirely of the men's own making: The botched attack, as the *New York Times* reported, was neither initiated nor directed from al-Qaeda in Pakistan, a position not clearly controverted by the later – and somewhat ambiguous – claim in the indictment and plea bargain of contact with known al-Qaeda operatives.[23] Or the president may have had in mind Bryant Neal Vinas, a convert to Islam and the son of immigrants from Peru and Argentina, who pleaded guilty to being trained in an al-Qaeda camp, but who, like several others, fought against American troops in the region rather than carrying out a plot within America's borders.

---

[22] Barack Obama, "Text: Obama's Address on the War in Afghanistan," *New York Times*, December 2, 2009.

[23] William K. Rashbaum and Karen Zraick, "Government Says Al Qaeda Ordered N.Y. Plot," *New York Times*, April 23, 2010. See also Sebastian Smith, "US Accuses Top Al-Qaeda Leaders in NY Bomb Plot," *New York Times*, July 7, 2010: "'The charges reveal that the plot ... was directed by senior al-Qaeda leadership in Pakistan and was also directly related to a scheme by al-Qaeda plotters in Pakistan to use Western operatives to attack a target in the United Kingdom,' the Department of Justice said in a statement.... All three 'organized' the Zazi plot, although only El Shukrijumah is charged, the justice department said." On September 22, 2010, the director of the FBI strikingly stated in his Congressional testimony: "The 2009 plot led by Najibullah Zazi to attack the New York subway was the first known instance since 9/11 that al Qaeda had successfully deployed a trained operative into the United States."

Later attempts displayed similar characteristics. The Christmas Day 2009 attempt by Nigerian Abdul Farouk Abdulmutallab to bring down an airliner near Detroit – even assuming it was seriously intended – was either an independent act or organized through a Yemeni group: It was not, according to the State Department's own spokesman, directed by al-Qaeda.[24] Similarly, the attempted bombing by Faisal Shahzad at Times Square, New York, on May 1, 2010 cannot be said to have been directed by al-Qaeda. Indeed, early claims of involvement by the Taliban in Pakistan were subsequently retracted, and despite Attorney General Eric Holder's initial statement that "he [Shahzad] was basically directed here to the United States to carry out this attack," later information showed that Shahzad was handed around by various Pakistani contacts,[25] thus prompting the ranking Republican on the Senate Select Committee on Intelligence, following Holder's closed-door testimony, to say, a propos any al-Qaeda direction: "I am not convinced by the information I've seen so far."[26] Whatever opportunistic use elements in Pakistan may have made of Shahzad, there is insufficient evidence to assert that they initiated and controlled his actions. Similarly, three local Muslims convicted in Britain for planning airline attacks in 2006 were said by prosecutors to have been directed by al-Qaeda operatives in Pakistan, but clear evidence that they initiated the plot was not forthcoming.[27] The testimony by CIA analyst Marc Sageman to the Senate in October 2009 remains valid:

It is interesting to note that for all the fear of al Qaeda, the organization managed only two successful plots in the West in the last twenty years! The fact that they were so deadly overshadows this truth. It appears that either we are getting luckier or this terrorist threat is diminishing. In the United States, the last casualty dates back eight years to 9/11/01. There has

---

[24] Jason Keyser, "Bin Laden Endorses Failed Attempt to Bomb US Jet," *The Washington Post*, January 24, 2010.

[25] David E. Sanger, "U.S. Pressure Helps Militants Overseas Focus Efforts," *New York Times*, May 7, 2010.

[26] Greg Miller, "Man Claims He Aided Times Square Suspect," *The Washington Post*, May14, 2010. On the Attorney General's claim, see Charlie Savage, "Holder Backs a Miranda Limit for Terror Suspects," *New York Times*, May 9, 2010. See also Art Keller, "Exclusive: al Qaeda Bomb-Factory Video," *Foreign Policy*, May 14 2010.

[27] John F. Burns, "3 Britons Convicted in Plot to Blow Up Airliners," *New York Times*, July 8, 2010.

not been even one plot that went to termination since then. In the rest of the West, there has not been a single casualty in the past four years.... [T]he majority of global neo-jihadi terrorist networks from 2004 onwards did not have any formal training from foreign terrorist groups, contrary to the statements of Intelligence agency chiefs on both sides of the Atlantic. They were purely homegrown.[28]

Even if the Times Square attempt involved core al-Qaeda in the Afghanistan–Pakistan border region, testimony by F.B.I. and Homeland Security officials indicated that no attack had been directed by al-Qaeda for as much as eight years following 9/11. Therefore the idea that al-Qaeda – as opposed to some of its imitators in Somalia and Yemen, or through "homegrown" terrorists in Canada, Europe, or the United States – has continuously promoted attacks on the United States from Afghanistan's borders is at best unproven.[29]

The central question that was not being asked, then, is: Why were there so few if any attacks initiated by and clearly attributable to al-Qaeda and similar organizations within the United States after 9/11? Indeed, what sociological assumptions made this question so difficult for officials to address?

The answer cannot possibly be that the terrorists had been pinned down in the Afghanistan–Pakistan border region or that Homeland Security had made us all safe. Surely the capacity of such organizations

---

[28] Marc Sageman, "Testimony to Senate Intelligence Committee" 2009. www.fpri.org/transcripts/20091007.Sageman.ConfrontingalQaeda.pdf. "In June, [2010] CIA Director Leon Panetta estimated that, 'at most,' only 50 to 100 al-Qaeda operatives were present in Afghanistan. His assessment echoed those given by other senior U.S. officials. In October, national security adviser James L. Jones said the U.S. government's 'maximum estimate' was that al-Qaeda had fewer than 100 members in Afghanistan, with no bases and 'no ability to launch attacks on either us or our allies'." Craig Whitlock, "Facing Afghan Mistrust, al-Qaeda Fighters Take Limited Role in Insurgency," *Washington Post*, August 23, 2010, A01. The same points were emphasized in the September, 2010 report to the 9/11 Commission.

[29] The involvement of al-Qaida from the Afghanistan–Pakistan border in later attacks is equally murky. Three British Muslims, said to have connections to al-Qaida, were convicted in July 2010 on secondary charges of plotting an attack after one jury failed to reach a verdict and a second acquitted the men on more serious charges. Burns, "3 Britons Convicted in Plot to Blow Up Airliners." Similarly, Norway arrested three men said to be connected to al-Qaida, Najibullah Zazi, and a plot in Manchester in April 2009: See Scott Shane and Eric Schmidt, "Norway Announces Three Arrests in Terrorist Plot," *New York Times*, July 8, 2010.

to send the occasional terrorist was and is not nil. And with US borders so porous that nearly 1.5 million illegal migrants are added to the country each year – including, by State Department estimates, some 14,500–17,500 forced labor or sex slaves[30] – and with drugs easily brought into the country and illegal weapons locally available the idea that suicide bombers could not be sent to wreak havoc on public parks, shopping malls, or sports arenas is untenable. Yet it has suited politicians not to ask why there have been no further attacks: They cannot afford to do so in case a subsequent assault makes them appear to have been naïve, insufficiently tough, or too cavalier about the threat. And while it is true that the leaders of al-Qaeda and its allies in southwest Asia were seriously affected by air and ground attacks, it is not clear whether (as Sageman further testified) "the threat against the West is degenerating into a 'leaderless jihad'" or if it has been morphing into the type of acephalous organization found in many tribal situations. By not addressing fully the reasons why no attacks organized by al-Qaeda, the Islamic Caliphate (ISIS, Daish, ISIL), or similar organizations may have occurred in the United States since 9/11 the risk is that policy becomes driven by unexamined myths and cultural assumptions, as was the case when it was believed that Saddam Hussein must have weapons of mass destruction or that Southeast Asian countries must fall like dominoes.

It is, therefore, worth considering a very different reason why there have been no further attacks by these groups on American soil, namely that public opinion in the Muslim (particularly the Arab) world would not support such attacks. It may seem ironic that America's safety has lain in the "Arab street" but to understand why that might be so one must return to the context in which the attack of 9/11 occurred and to the failure of the administrations of that time and later to consider certain anthropological insights.

At the outset of his presidency, George W. Bush made it clear that, unlike Bill Clinton, he would not involve himself deeply in the Arab–Israeli dispute and would simply leave matters in the hands of the then Prime Minister of Israel, Ariel Sharon. To ordinary Arabs, this was tantamount to saying he did not regard them as real men. Two factors are crucial here – the way in which manhood is achieved and the way

---

[30] Joseph Berger, "Despite Law, Few Trafficking Arrests," *New York Times*, December 4, 2009.

direct threats to it are commonly managed in the Arab world. In the Muslim countries of the Middle East, there are essentially no religious rituals that advance a man to adult status. Rather, what one must do – particularly in the Middle Eastern/Southwest Asian variants of Muslim cultures – is demonstrate that one can put together a network of people with whom one has a range of mutual obligations: Society, like an electrical system that only works through pluses and minuses, is held together by the running imbalance of indebtedness. And the moment when this is most fully demonstrated in a young man's life is at the time of marriage. That is the time when alliances must be made by and for the groom, a time when a man may be said to have proved his capacity to maneuver in a world of relentless contingency. Moreover, all social ties must be constantly serviced and their capacity to be precipitated recurrently demonstrated; as an ally a man is, in this cultural system, only as reliable as his last performance.[31] And one of the crucial indicators of this capacity to create safety in relationships is revealed in the way disputes are commonly addressed.

Disputes have an almost ritual-like pattern: Opponents will raise their voices enough so that others gather around and then, turning at an angle to each other, make their case to the assembled crowd. If, however, someone turns his back to the other it may mean he does not regard him even as a worthy opponent.[32] Just as in poker, where your cards are a function of the other person's cards, so, too, in these cultures, it is often acknowledgment by an enemy that is vital to acceptance as a leading figure in one's own group. This pattern became evident in the weeks following 9/11, for the statement commonly heard in the "Arab street" was that President Bush, by refusing to involve himself in the region, had turned his back on the Muslims as if they were unworthy of engagement as adult men. As a result,

---

[31] These points are elaborated in Lawrence Rosen, *Bargaining For Reality: The Construction of Social Relations in a Muslim Community* (Chicago: University of Chicago Press, 1984).

[32] Conflicts may, of course, be negotiated in a wide range of ways in Muslim cultures. See, e.g., Victor F. Ayoub, "Conflict Resolution and Social Reorganization in a Lebanese Village," *Human Organization*, 2 (1965): 11–17; Frederick Charles Huxley, *Wasita in Lebanon* (Ann Arbor: Museum of Anthropology, University of Michigan, 1978); Ido Shahar, "Legal Pluralism and the Study of Shari'a Courts," *Islamic Law and Society*, 15, 1 (2008): 112–41; and Baudoin Dupret, Maurits Berger, and Laila al-Zwaini, *Legal Pluralism in the Arab World* (The Hague: Kluwer Law International, 1999).

Osama Bin Laden no doubt understood very well that the people whose approval he needed were prepared to license an attack that they might not otherwise have been willing to tacitly support. The reaction, though strongly felt, was nevertheless transient: Once the United States did re-engage people of the region – even in an oppositional way – popular legitimization for further attacks declined. Additional attacks would not only lack such validation but would most likely be seen as counterproductive: Attacking the United States and its civilians could only lead local regimes to tighten their controls, encourage Western nations to replace interaction with force, and undermine any man's claim to be a serious interlocutor. Here, then, may be another example of faulty anthropological assumptions at work in the war, for both the Bush and Obama administrations seem to have accepted the idea that Bin Laden's al-Qaeda was sociologically self-contained, that it was not really connected or responsive to a particular constituency since that "imagined" constituency was neither highly localized nor institutionalized. A more holistic approach, however, would have suggested that the construct within which such terrorist groups operate is not unconnected to the virtual community upon which a portion of its legitimacy depends. The anthropological assumptions of the Bush and Obama administrations left both of them strangely unaware of the forces at work in the region – the Bush people because they chose to willfully ignore such factors, the Obama administration because of its reluctance to consider the broader rationale that may account for the absence of further attacks on the US mainland.

By failing to understand why people in the region believed the United States had turned its back on the Arabs – or by simply regarding Arab rhetoric as meaningless exaggeration – both administrations missed the import of what was being said. It is identical to assuming – as some in the administration and press did – that various regimes in the Middle East are regarded by their people as illegitimate when, in fact, a proper understanding of how legitimacy is attributed would lead to the more supportable conclusion that such regimes are often disliked but that the way any given leader accedes to power – by establishing a network of dependents – is the way anyone should do so, and hence that anyone who succeeds in putting together such a political network is ipso facto legitimate. This failure to understand what American actions have meant to people in the region obscured an understanding of why Bin Laden – whose primary target was not the United States but the nearby Arab regimes – had popular support for 9/11 but not later. And failure to even ask why there were no more attacks on American soil by Bin Laden or successor organizations only perpetuated the myth that we were continually under attack from their bases.

## Suicide Bombers Are Motivated by Their Hatred and Envy of Us

Speaking of Islamic extremists, George W. Bush always said that "they hate us" – indeed "they hate our freedom." Various experts – few of whom spoke the languages or lived for extended periods in the region – have claimed that suicide bombers act only when provoked by foreign invaders,[33] that because they come from all socioeconomic classes they are not motivated by poverty or relative deprivation,[34] that they are protesting their countries' lack of civil liberties,[35] that they are psychologically affected by their powerlessness,[36] or that they kill themselves to achieve religious martyrdom,[37] solidarity with fellow jihadists,[38] or fulfillment as cultural heroes.[39] Once again, the myths obscure the local dynamics, and the various administrations accepted uncritically

---

[33] Robert A. Pape and James K. Feldman, *Cutting the Fuse: The Explosion of Global Suicide Terrorism and How to Stop It* (Chicago: University of Chicago Press, 2010).

[34] Olivier Roy, *Globalised Islam: The Search for a New Ummah* (London: Hurst, 2004).

[35] Alan B. Krueger, *What Makes a Terrorist: Economics and the Roots of Terrorism* (Princeton: Princeton University Press, 2008).

[36] See Jerrold M. Post, *The Mind of the Terrorist: The Psychology of Terrorism from the IRA to al-Qaeda* (New York: Palgrave Macmillan, 2007); Ariel Merari, *Driven to Death: Psychological and Social Aspects of Suicide Terrorism* (Oxford: Oxford University Press, 2010); and Mohammed M. Hafez, *Manufacturing Human Bombs: The Making of Palestinian Suicide Bombers* (Washington, DC: United States Institute of Peace Press, 2006).

[37] David Bukay, "The Religious Foundations of Suicide Bombings." *Middle East Quarterly* 13, 4 (2006): 26–36.

[38] Marc Sageman, *Understanding Terror Networks* (Philadelphia: University of Pennsylvania Press, 2004).

[39] For a variety of explanations, see, generally, Armando Spataro, "Why Do People Become Terrorists? A Prosecutor's Experiences," *Journal of International Criminal Justice*, 6, 3 (2008): 507–24; Jessica Stern, "5 Myths about Who Becomes a Terrorist," *The Washington Post*, January 10, 2010, B4; and Sarah Kershaw, "The Terrorist Mind: An Update," *New York Times*, January 9 2010.

the underlying anthropological assumptions embraced by these theories. The reality, it may be argued, is rather different.

If being a man means forming a network of indebtedness, then the removal of those resources necessary to create such an index of one's manhood can have very serious repercussions. Older men will have established their ties and hence their standing as men, so they have nothing to prove by suicide bombing. Men of any age may participate vigorously in funeral processions to demonstrate involvement in their networks. Younger men, however, may need to prove they stand at the center of some network, in part through the elaborate process of negotiating a marriage.[40] Nowadays, however, in many parts of the Middle East, younger men cannot easily get married because they do not have the financial wherewithal or other means by which to build the requisite obligational bonds. Indeed, the average age for marriage has climbed well into the thirties for men and into the mid-to-upper-twenties for most women. In Iran, 38 percent of men aged 25–29 remain unmarried, while the cost of marriage in Egypt, for example, is as much as 11–15 times annual per capita household expenditure.[41] Barred from the usual avenues for substantiating adult status, some men may choose, however, to demonstrate that they have formed bonds of indebtedness by being attached to a terrorist group. More than that, since any man's network is only as good as his capacity to maintain it, there is always the risk that his allies will not be there when needed.

But if a man kills himself in pursuit of a holy endeavor he fixes, both in religion and in the public eye, that he did indeed have a network – and

---

[40] As a recent report states: "Marriage ... is widely perceived [in Muslim cultures] as the main marker of adulthood." Ragui Assaad, Christine Binzel, and May Gadallah, "Transition to Employment and Marriage among Young Men in Egypt," The Middle East Youth Initiative, Working Paper No. 12 (Washington, DC: Brookings Institution Wolfensohn Center for Development and Dubai School of Government, October 2010).

[41] See Brian Whitaker, *What Really Went Wrong* (London: Saqi Books, 2010); Assaad, et al., "Transition to Employment"; Diane Singerman, "The Economic Imperatives of Marriage: Emerging Practices and Identities among Youth in the Middle East," Middle East Youth Initiative Working Paper Number 6 (Washington, DC: Brookings Institution Wolfensohn Center for Development and Dubai School of Government, 2007); and Michael Slackman, "Stifled, Egypt's Young Turn to Islamic Fervor," *New York Times*, February 17, 2008.

that, unlike ordinary men whose networks are subject to constant uncertainty, his own network now lies beyond risk of revision.[42] It is not that "they" hate or envy us: It is that if men in this part of the world are not able to negotiate their webs of relationship freely, there is no way they can see themselves as real men. The American administrations have continued to assume that suicide bombing is an individual act, that it is attached to issues of religious fervor and resistance to foreign occupation. As a result, the focus remains on personal disaffection rather than society's situation. Such assumptions preclude consideration of the broader array of cultural implications that may lead to suicide bombing. But it is only if the forms of social arrangement in which these men become more recognizably adult – with jobs and other opportunities to build alliances – that their sense of free movement will be reaffirmed. In the absence of such opportunities – and with US policies aimed more at the suppression than the maturation of young men in the region – inappropriate anthropological assumptions can only lead to inapposite political results.

## Many Bombers, Though Potentially Very Dangerous, Have Failed in Their Attempts

The factors that apply to clearly intended bombing attacks within the United States apply as well to those that have failed. From the Shoe Bomber to the Christmas Day Bomber to the Times Square Bomber, attempts have generally been unsuccessful. Chance, incompetent training, and possible loss of nerve may all have played a role. But success is a cultural construct, not just an explosive result. From their perspective, the bombers' success may lie primarily in the meaning of the attempt itself. Consider, in particular, two factors common to most of the bombers who have been captured and interrogated: the ready confession of involvement and the willingness to implicate others.[43] If the goal is to sacrifice oneself to the destruction of American targets, why would these bombers so quickly admit guilt and inform on their

---

[42] See Lawrence Rosen, "Why Do Arab Terrorists Kill Themselves?" In Lawrence Rosen, *Varieties of Muslim Experience* (Chicago: University of Chicago Press, 2008), 39–46.

[43] See, e.g., Associated Press, "Pakistan Detainees Proud of Role in NYC Bomb Case," *New York Times*, May 22, 2010.

coconspirators? The answers may lie in a fuller understanding of the cultural context of these acts.

My own interviews with Muslim judges as well as individual instances collected by other scholars indicate that, career offenders aside, criminal defendants quite frequently plead guilty.[44] They do so not out of coercion or plea bargaining, however, but because they believe their acts to have been justified, and they know that, unlike American proceedings that end when a guilty plea is entered, in their own cultures they will generally still have the opportunity to explain their reasons in court. For example, Zacarias Moussaoui, sentenced to life imprisonment for aiding terrorists, pleaded guilty – to the mystification of his American attorneys and the judge in the case – but was outraged when he was not allowed by the rules of evidence to tell the jury his story in his own fashion.[45] Similarly, terrorists may implicate others because, if their acts are to have meaning, they must demonstrate that they have indeed constructed a network of associates, a far more significant indicator of their adult status than the anonymous completion of their terrorist acts. A bombing attempt, then, need not necessarily result in a deadly explosion in order to prove that most important of factors – that the bomber is embedded in a network of consequence. And the admission of involvement is a statement of the justifiable basis for the attempt and hence a statement of one's standing as a rational man. Once again, if the implicit anthropological assumption is that the meaning of an act is a shared human phenomenon immediately accessible to all regardless of cultural variation, the nuances of local meaning – and the mistakes attending such incomprehension – may have very serious consequences. Failure to appreciate what passes for reason and success in this cultural frame can, therefore, easily lead government officials and media commentators to misunderstand the very nature of the terrorists' acts.

---

[44] See, e.g., Herbert J. Liebesny, *The Law of the Near and Middle East* (Albany: State University Press of New York, 1975), 234–39, and Rudolph Peters, *Crime and Punishment in Islamic Law* (Cambridge: Cambridge University Press, 2005).

[45] See Lawrence Rosen, "Trying Terror: Zacarias Moussaoui and His Culture on Trial," In Lawrence Rosen, *Islam and the Rule of Justice* (Chicago: University of Chicago Press, 2018) 136–65.

## If We Build Safe Settlements, Others Will Want to Emulate Them

This has been a key doctrine of the counterinsurgency (COIN) litany. But it fails to recognize the tremendous range of differences among regions and groups in this part of the world, the constant fractionation that is at once a hedge against centralized power and a vehicle for keeping open the range of ways a man may build his personal network. Far from wishing to emulate aspects of other settlements, emphasis is often placed on ways to distinguish oneself and one's group. The rivalry of cities and locales is a keystone of Middle Eastern cultures, differentiation being crucial to individual and collective identity. Thus the COIN attempt to establish baseline settlements is often undercut from the outset. American military personnel, many of whom continued to refer to the Afghans derisively as "hajjis," were not, as Nir Rosen argued, even capable of carrying out their own professed COIN policy:

The troubles with COIN are institutional. The American military and policy establishments are incapable of doing COIN. They lack the curiosity to understand other cultures and the empathy to understand what motivates people. Counterinsurgency doesn't make sense. It asks soldiers, concerned primarily with survival, to mix Wyatt Earp and Mother Theresa. In public they pay lip service to COIN because that is the way to advance. Less publicly, officers speak of going into villages and "doing that COIN shit."[46]

Indeed, the guidelines were so inchoate that, as one army captain put it, "the word 'counterinsurgency' is like a Potemkin village satisfying the curiosity of a typical stranger but upon close examination by a serious interrogator, falling apart."[47] Or, as Marc Sageman told the Senate:

The proposed counter-insurgency strategy in Afghanistan is at present irrelevant to the goal of disrupting, dismantling and defeating al Qaeda, which is located in Pakistan. None of the plots in the West has any connection to any Afghan insurgent group ... Taliban return to power will not mean an

---

[46] Nir Rosen, "Something from Nothing: U.S. Strategy in Afghanistan," *Boston Review*, January/February, 2010. See, generally, Nir Rosen, *Aftermath: Following the Bloodshed of America's Wars in the Muslim World* (New York: Nation, 2010).

[47] See Timothy Hsia, "Counterinsurgency – All Things to All Men," *New York Times*, May 21, 2010, and Kalev Sepp, "Best Practices in Counterinsurgency," *Military Review*, May-June, 2005: 8–12.

automatic new sanctuary for al Qaeda. [C]ounter-insurgency in Afghanistan has little to do with global neo-jihadi terrorism and protecting the
homeland.[48]

But even where safe havens were constructed, the belief that others
would seek to emulate them was misguided. The assumption of relative uniformity among local groupings in the region and the concomi-
tant assumptions that successful economic and security advances for
one will become the object of envy for all simply fly in the face of local
diversity. Indeed, in the cultures of the region, it is precisely in such
diversity that some degree of safety resides: By being able to reach out
in all directions to a wide range of possible allies, one retains a significant degree of maneuverability that is lost in constraints of social
uniformity and state-controlled regularization. In the Quran (V: 54),
it is said: "If God had willed, He would have made you one nation."
Or, as a Muslim character in a Conrad novel explains: "In the variety
of knowledge lies safety" – knowledge of others' customs and contacts being the crucial knowledge to garner. It is precisely in difference, then, that men, imbued with God-endowed reason, are expected
to make their way, and reveling in difference is an integral part of
the cultural pattern that characterizes the area. The assumption that
everyone would want to follow the model of an American-created
settlement simply ignores the crucial value placed on differentiation
throughout the region.

## Underneath, We All Really Want the Same Things and Are All Really Alike

This was President George W. Bush's rationale for not having to think
about what happens after the former regime is removed. For him it was
as much a matter of natural law that, wanting to be like us, the Iraqis
and Afghans would simply welcome American troops with flowers and
candy and would then proceed automatically to welcome our institutions and our goals (Figure 5.1). Just as Bush believed that the market
is always self-regulating so too the political thicket, once cleared of the
brush, was thought to yield a "human terrain" in which democracy
would seed itself and (as Ron Chernow has said of the Marquis de

---

[48] Sageman, "Testimony to Senate Intelligence Committee," 2009.

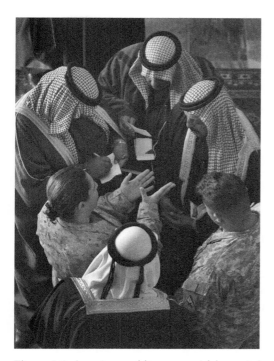

**Figure 5.1** American soldiers meet Afghans. John Moore/Getty Images.

Lafayette's attitude toward the Terror following the French Revolution) "that liberty would somehow thrive in the vacuum."

President Obama did not subscribe to Bush's natural law vision, but he did appear to accept a functional equivalent – that everyone who wants safety must want it in much the same way. This is a truly remarkable position for someone who, in many other respects, has followed in the intellectual footsteps of his anthropologist mother. As he stated in his letter of July 8, 2009 celebrating the award of the James Smithson Medal to anthropologist Claude Lévi-Strauss: "My mother earned her Ph.D. in anthropology and instilled in me a deep appreciation for finding the universal common ground among all people and societies, while at the same time studying and celebrating what makes each unique."[49] Indeed, in a number of other instances, the

---

[49] On President Obama's connections to anthropology, see Ruth Behar, "The Anthropologist's Son," *The Chronicle of Higher Education* 55, 14 (2008): B99.

president clearly demonstrated his anthropological orientation: His near-yet-distant way of choosing his religious and ethnic attachment is consonant with the anthropologist's pose of participant/observer; his partial apology for his countrymen's past deeds bespoke his relativist propensities; his bowing to the Emperor of Japan and the Saudi king demonstrated not the abasement of his office but engagement in others' practices without accepting their meanings as his own. Yet on some continuum running from the universal to the particular, President Obama tended to lean toward the former orientation in most instances. By ignoring the differences encountered in Afghanistan, he set most of the particularistic tendencies of anthropological theory aside and directed the army to engage in community development as if those communities could be anywhere in the world.[50]

It is true that in his Nobel lecture, President Obama noted that "somehow, given the dizzying pace of globalization, the cultural leveling of modernity, it perhaps comes as no surprise that people fear the loss of what they cherish in their particular identities – their race, their tribe, and perhaps most powerfully their religion." But he prefaced that remark by saying that "we'er all basically seeking the same things."[51] Clearly the president was trying to walk a fine line between the universal and the particular, individual desires and group identity, respectful relativism and the need to make choices as commander-in-chief. The American propulsion to regard everyone as basically the same may make Americans feel that we are really just being "friendly" and selfless. But trying to have it both ways, we set ourselves up to be shocked and disappointed when we discover that everyone does not, in fact, always want what we want. By focusing too much on the universalistic side of the anthropological equation, one may readily slide into the myth that the likable American is simply helping those who naturally want to be just like us.

* * *

---

[50] Obama began his career as a community organizer in Chicago, and it is unclear to what extent that experience, based on Saul Alinsky's model, led him to see such organizing in rather more universal than particularistic terms. See, generally, Serge Kovaleski, "Obama's Organizing Years, Guiding Others and Finding Himself," *New York Times*, July 7, 2008.

[51] Barack Obama, "Remarks by the President at the Acceptance of the Nobel Peace Prize," Washington: The White House, Office of the Press Secretary, December 10, 2009.

Presidents Bush and Obama allowed their policies to become associated with unarticulated orientations in anthropology that are substantially outmoded: The kind of holism and functional anthropology to which their administrations attached themselves is seriously flawed. Holism's assumption that everything is connected to everything may have influenced the administrations' attempt to solve multiple issues of domestic policy, economic structure, and international relations simultaneously, but in truth, all parts of a cultural system do not cohere equally: One cannot simply change the structure of centralized power and expect all concepts of, say, personhood and morality to fall into line accordingly. And functionalism's assumption that everything works to the maintenance of the totality fails in its incapacity to account for historical change and thus negates any serious consideration of the relevance of cultural history in the assessment of one's actions in the region.

The Obama administration in particular (including the top echelon of the military) would appear to have accepted several cultural assumptions that are highly questionable: (1) that tribes are structurally rigid entities and/or obdurate precursors to desired democratic governance; (2) that under the policy of "clear, hold, build" (which Mr. Obama preferred to call "target, train, and transfer") the example set in one village will be readily transferable to any other village since they share a common aspirational and organizational structure; and (3) that in a supposed age of globalization, the local is either unimportant or will be overwhelmed by the need or desire of local people to be incorporated in a process of ineluctable uniformity. The first assumption is grounded on a view of tribal organization that is at least fifty years out of date, the second on a belief that there is very little variation among indigenous groupings, and the third on the assumption that the local is overwhelmed by the global when in fact the human quest for variation renders such uniformity illusory. The Human Terrain projects – which involved anthropologists as key figures in discerning local leadership and patterns of opposition – were favored by both Secretary of Defense Robert Gates (who served in that role under both presidents) and General David Petraeus.[52] Even if we leave aside the

---

[52] As Petraeus has stated: "The human terrain is the decisive terrain." Mark Bowden, "The Professor of War," *Vanity Fair*, May, 2010. See also Human Terrain Team Handbook, 2008. www.vho.org/aaargh/fran/livres9/

propriety of anthropologists' involvement in such operations, it is, however, clear that the assumptions that received favor in the manuals and implementation were highly questionable and dangerously unreliable from the outset.

War tests our theories, no less than our received assumptions, our creativity, and our courage. Whether knowingly and hopefully or naively and dangerously, whether as the rationalization for a planned withdrawal or a sincere belief that we could do an end-run on the Afghan government and build decentralized communities in strategic locales (implanting what then commanding General Stanley A. McChrystal called a "government in a box"), what was left on the table were many of the same sociocultural assumptions that had endured since at least 9/11.[53] Moreover, these assumptions became entrenched in military doctrine as the war was seen as an instance in which US forces were withdrawn but not defeated, leading a generation of future commanders and cadets to a misguided view of anthropology's contribution to COIN ideology. Without an understanding of why we were attacked and why actions do not mean the same to our opponents as we assume they must to any human being, it is unsurprising that we often wind up as mystified by our lack of success in this part of the world as we have often remained insensible to our failures in other such localized wars.

By the summer of 2021, when the lights were turned out at the massive American airbase at Bagram, as President Biden ordered the

humterrainhandbo.pdf. See, generally, David Axe, "Social Scientists under Fire," *Miller-McCune*, (March/April, 2010): 58–69; George R. Lucas, Jr., *Anthropologists in Arms: The Ethics of Military Anthropology* (Lanham, MD: AltaMira Press, 2009); and George Packer, "Knowing the Enemy: Can Social Scientists Redefine the 'War on Terror'?" *The New Yorker* (December 18, 2006): 58–69. For critiques of anthropologists' involvement in human terrain projects, see Roberto González, *American Counterinsurgency: Human Science and the Human Terrain* (Chicago: Prickly Paradigm Press, 2009); Roberto González, "Going 'Tribal': Notes on Pacification in the 21st Century," *Anthropology Today* 25, 2 (2009): 15–19; and Network of Concerned Anthropologists, *The Counter-Counterinsurgency Manual* (Chicago: Prickly Paradigm Press, 2009).

[53] On setting up local governments, see Maureen Dowd, "The Evil of Lesser Evilism," *New York Times*, May 11, 2010: "A Pentagon report also shows that General McChrystal's boast that he could wheel 'a government in a box' into Marja was premature." General McChrystal was fired by the president after remarks the general and members of his staff made were reported in Michael Hastings, "The Runaway General," *Rolling Stone*, June 22, 2010.

end of war and the Taliban were again surging, the American vision of tribes and of nation-building was once again drifting in the absence of an acceptable understanding of what went wrong. Anthropology as a discipline is not well equipped for application, notwithstanding a subfield that has appropriated the term and the numerous anthropology degree holders who have taken positions in the private sector. But if less than perfect is better than a misguided need for certainty and if anthropology is to continue to be employed in the armature of warfare, a clearer view of presuppositions and their history may yet prove indispensable, if ultimately incomplete.

# 6 | Aging Out?
## Moroccan Youth in the Aftermath
## of the Arab Spring

*When discussions about the Arab Middle East turn to its prospects for liberalization, Morocco is frequently one of the countries to which analysts point most hopefully. A nation of apparent moderation with a history of broad political party activism and economic decentralization, its 37 million people value education and independence in equal measure. Under the guidance of recent kings who, whatever their failings, cannot simply be characterized as unmitigated tyrants, expectations for political and economic development are enticing.*

*King Hassan II, who ruled from 1962 to 1999, was a master at playing parties against one another, and the truth and reconciliation commission founded by his son and successor, Mohammad VI, though allowing no direct criticism of the monarchy, did grant amnesty to thousands of former prisoners. Despite each monarch's illiberal actions, political discussion at the local level is relatively open. The success of some Islamist parties who now vie for an electoral role – while others who reject the monarchy are kept outside – nevertheless continues to depend on their willingness to accept this brand of authoritarianism. King Hassan used to say that "Moroccans are not a people of excess." But like his revered father, Muhammad V, he also said that Morocco is like a lion to whom he was tethered: "Sometimes you ease up on the leash and sometimes you have to rein it in tightly." Following the events of the Arab Spring, with many Arab states backing away from their modest pronouncements about liberalization, the Moroccan lion and its keeper, irretrievably linked, continue to lurch back and forth. Who will be pulling who continues to breed uncertainty. Particularly for the country's young.*

\*

Imagine that you are a young man living in Morocco. You are not malnourished much less starving; you are not mired in an endless civil war nor are you surrounded by hostile forces that regard your form of Islam as heresy. You probably know that yours is a nation in which over a quarter of the population is under thirty nor would you be shocked to learn that 28 percent of the population of the entire Middle East is aged between fifteen and twenty-nine, the largest number in the history of the region. As a Moroccan you are a citizen of a country with an overall male literacy rate of about 80 percent, though the numbers fall significantly among the 43 percent of the nation that live outside of cities. From the nearby shantytowns and decrepit old medina dwellings you could have guessed that roughly one in five of your countrymen lives below the poverty line. You may think it regrettable that your country has no oil wealth, even though you are not sure that resource has proven such a blessing to Libya or Algeria or Iraq. You may not know with statistical precision that your country's agricultural sector accounts for only 14–17 percent of export income while occupying 40–45 percent of the labor force, but you certainly appreciate that the highly variable annual rainfall has a dramatic impact on the nation's sense of economic well-being. You can see that textiles, phosphates, and (at least before the COVID-19 pandemic) tourism continue to play a big role in what most analysts describe as a relatively free market environment. At the same time it would not surprise you that judicial corruption, inefficient land titling, and a bloated bureaucracy contribute to *The Index of Economic Freedom* ranking Morocco 86th out of 180 nations.

On a more personal note, as a young man you certainly know many others who are struggling for a regular income, that a hundred thousand people swell the unemployment ranks each year while 400,000 graduates continue without work. You have even seen, over the course of many years, the heartbreaking protests by jobless graduates in front of the Parliament building and find it ironic that unemployment in most Arab countries is actually higher for those who finish college than for the less well educated. You will have been shocked, in the years since the Moroccan reactions to the Arab Spring, by the self-immolation of nearly a hundred young people whose act of desperation mirrored their loss of all confidence in a future.[1] While not

---

[1] See John Thorpe, "Self-Immolation Attempts Shock Morocco," *The National*, January 21, 2012. www.thenational.ae/world/africa/self-immolation-attempts-shock-morocco-1.390292.

inherently indolent, studies show that 80 percent of your time is spent just hanging out, and that civic or recreational institutions that might absorb your energy are few in number.

More poignantly, throughout the Middle East and North Africa, you will have sensed that the average age of marriage for men is now over thirty-four. Indeed, issues of sex and marriage weigh heavily on you. No doubt you think how wonderful it would be to marry a foreign girl and get a permit to live in France or America.[2] In the meantime, you try to contact women online but are less likely than in the past to have your mother scout out prospective brides in the public baths since the wherewithal to get married so often seems out of reach. Although you yearn for sex, you may be ashamed when you see other young men exhibiting themselves to unveiled women in public or working as gigolos for middle-aged European women who treat your country like a stop along the sex tour route usually ascribed only to men. You know that an independent income is essential to getting married and having sex, but even though you do not for a moment believe the official unemployment rate of 10.6 percent and are not surprised that four out of five unemployed men are in your age bracket, somehow – whether by cobbling together part-time work or continuing your studies – you have, against all odds, preserved some degree of optimism about your own future.[3]

As limited as your prospects may seem, at each juncture, you have not been without choices. For even though the range of realistic alternatives

---

[2] Avi Spiegel, without citing a source, says: "During one typical year in the 2000s, 100,000 attempted to cross illegally into Spain," while, again without citation, he says: "One poll found that more than 90 percent of young people expressed a desire to emigrate from Morocco, and more than 70 percent of university graduates hoped to settle abroad." Avi Max Spiegel, *Young Islam: The New Politics of Religion in Morocco and the Arab World* (Princeton: Princeton University Press, 2015), 85 and 84. Numbers seem to vary a good deal: A Gallup poll of 2010 shows that before the Arab Spring a quarter of North African men said they would like to emigrate. Neli Esipova and Julie Ray, "One in Four in North Africa Desired to Migrate before Unrest," *Gallup News*, April 29, 2011. http://news.gallup.com/poll/147344/one-four-north-africa-desired-migrate-unrest.aspx.

The nearly four million Moroccans living abroad remit some $6.4 billion each year.

[3] For recent statistics, see Trading Economics, "Morocco Unemployment Rate," Tradingeconomics.com. See also Lahcen Achy, "Moroccan Youth Struggle to Find Employment Opportunities," *Al-Monitor*, June 30, 2013. al-monitor.com.

available to you may, from the perspective of an outsider, seem very limited that is not quite the way you are likely to see matters. In Moroccan society, one always had considerable leeway in negotiating relations with others – within as well as beyond one's immediate kinfolk. Indeed, it was taken as the mark of a mature man that he had constructed a network of people with whom he had forged reciprocal obligations. In a society in which there are no rites of passage to adulthood, the nearest analog is marriage – but not as the result of any sacralizing ceremony but because in order to get married, one must raise the necessary bridewealth payment, and that, in turn, requires forging a web of indebtedness that is proof of one's being a person whose actions have consequences in the ongoing game of searching for and servicing a network of persons who may be called upon for various needs.

In forming such a network, one could draw – at least in the past – upon several different resources, any one of which might suffice to build alliances. So, for example, an economic "favor" done for someone can be called up in another form at a later time. Alternatively, you might have a fine grasp of language – even of poetic language – through which you could define a given situation in such a way as to allow or preclude the use of competing resources and the relationships they might entail. For instance, you know of situations in which a rich man claimed that he need not perform the yearly work cleaning a settlement's irrigation canals, instead proposing to hire another to do the job. But a poor man then publicly humiliated the wealthy man into performing such a duty himself by defining the situation as one of settlement solidarity rather than worldly wherewithal. As one builds a greater or lesser web of obligation similar mechanisms will be employed, whether the resultant constellation is as small as the choice of who among others to depend upon or as large a constellation as embraces great power over others. Still, like so many other young men, you will no doubt be wondering how much this pattern really applies to you: In the present social and economic environment – where, as one saying goes, what used to be based on kinship, and then on friendship, now depends only on money – how much choice can you realistically exercise as you try to build a network, a life, of your own?

Now imagine, instead, that you are a young Moroccan woman. By comparison to your male counterparts your gender's overall literacy rate is about 62 percent, but significantly less in rural areas. Notwithstanding the pressures to which you may be subjected by your family, you are well aware that the average age of marriage for women like yourself is approaching thirty, which like that for men is the highest of all African countries. It is also true (and not for the first time in the country's history) that about 12–15 percent of women live alone and that one out of every six marriages ends in divorce. You know, too, that women are having far fewer children than was the case for your parents' generation, so while you may not actually know that the birthrate in Morocco has dropped below replacement levels in the cities and barely above it in the countryside such numbers would hardly surprise you. After all, you probably would not be shocked to learn that over 60 percent of Moroccan women in their childbearing years are using contraceptives. In terms of such birthrates, your experience will not be so different from that of other Muslim countries: Fertility rates in Pakistan, for example, have dropped from 6.4 to 3.4 children in the past generation (and are expected to go to 2.4 in the near future), while in Iran the rate has crashed from 6.5 in the early 1980s to just 1.6 by 2017.[4]

As a young female you are also not so naïve as to imagine that marriage is the solution to all of a woman's problems. According to the Moroccan Ministry of Social Development, roughly one in three women has been the victim of domestic abuse.[5] Thirty-eight percent of young women are unemployed, but even if you do have an urban job it is likely to be in the textile industry where conditions are harsh and work-induced ailments common.[6] Because you tend to do better in school than the boys you have a good chance for a job in the public sector and are aware that if you succeed there you will have reasonably good pay, job security, and benefits. You even know that a number of judges and nearly a quarter of the lawyers are now women, and that the government is prepared to allow women to be employed as court notaries notwithstanding the objection of traditionalists who oppose women serving equally with men as witnesses.[7] In public you are most

---

[4] *The Economist*, November 11, 2017. See, generally, David Ignatius, "A Demographic Shift in the Muslim World," *Washington Post*, February 8, 2013.

[5] Bikya News, "Morocco: Women Battle against Domestic Abuse," *Women Living under Muslim Laws*, May 13, 2013. wluml.org.

[6] Jules Crétois, "Moroccan Women Face Hardships in Textile Factories," *Al-Monitor*, April 15, 2013. al-monitor.com.

[7] Women have also been admitted to the imam training program, though not permitted to serve as actual prayer leaders. But as the head of Al Adl's political

likely to wear a headscarf rather than a full-face veil, and perhaps you were sympathetic to the women who took to the streets to protest the trial of two young women for being insufficiently covered when walking through the marketplace in Agadir. And though you are correct that the deck is stacked against you as a woman in many ways, you may be intrigued to learn that, as in other Muslim countries, you are likely to win most or all of any family law case you see through to judicial decision anywhere between 65 percent and 95 percent of the time.[8] Thus, in a number of ways – attitudinal, circumstantial, and institutional – you, too, will not be without certain choices as you go about forging your personal and public life.

Young men and women like yourselves will also have followed the events of the Arab Spring and its aftermath. Like many outsiders, however, your image of those events may not be entirely accurate. You are likely to view what happened in Cairo's Tahrir Square in late January 2011 as a series of protests in which masses of young Egyptians took over that space. You may also picture unemployed youth by the thousands using Facebook and Twitter to topple an aged tyrant and revolutionize their country. If so, you may have been somewhat misled. In this you will not be alone.

Juan Cole, for example, in his study of the Arab Spring is one of those commenters who accept such images as accurate.[9] Best known for his wide-ranging blog on Middle Eastern developments, Cole argues

circle noted, determining which roles women may play is yet another clever way by which the king asserts his control over the religious field. The regime has exercised similar control when it has shut down a number of informal mosques operated by Islamists. Spiegel, *Young Islam*, 138–39.

[8] See Lawrence Rosen, "Why Do Women Usually Win in Islamic Family Law Courts?" In Lawrence Rosen, *Islam and the Rule of Justice* (Chicago: University of Chicago Press, 2018), 28–62. Muslim women can be seen speaking up quite forcefully in court in such films as *Divorce Iranian Style*, available at https://freedocumentaries.org/documentary/divorce-iranian-style#watch-film; *Divorce Shari'a Style*, which concerns an Islamic court in East London and can be seen at https://vimeo.com/18622831; and *Justice at Agadez*, which follows an Islamic law judge in Niger and is available in French at www.dailymotion.com/playlist/x28sdx_mgm_lacoste_justice-a-agadez/1#video=xtqqzo. *A Separation* is a highly accurate though fictionalized courtroom drama from Iran that can be downloaded from http://putlocker.is/watch-a-separation-online-free-putlocker.html

[9] Juan Cole, *The New Arabs: How the Millennial Generation Is Changing the Middle East* (New York: Simon & Schuster, 2014).

that the new generation of Arab youth – sometimes called "Gen Y," sometimes "the millennials" – is quite unlike its failed predecessors and, like many other commenters, he attributes much of their success in organizing the Arab Spring to their use of social media. In support of his view he notes, for example, that the number of Tunisians online doubled to 1.7 million between 2006 and 2008, and doubled again within a year, by which time 90 percent of the citizenry had cell phones and nearly a million of the country's 10 million people were Facebook users. In Egypt, 46 percent of urban dwellers were online by 2012, 40 percent having Internet-capable mobile phones. Libya, the third country on which Cole focuses, was much less connected, but its youth still figured prominently in the uprising against Col. Muammar Qaddafi. By communicating pictures of police assaults and witnesses' statements of torture, by texting where marches were forming and relaying the protest lyrics of popular singers, demonstrators were able to rally their cohort and overcome their fear of moving into the street.

But demography is not destiny, and Cole is far too good an historian to suggest as much. Yet at each point, despite more problematizing evidence, Cole stakes his claim to the transformative power of the new generation. He properly shows that anywhere from a quarter to a third of young people were unemployed, a rate that only increases with levels of education; that 8 million Egyptians applied for the US immigration lottery in 2006 and that by 2008 nearly half of the young said they wanted to go abroad. He rightly stresses the role of the Egyptian unions and lower-class youth in the events leading up to Mubarak's resignation, as well as the effects of a world-wide recession and regional droughts on jobs and bread prices – all of which certainly helped to mobilize the twenty-somethings of Egypt and Tunisia.

But look closely at the photos from Tahrir Square and you will see a lot of gray hair (Figure 6.1). As the Cambridge University YouGov poll showed: "Indeed, in contrast to those who have portrayed the participants in the Arab Spring as predominantly young, educated and unemployed – the 'youth bulge' explanation for the uprisings – the results we've seen indicate that in most (though not all) countries, those over 35 years old are slightly more likely to take part in protests than those under 35."[10] Whether it was parents furious at a regime

[10] University of Cambridge, "The Myth of the Arab Spring," October 18, 2011. www.cam.ac.uk/research/news/the-myth-of-the-arab-spring. Reporting from

**Figure 6.1** Older protesters during Arab Spring, Tahrir Square, Cairo. John Moore/Getty Images.

that undermined their children's education, for which they sacrificed so much, or workers who were more concerned with their pay packets than changing the structure of government, the sources of frustration went well beyond those of the young alone. Cole never discusses the corrosive nature of everyday corruption – in which one has commonly had to bribe a child's teacher for advancement, a hospital orderly to visit a relative, or a postal clerk to get an ordinary form. Adults were made complicit in this ever-present corruption and felt themselves dirtied by it. When the time came, it was the youth who precipitated events, but it was the parents who made those events unstoppable.

Cole's references to the importance of social media also do not point in a single direction. He calls use of the Internet "formational" but notes that "the rise of the Internet may not have been

the scene at the beginning of the occupation of Tahrir Square, *New York Times* correspondent David D. Kirkpatrick, *Into the Hands of the Soldiers: Freedom and Chaos in Egypt and the Middle East* (New York: Viking, 2018), 37, wrote: "Men and women mingled freely, and safely, by day and by night, in galabiyas and suits, niqabs and V-necks. Most were under forty. But there were plenty of older people, too, both rich and poor."

as central to these social movements as some Western press coverage assumed." Indeed, his own description shows that information disseminated by pamphlet and word of mouth was usually more important than the ether. He makes a common mistake when he says that the younger generation took over "public" spaces like Tahrir Square. But there is no concept of "public" space for which individuals feel responsibility in the Arab world: Space is either private or government-controlled. Indeed, on his own evidence, the occupied plazas were treated like private space, where (until government thugs broke in) women were safe and unveiled, where tea was offered entrants, and where people cleaned up any garbage. Critics say the youth revolution lacked leadership. But private space requires no leaders, since everyone knows how to act in an area that is likened to one's home.[11]

It is also an open question whether the demonstrators imagined a truly different relation to the state. T. E. Lawrence once said that Arabs believe in persons, not institutions. In a political culture of intense personalism – where roles are not segregated from networks of indebtedness and corruption is seen less as abuse of office than as failure to share with your dependents – reciprocity is crucial. However, the state is not an entity with which one can have the sort of reciprocity as with someone encountered face-to-face: Indeed, as I have suggested elsewhere, the state is *un*reciprocity incarnate.[12] And this is where the younger generation failed to differentiate itself from its predecessors. Young men wanted to prove their adulthood in a culture that lacks any other rite of passage than collecting the allies necessary to fund a marriage. But with jobs and housing scarce the average age of marriage for both genders had been pushed into their late twenties and thirties. Sexually and sociologically frustrated, unable to genuinely imagine that authorities could separate personal ties from official duties, the younger generation was unable to effect the one thing (as

---

[11] For an elaboration of this argument, see Lawrence Rosen, "Justice and the 'Arab Spring': A Guide to the Arab Street," In Rosen, *Islam and the Rule of Justice*, 99–107. Robert Worth, in his book *A Rage for Order: The Middle East in Turmoil, from Tahrir Square to Isis* (New York: Farrar, Strauss and Giroux, 2016), 29, notes: "The square was officially leaderless throughout its eighteen days."

[12] Lawrence Rosen, "The Culture of Corruption in the Arab World," in his *Islam and the Rule of Justice*, 99–107.

Hannah Arendt noted) necessary to make a revolution – not just a change in ways of thinking but a change in ways of relating.

Ultimately, Cole concludes that these young people "forever changed their societies" (indeed, "forever changed the world") and that however matters have developed since the heady days of the Arab Spring "it seems unlikely that we have heard the last of the Egyptian millennials." But while Tunisia may for a time have proved the exception, Michelet's description of the Champs de Mars after the French Revolution sounds hauntingly like the "revolution" of Tahrir Square, which in the light of subsequent events "has for her monument empty space… this sandy place, flat as Arabia." The private space is gone, the public space has yet to be created, and areas like Tahrir have reverted to government space.

Still, what happened is not insignificant. The people in the Arab Street sank to the depths of cultural discomfort and then extricated themselves through practices that felt both familiar and authentic. The millennials were unable to shift the categories by which they grasp the world, but for a time they were a catalyst for rebellion, altering their surround while themselves remaining largely intact. The New Arabs may not have succeeded in revolutionizing their societies, but they may have sensed the possibilities of a new world and the solidarity it will take to achieve it. Their interest, much less their commitment, to a form of democracy, however, is open to question. A good example is the experience related by a visiting professor from the West in the Gulf States.

Joshua Mitchell is a professor of political theory at Georgetown University.[13] He offered a course, not unlike the one he usually teaches at his home institution, about democracy and the works of Alexis de Tocqueville to students at Georgetown's extension in Doha, Qatar. Tocqueville famously argued that "democratic man" would always be a separated creature, disconnected from a set of relationships of the sort that were at least provided by an aristocratic order, living (in Mitchell's terms) "lonely, delinked, and homeless in an ever-changing world" (p. 109). Mitchell takes this stance as the basis for a personal exploration of the twinned gaps that separate his generation of the late 1960s from that of his current university students, and that which separates the

---

[13] Joshua Mitchell, *Tocqueville in Arabia: Dilemmas in a Democratic Age* (Chicago: University of Chicago Press, 2013).

young people he teaches at Georgetown in Washington, DC, from those he encountered in Doha. In each instance, his reading of Tocqueville's *Democracy in America*, along with texts by Plato, Adam Smith, and Marx, constitute the common touchstone through which he engaged the two groups of students in a wide ranging discussion – including aspects of sexuality, the relative merits of different governmental forms, and the meaning of sin and suffering – that test the students' responses to their own perceived situation. The result is neither a formal survey of attitudes nor a controlled experiment in response to identical texts. Rather it is a highly personal account of the problems and prospects outlined by Tocqueville measured against the students' classroom thoughts and the author's impressions of them.

In the course of describing his teaching, Mitchell offers a clear synopsis of a number of Tocqueville's central points. Although it is not possible from the book alone to tell precisely how Mitchell presents the Frenchman's arguments, it is clear that he emphasizes the isolation of the individual over Tocqueville's reciprocal emphasis on the ways in which Americans counter their isolation through participation in voluntary associations and national institutions. For Tocqueville not only said of man that democracy "constantly leads him back to himself alone" but "I remarked a hundred times that, when needed, [Americans] almost never fail to lend faithful support to one another," that "Americans of all ages, all conditions, all minds constantly unite," that "they seek each other out," that "[i]n democratic countries the science of association is the mother science," and that in regard to the family, "[d]emocracy loosens social bonds, but it tightens natural bonds. It brings relatives together at the same time that it separates citizens."

Given his emphasis on those aspects of isolation in Tocqueville's analysis, Mitchell sees his American students' use of computers and social networks as evidence that "[i]n their outreach to their 'friends,' they live within themselves" (p. 67) and that "[i]n their friendships and in their romantic life, it scarcely occurs to them that they should arrest an affection that their heart declares" (p. 55). He argues that for these young Americans, "irrespective of the *personal* struggles they endure, the social and historical struggle of ideas is largely over, and all that remains is to implement 'social justice'" (p. 73). Moreover, the students do not appreciate that they live in a world of mutual indebtedness (p. 89), engaging in "[s]exual intimacy without the burden of reproduction: a formula by which the current generation proclaims that it owes little or nothing to future generations" (p. 135). Instead, "many of them want to go into 'financial services' – that euphemism for making money without producing anything" (p. 111), further underscoring that "what occurs in many of our colleges nowadays amounts less to higher education than to 'higher certification,' perhaps even 'higher stupefaction'" (p. 76).

At times, however, Mitchell appears to contradict himself: "One of the remarkable things about my students on the main campus is how many of them 'herd' together in groups rather than break apart, publicly, into couples" (p. 128) – an observation he could have followed up by considering whether 'hook-up' culture is a sign of loneliness or 'herding' a sign of conviviality. He also complains that American students know little of suffering (an odd view to hold about modern adolescence) and that they seek no religious depth in this regard given that, from his own Christian perspective, "When I look at my young students … who among them will have faith strong enough to declare that their suffering is a testimony to God's glory," (p. 149) or recognize that "[r]eligion is the deepest thing" (p. 175) and "our lives must be made with a view to and from Eternity" (p. 176). He even indicates (rather like Tocqueville) that absent such a religious emphasis "I suspect liberty in America cannot long be saved" (p. 178), especially if religion is reduced to some generalized "spirituality."

Mitchell's description of the students in Doha risks being perceived as equally thin. He presents his students in Doha as exclusively embedded in family structures and says nothing about the ways in which individuals in the Arab world must create networks of obligation that are not readily passed from one generation to the next. Doha, it should be remembered is a very atypical place even in the Arab world, a country that is wholly reliant on foreign laborers who can never become citizens. The result is less a nuanced analysis of the reaction of students to the full array of Tocqueville's observations and more an exercise in limited stereotypes. Perhaps his Arab students do "recur either to dreamy ideas about a past that cannot be retrieved or to revolutionary ideas that dispense with the whole of their inherited history" (p. 40), are "neither quite able to embrace nor repudiate the world that is now upon them" (p. 38), and "approach Tocqueville's *Democracy in America* with a sense of urgency … for few things are more haunting to them than the specter of loneliness" (p. 43). But far more detail or reference to others' studies of the region would go a long way toward supporting such assertions. One might at least inquire whether the Doha students' rejection of democratic 'liberation' is due to their inability to "imagine living in a world that presupposes infinite possibilities" (p. 52) or because they have thus far benefitted from the superior position men of the region possess over their subordinates.

Nevertheless, Mitchell's account underscores several key points: First, the younger generation must, like its forebearers, find a way to construct a network of obligations in order to secure themselves in the world. Even those who take jobs in the bureaucracy find that this spoke-and-wheel pattern of interpersonal obligations often characterizes the agency itself, rather than a rule-bound, organization table, knowledge-based structure of duties and roles.[14] Second, the pathway is cleared to corruption, if we accept their concept of corruption as the failure to share largesse with one's network of affiliates. And third, as studies like that of Mitchell and others suggest, the distinction needs to be made between a revolution and a rebellion, the latter being a demand to be included in the existing system, not, as the former implies, a desire for it to be overturned. Mitchell's students, like many other young people in the region, want their share of the existing system and find little in the institutional structure of democracies to attract them. Under such circumstances, their rebellion will likely reinforce, rather than alter, the status quo. This is also evident as one considers, at least in the Moroccan case, the place of youth in the apparatus of the political parties.

In a recent study, Avi Max Spiegel analyzes the choices of young people in Morocco, particularly their decisions as to which, if any, grouping to be affiliated as they explore their own political awareness.[15] Indeed, as the choices play out, how, he asks, does this affect the Islamist organizations that are vying with one another for young members? Spiegel was, of course, somewhat less able to study the young women than the young men of the country, but through his careful research, his frequent citation of the work of (mostly female) scholars who have worked with women in the Muslim world, and his

---

[14] This pattern is clearly illustrated in the case of Saudi bureaucrats in Steffen Herzog, *Princes, Brokers, and Bureaucrats: Oil and State in Saudi Arabia* (Ithaca: Cornell University Press, 2011).

[15] Spiegel, *Young Islam.*

unusual willingness to follow his informants over a number of years we have a rare opportunity to see the process and consequences of the political choices being made by these young Moroccan Muslims.

Spiegel argues that "everywhere the dilemma confronting young Arab Muslims has become not *whether* Islamism, but rather, *which* Islamism" (p. 6, original italics). Indeed, where Islamic-oriented political organizations are concerned "the age of competing Islamists is officially upon us" (p. 6), a competition that, far from leading to the elimination by one of the others, actually spurs each of them to find ways to appeal to younger people. Contrary to some stereotypes, he says, "young activists are neither blind followers to those supposedly directing them nor passive spectators to events unfolding around them" (pp. 12–13). Instead, they actively shop around among alternative attachments, sometimes affiliating themselves only with the political or spiritual arm of a group, sometimes freely moving back and forth between competing groups, sometimes availing themselves of the fact that these organizations are not "selling organizational rigidity – firm lines of hierarchy and control – but rather promising and preaching personal choice, autonomy and freedom, by offering the ability to carve out what young people want: their own individual identities" (p. 8).

But what exactly does it mean to say that what young people want are their own identities? Are the ways young people hope to achieve that end significantly different from those of their predecessors? Or are they effectively drawing on the same repertoire of relational possibilities as their cultural forbears, not always replicating exactly the same patterns and structures but partaking of the same mechanisms of personal identity and network formation? And if they are truly operating in a different way than their parents – whether in what they desire or how they go about achieving it – is this apparent in multiple domains of their lives or only in the religious–political sphere?

Spiegel approaches these issues by first offering a roadmap to the complex history of Islamist organizations presently contending for the youth in Morocco. It is not a deep history he offers – one that seeks the organizations' sources, language, and integration with other aspects of Moroccan culture or one that describes the background of pan-Arab or religious brotherhood politics during the precolonial and colonial periods. Indeed, it remains an open question (at least, absent such consideration in Spiegel's analysis) whether that deeper history would alter the picture the author presents of the present. What we do get, by way of introduction, is a careful and lucid account of the development of the two main organizations now claiming Islamic legitimacy, Al Adl and the PJD.

Al Adl (whose full title is Al Adl wa Ilhsane, or the party of "Justice and Spirituality") grew out of the 1971 break between its founder Abdesslam Yassine and the head of Boutchichiya, a Sufi religious brotherhood, when the order's leader chose his own son as his successor rather than Yassine. Unlike the Sufis, Yassine believed that one had to combine political and religious goals, and in 1974, he published a direct attack on the claim of the monarchy as the final arbiter of matters religious.[16] For more than a decade, he continued his dissent and, in 1987, formed Al Adl to further his program. As a result of his attacks on the monarchy, Yassine was condemned to three years in a mental hospital in the late 1980s followed by house arrest until his release by the present king in 2000. Throughout the years when he was not free, Yassine continued to build his organization, to publish over twenty books, and, though he had renounced violence, to voice his belief in a state divested of a king claiming full religious authority.

By comparison, the PJD (Party of Justice and Development) grew out of several small political groupings and was, from the outset, much more purposely constructed as a party hoping to participate in the political system of the country. Like Al Adl, it kept its religious and political wings more or less separate, and in the early years, it was not uncommon for some members to attend meetings of both groups. But unlike Al Adl, the PJD was committed to working within the system and did not attack the monarchy directly. As one leader phrased their distinction between the political and the religious: "We should not confuse the relative with the absolute" (p. 52). The powerful interior minister at that time, Driss Basri, backed the party's recognition in time for it to put forth a limited slate of candidates in the 1997 parliamentary election. Under the leadership of Abdelilah Benkirane, the party gradually increased its representation in parliament, winning 42

---

[16] Yassine was a descendant of the Prophet (*cherif*) in the Drissi line, as opposed to the Alaoui line that has held the Moroccan throne for nearly half a millennium. While there is no indication that Yassine, unlike some earlier rebels, claimed that his should be the proper line of royal descent, being a cherif may have added to his overall store of charismatic authority.

of the 325 seats in 2002, 43 in 2007, and then 107 in 2011. As a result of that latter victory, the PJD forged an alliance with three smaller parties and, at the King's invitation, formed a government with Benkirane as Prime Minister. He served in that post until after the 2017 elections when, following months of stalemate in forming a working coalition, the King turned to Benkirane's PJD rival Saad Eddine El-Othmani, a medical doctor and psychiatrist, to fill the Prime Minister's post.

In many respects, the electoral success of the PJD can be attributed to the government using it as a foil for the events attendant on the Arab Spring. Protests in Morocco – which drew a number of young people – had prompted the King to revise the constitution so as to allow a party gaining a plurality of parliamentary seats to form a government. But as so often in the past, the palace created or co-opted a party to the purpose, this time funding the PJD as a vehicle for appealing, in part, to rebellious youth and those who regard themselves as supporters of both the monarchy and a party oriented toward Islam. Thus, whatever their similarities, the differences between the two Islamic parties have remained sufficiently sharp to present young people seeking an affiliation a distinct choice.

Two themes emerge from Spiegel's analysis of Al Adl and the PJD: (1) that while neither organizationally nor ideologically has either movement fully done so, a distinction is made between their spiritual and political aims such that members can choose attachment to either or both as they find themselves within any one organization's embrace; and (2) the stereotypes of each – whether that it is populated only by men with long beards or that it is simply the puppet of the regime – misses the diversity of each group's membership and aims while obscuring the freedom they offer young people to find their own way within and beyond the organization. Thus, it is mainly between these two parties that, Spiegel says, young people may choose, and the differences these organizations represent become a key part of both the decisions young members make and the ways in which their own ideas of themselves are mirrored by each of these movements.

What, then, is it that young people want such that they might sign on with one or another of these Islamist organizations? Spiegel rejects several of the theories that analysts have offered. Young people, he says, are not attracted to Al Adl or PJD out of a feeling of religious obligation or because they have rationally calculated that the advantages of attachment that may accrue to them are so alluring. Neither, he argues, do they come for the free services these movements offer or because of some generalized sense of solidarity with others. Through a series of vignettes of individual young men and women he suggests, instead, that, in their highly individualistic experimentation – described as "fluid and relational," a process in which people "dabble and identities intersect" – each is "looking for nothing less than a new sense of self" (p. 88). Similarly, he refers to their "pursuit of self-betterment," to PJD's new members as people who "are trained not necessarily to be better people or better Muslims, but to be independent individuals" (p. 99), and to that personal sense of sacrificing for the good of others that Al Adl recruits feel when they risk their freedom and safety by joining the organization.

By definition, those attracted to these Islamist organizations dissent from the mainstream of Moroccan Muslims. Whereas the vast majority, for whatever reasons, strongly support the monarchy and, whether eagerly or with their fingers crossed (so to speak), accept the King's claim as Commander of the Faithful to be the ultimate font of religious authority, these young people are put off by the assertion (in the wording of the 2011 constitution) that the monarchy is "inviolable."[17] They are also only too familiar with the ways in which the monarchy regulates religion. King Hassan II, who was succeeded upon his death in 2000 by his son Muhammad VI, used to quote his own father as saying that Morocco is like a lion on a leash: Sometimes you have to ease off and sometimes you have to jerk it back hard. In that vein, the present king, though far less brutal than his father, alternately relents and restrains both organizations.[18] So, at times he will permit meetings of Al Adl members even though the organization is formally outlawed, and at other times he will close down a meeting of the PJD or bar a candidate from the party running for office (as was the case in 2017 with Hammad Kabbadj, who was deemed an "extremist" and thus barred) if he feels members of the movement are challenging the monarchy too directly on religious matters. Spiegel calls this "selective suppression" (p. 129), though one may question whether it might not equally be denominated selective co-optation.

[17] Following events elsewhere in the Arab Spring, the wording of the Moroccan constitution was actually changed from the prior "sacred and inviolable."
[18] See, generally, Marvine Howe, *Morocco: The Islamist Awakening and Other Challenges* (New York: Oxford University Press, 2005).

Indeed, the question of co-opting is complex. Spiegel is perfectly well aware that there is reason to claim that this is exactly what the monarchy has done with the PJD. After all, at least since it began participating in elections in 1997 the party has been receiving major funding from the government (Spiegel says "millions of dollars"), it has held both the Prime Minister's position and a number of other ministerial posts, and its publications are only occasionally confiscated (p. 131). At the same time, the PJD is not allowed to campaign in mosques or otherwise seem to be challenging the religious legitimacy of the regime. The party may bring a Moroccan rock star to one of its conventions or invite the renown Egyptian cleric Yusuf al-Qaradawi as a speaker, but it is the king's picture that dominates such meetings and his nationalization of religious symbols that trumps any uses to which the party faithful may put them. Indeed, Spiegel notes: "The final day of the 2012 PJD convention was broken up by authorities after activists criticized the relationship between party elites and the monarchy" (p. 197). Similarly, Al Adl may have to charge a higher membership tax because, unlike the PJD, they are not subsidized by the government even though they may be allowed to help the poor through a variety of social service programs. However, the moment the government senses that they are assuming too much religious authority, they are quickly reined in.

But does this really mean that the PJD has been rendered the house Islamist party, the creature of the government? Does it mean that Al Adl is viewed as 'purer' for being banned by the regime? Here, matters turn on the interpretations rendered by each party's adherents as well as by Spiegel himself. For his part, the author claims that the PJD is not, in fact, the lap dog of the regime, notwithstanding its inclusion in elections and financial support from the king. His argument turns more on the subjective views of the young members as he understands them than on any objective data or theoretical orientations (p. 159). He points not only to the absence of subservience by young members to the organizations and their leaders but also detects "signs of ambiguity, multiplicity, and even inconsistency" (p. 153) in the organizations' and their members' own approaches to religion. Indeed, in the religious wings of the parties, he says, no straight line exists between doctrine and action: "Not only are young people constantly reinterpreting for themselves what religion means, but doctrinal specificities of their so-called leaders are also difficult to pin down. Divining a

single ideological marker for their individual movements is thus neither straightforward nor salient" (p. 70).

The ambiguities of ideology are mirrored in the parties' formal organization. When young members were asked to diagram the organizational chart of their movements Spiegel obtained widely divergent
illustrations: "this hodge-podge – this ambiguity, this seeming jumble –
represents a new and significant development in understanding Islamist
mobilization. *The lack of a pattern was a pattern*" (p. 154, original
italics). For Spiegel, it is the "individuation" that bears highlighting:
"No two individuals I met shared identical views, regardless of their
choice of movement" (p. 66). As one young man told the author about
choosing who to follow: "each member highlights the strongest points
depending on the personality of the candidate" (p. 153), so that, as
Spiegel puts it, "religious authority is progressively constructed as
permeable ... crafted to fit new realities ... adjusted and understood
to fit each person's own aims – not the other way around" (p. 156).
Noting the separation of the religious from the political aspects of
the movements, he concludes "that the representations of religion in
young Islamists' lives are not the product of prevarication, but rather
of personalization" (p. 178).

Spiegel's analysis thus raises a host of issues vital to an assessment of
the place young people occupy in the Islamist movements of Morocco,
and, perhaps by extension, to other such movements elsewhere in the
Middle East and North Africa. Clearly the backdrop against which the
author poses his study is that of Islamist organizations being viewed as
rigidly guiding the religious views and political actions of their adherents, organizations that often expect close adherence to a charismatic
leader and his agenda. To this view, Spiegel consistently demurs: His
emphasis on the tendency of these organizations not only to adapt to
the flexible approaches of their youthful members but also to respond
to the competition posed by alternative parties yields a far more varied
set of individual views than common stereotypes would suggest. It is a
reading with which one can be very sympathetic – but not necessarily
for all of the reasons offered.

Take, for example, the assertion that involvement in these organizations by young people is often a personal exploration aimed at
self-improvement. Like many of Siegel's claims, on its surface this is
appealing: Is that not what young people commonly do, so why should
we be surprised if, instead of slavishly following their elders, that is

what they do in Morocco? The problem is not the proposition but its lack of specific content. What, substantively, is the actual range of identifiers to which these younger members become attached? For just as you cannot have language but only some language, and you cannot have religion only some particular religion, so, too, these young people must have some content to their range of possible identities. Yet we are given no indication of what that is. To the contrary, in his insistence that everything is individualistic, the author repeatedly says that there are no patterns to be discerned (pp. 152–55). Admittedly, we are here in the domain of interpretation rather than scientifically testable hypotheses, but from Spiegel's own limited range of evidence – and more particularly if we see the situation of young people not against the stereotype of Islamic organizational rigidity but Moroccan culture as described by a number of social scientists to whose work Spiegel has no reference – an alternative reading can surely be considered.

Earlier, it was noted that Moroccan men must build a network of obligations in order to be regarded, by themselves and others, as truly adult: Worldly consequence is the measure of being a man in the world, and that comes about by having effects on one's own and others' webs of indebtedness. Seen from this perspective, what the subjects of Spiegel's study are doing is not altogether new. To the contrary, old patterns could be seen as replicated among the younger generation as well as by these religious parties, patterns scholars have noted over the years. Among the key features of such patterns are not only the need to construct and constantly service a set of potential allies but a tendency to undermine the consolidation of power in too few hands for too long a period of time. Everything from rituals of reversal to styles of joking underscore to the momentarily powerful that other sources and candidates than those they have relied upon for their own success may challenge at any time. Thus, when Spiegel cites studies that point "to a fragmentation of authority, a move away from a monopoly of religious authority nestled in the hands of a selected group of religious scholars or 'ulama'" (p. 160), he is actually touching on a series of orientations that reverberate throughout Moroccan history and culture. The constant use of phrases invoking the name of God in Moroccan linguistic usage is not, as the author suggests, simply an indication that religion and politics cannot be separated (p. 158): If one looks to context it is clear that, among other meanings, these phrases often carry the implication that, even if supernatural oversight is not invoked, the interlocutor needs to be reminded, in any relationship subject to constant servicing and renegotiation, that power is not always where the listener may imagine it to be.[19]

Nor is the argument that authority is now fragmented without resonance in Moroccan cultural history (p. 160). To the contrary, the sources for building a power base being multiple and scattered it is the test of any leader that he be able to assemble his following if his claims to authority are to be seen as legitimate. Indeed, whoever builds such a network of dependencies will be regarded as legitimate until and if another can do so more effectively.[20] This is as true in the realm of religious organizations as in the expression of political power. The question, then, is not one of slavish adherence to a leader but of how, given the overall cultural focus on personal attributes and associations rather than institutions as depersonalized structures, one can build a following. Indeed, part of the freedom Moroccans have always imagined themselves to possess is that power of weakness that allows one to choose the persons upon whom one will be dependent. The young members of the organizations in question could, therefore, be seen not as representing (as Spiegel claims) a wholly revolutionary shift in Moroccan Islamic attachments but a replication of cultural patterns they learned early on.

It may also be worth recalling here the distinction that Ernest Gellner made between revolution and rebellion. The former, he noted, is an attempt to change the entire system, the latter to enter into it.

---

[19] For a telling example of this process, see Lawrence Rosen, *Bargaining For Reality: The Construction of Social Relations in a Muslim Community* (Chicago: University of Chicago Press, 1984), 40–47. Similarly, the meaning of the headscarf is more complex than the author indicates. It is, for many women, a statement of power – both the power to disrupt men's actions toward them and to make a characteristic comment on power being relativized. In Morocco, the headscarf is also a compromise between the face veil worn by their grandmothers and no covering worn by most young women in the 1960s and 1970s, a meeting of all three generations of women who previously strolled down the street together in three distinct garbs.

[20] Thus the statement of a Yemeni political figure – "No ruler in the region sees himself as legitimate. So they all constantly look over their shoulders, scheming against their rivals, because they see no reason why their rivals should not be in their place" – is, therefore, only half right. Legitimacy flows from putting together a successful network, so anyone who does replace a rival is ipso facto legitimate, however insecure his station. The quotation is from Worth, *A Rage for Order*, 7.

So, on numerous occasions in Moroccan history – whether it be during the Rif rebellion following independence (when what was sought was representation at the ministerial level in the government) or in the more recent demands for inclusion in the wake of the death of an ordinary fisherman in that region[21] – it is not wholesale change but inclusion that is at issue. Similarly, one could read many of the points raised by Spiegel's young informants as indications that they want into the system – rather than a wholesale alteration of the system – and find both of these Islamist organizations vehicles for that goal.

Indeed, we also know that many protests in Morocco are not (or are not mainly) about their asserted purpose but an attempt to demonstrate that people can be rallied notwithstanding government attempts to control when and if such demonstrations occur. This has long been true, whether it concerns labor demonstrations (like those of 2012–14) or those on behalf of the monarchy but not instigated by them (as occurred at the time of the Green March or the first Iraqi war). Once again this is part of a very typical Moroccan pattern in which one must show that one's network is really there to be called on, and the only proof of that is by actually precipitating it. Any leader is only as good as his last act, so he may find it necessary, as Gellner once remarked: "to strike a match to see if it will work when the day comes, or he may wish to show his opponents what good matches he has." Thus, when Spiegel refers to the adherents of Al Adl as attending to the "needs" of others one wonders what word they are using and whether what is really involved is trying to show that one has built a network of one's own, rather than engaging in purely altruistic acts for which no reciprocation would ever be expected.[22] Joining one of the Islamic parties may not be an act of free-floating solidarity – an explanation Siegel rightly rejects – but a culturally characteristic vessel (among others) through which one builds personal attachments.

Spiegel says of these young people that "With their choices, they are actively charting their own futures, or at least feeling that they

---

[21] Aida Alami, "Morocco's Stability Is Roiled by Monthslong Protests over Fishmonger's Death," *New York Times*, August 26, 2017.

[22] Spiegel's main example is drawn from the statement of just one young man who says that he is "different" from others because other people his own age have no worldview: "And 'different,' in this case, was code for 'more independent.' But it was also often code for 'more powerful' and even 'more aware of the needs of others'." Spiegel, *Young Islam*, 99–100.

are – something they had not previously been able to do" (p. 96). Leaving aside the highly subjective nature of this assertion, young people are not, it may be argued, charting their own course for the first time in Moroccan history. Not only have younger people always fashioned networks of their own – and thereby formed directions of their own – but it is not clear exactly in what ways the author can demonstrate that these young people are doing so within their own organizations. He does not offer instances in which any of these organization has changed in response to its young members – whether organizationally or doctrinally. Nor does he offer examples of when members overstep the bounds and are sanctioned by these organizations. Just as the Arab Spring was not simply a youth revolution (much less a Facebook Revolution), we would need a circumstantial account of how the younger members are forcing changes on their movements to be persuaded that they are having such an effect.[23] Absent such data, one cannot simply take the author's assertions at their face value.

A number of factors thus complicate an understanding of the religious orientations of the younger generation of Moroccans. Surveys show that young people are joining Sufi groups at a much greater rate than political parties. The explosive growth of the Boutchichiya since the turn of the century and its support by the regime would suggest that the choice many youths are making is of a rather more non-worldly spiritual nature than one attached exclusively to partisan goals.[24] The recent government ban on the production and sale of

---

[23] See, in refutation of the argument that the Arab Spring was predominantly a youth and Facebook Revolution, Rosen, *Islam and the Rule of Justice*, 108–23. Those who claim the Arab Spring in Egypt was a Facebook Revolution should note that David D. Kirkpatrick (*Into the Hands of the Soldiers*, 32), speaking of the beginning of eighteen days of occupation by protesters of Tahrir Square, observed firsthand: "We awoke on Friday, January 28 [2001], to discover that the government had shut down all internet and mobile phone service." Indeed, he reports, the Internet remained down for an entire week, though satellite communications were available. *Ibid.*, 36. President Obama said at the time: "What I want is for the kids on the street to win and for the Google guy to become president" – referring to Wael Ghonim, a Google executive in Cairo with an American wife and degree from American University. "That image of the revolution," says Kirkpatrick, "was as much about Western narcissism as it was about Egypt." *Ibid.*, 41.

[24] Indeed, after the Casablanca terrorist bombing of 2003, the King specifically commended Sufi orders to young people and appointed a noted Sufi adept, Ahmed Tawfiq, as his Minister of Religious Affairs. See Khalid Bekkaoui,

full-body coverings for women – particularly the burqas of the Arab East – has not met with significant resistance by young women.[25] Certainly younger people have good reason to be disaffected from the state-run schooling system. As studies show, students are not only being graduated who are illiterate in several languages, lacking in real job training, and often subject to corrupt teacher practices (when the teachers actually show up), but at the mercy of an exam system in which the government may change the percentage passing at the last moment in order to make it appear that fewer graduates are unemployed.[26] Spiegel's central argument "is that Islamist groups that emerge from this dynamic marketplace – from this wild, disordered arena of inter-Islamist contestation – will bear little resemblance to the Islamists of yesteryear" (p. 6). Whether that will prove to be true and how a younger generation will address these problems, as Spiegel's study so clearly demonstrates, remain to be determined.

None of these questions takes place outside of a particular history. Moroccan youth, like many of their counterparts throughout the region, find them themselves in a dilemma, tied to a cultural history that makes enough sense to seem natural, bound to a political history they cannot simply rebuff. Like most of their parents and grandparents, they are heir to a colonial history they have, ironically, come to reinforce. Whether that superordinate power was French or Spanish (as in the Moroccan case) or British (as in many countries of the Arab East), the independent governments that replaced the colonial administrations adopted as the basis of their own legitimacy many of the same sources

Ricardo René Larémont, and Sadik Rddad, "Survey on Moroccan Youth: Perception and Participation in Sufi Orders," *The Journal of the Middle East and Africa*, 2, 1 (2011), 47–63; and Khalid Bekkaoui and Ricardo René Larémont, "Moroccan Youth Go Sufi," *The Journal of the Middle East and Africa*, 2, 1 (2011), 31–46. It is also worth noting that this latter study shows that 68 percent of the information young people get about Islam comes from programs generated outside of Morocco.

[25] See Aida Alamijan, "Morocco Said to Ban Sale of Burqas, Citing Security Concerns," *New York Times*, January 11, 2017; and Moha Ennaji, "Why Morocco's Burqa Ban is More Than Just a Security Measure," U.S. News, February 1, 2017; reprinted from *The Conversation*, January 31, 2017. http://theconversation.com/why-moroccos-burqa-ban-is-more-than-just-a-security-measure-72120.

[26] On the poor quality of the educational system, see Charis Boutieri, *Learning in Morocco: Language Politics and the Abandoned Educational Dream* (Bloomington: Indiana University Press, 2016).

that informed their predecessors' regimes. In each case – whether operating through a pervasive bureaucracy as in the Continental models or a system of indirect rule as in the British – officials took over the structure and the claim to authority of those European systems.[27] In the Moroccan case, the adoption of the colonial administration's legitimacy was compounded by reinforcement of the indigenous emphasis on the Sultan's religious authority, thus rendering a pattern that combined, in Weberian terms, elements of both rational and charismatic authority. Most particularly, the independent regimes fell heir to the one institution that gave the colonialists their power, namely a modern army, aided by control over the mass media of communication. The result, in both Morocco and Egypt, was for the next generation to accept the army as a legitimate institution when others – like government ministers and even the head of state – were regarded as having squandered whatever legitimacy they possessed. And because legitimacy comes not simply from the barrel of a gun but from building up a network of dependent allies superior to that of any opponent – a style of network formation that, in a smaller or larger constellational fashion, characterizes how everyone goes about establishing their place in the world – the young have replicated, or been frustrated in trying to replicate, in establishing themselves in the world.

Rebellion rather than revolution manifests itself in many cases, then – in the protests in front of the Parliament in Rabat, in the takeover of space they treated as elaborated private space rather than public space at Tahrir, and in those demonstrations that did not seek the overthrow of the army but of particular individuals at the top of the government.[28] The younger generation in many such instances has, in short, bought into the country's military-extractive complex rather than seeking its

---

[27] For just such a story of a Berber who fought the French and then accepted a post under the French – and who the current administrator pointed to as vital to his own line of legitimacy – see Edmund Burke, III, "Mohand N'Hamoucha: Middle Atlas Berber," in his edited volume, *Struggle and Survival in the Modern Middle East* (Berkeley: University of California Press, 1993), 100–13.

[28] Thus even in Egypt, when the army turned on demonstrators (in the Battle of the Camel in February 2011) and then on the Muslim Brotherhood (in the massacre at Rabaa al-Adawiya Square in August 2013), the mass of young Egyptians did not lose respect for the army. See Worth, *A Rage for Order*, 127–69. See also Kirkpatrick, *Into the Hands of the Soldiers*.

replacement, whether by another failed socialist model or one drawn from Western democracies.

The uncertainties with which young people cope are, therefore, as much political and religious as they are economic and social. Akbar Ahmed has suggested that the dilemma facing many Muslims in the current age – particularly the next generation of young people – is how to live in a world of radical doubt.[29] And Clifford Geertz once remarked that the dilemma of many contemporary religionists is less about *what* to believe than *how* to believe it. Doubt and expression may, therefore, form the twinned bases upon which more specific questions will have to be addressed by the next generation of Islamists. What rituals – whether of the mosque or the state – will best reflect their felt sensibilities? What symbols will convey a recognition of the orderliness of their world? What words will have to be suffused with new overtones if meaning itself to survive? What deep-seated cultural practices and values will they carry, consciously or not, into the patterns their own lives take? Will the competition among groups be so different from patterns of the past as to be truly revolutionary, or will the gravitational pull of those cultural patterns continue to inform the content and shape of the struggle for the hearts and minds of a new generation? Like others before and after them it may, as James Thurber once said, be better to ask some of the questions than to know all the answers.

[29] "Fundamentalism is the attempt to resolve how to live in a world of radical doubt." Akbar Ahmed, *Postmodernism and Islam* (London: Routledge, 2004), 13.

# 7 | Missionary Encounters
## Moroccan Engagement with the Western Other

Encounters with missionaries in the Middle East, as in so many other parts of the world, have not always gone well for either side. From the missionaries' perspective, the unwillingness of the local population to accept Jesus as their savior smacks of the perverse refusal of a self-evident truth; for Muslims, the missionaries may be seen as another invasive force, often backed by a colonial power, who need to be outlasted if not outlawed. And yet, the encounter is more complex than of one faith attempting to displace another, for often both sides are not only affected by their mutual engagement but the lingering effects of their encounter go well beyond their own divergence.

In the Moroccan case, I was able to observe the last days of a missionary encounter that had lasted some seven decades and to see, in the accounts the proselytizers left behind and those of local Muslims who knew them well, the implications for each of their encounter. That almost no converts were made is not the key point; that both were affected by the other is. It was Dame Margot Fonteyn who once said: "Minor things can become moments of great revelation when encountered for the first time." And the encounter of Muslim and missionary was precisely one of those initial meetings that revealed so much about each of them.

*

## Sefrou, Morocco, 1965

"No!" My denial was, perhaps, too strong. But when my Moroccan interlocutor asked if I was with the American Christian missionaries in town I was intent on stating unambiguously that I had nothing whatsoever to do with them. I think I even went so far as to describe them as people who "buy and sell God." To my surprise I was brought up short by the

132

gentleman when he said: "They were very good people. They gave us medicines, helped with the children, and didn't bother anyone." Over the course of several decades I was to hear similarly positive remarks from quite a wide range of people.

## Gospel Missionary Union, Smithville, Missouri, 1970

I had flown out to see the records of the Gospel Missionary Union who operated in Sefrou from the early 20th c. until the mid-1960s. Greeted at the airport by its director – himself a former missionary in Morocco, speaking excellent colloquial Moroccan Arabic – I was taken to their headquarters and put up for the night in the retired missionaries home. They even prayed for my work at dinner. The next day, while looking through the organization's records, the director said to me: "I am convinced the Quran is the perfect instrument of the devil." "Oh," I said, "in what way?" "Well," he replied, "whenever I would mention Jesus they would say 'yes, he's right here in the Quran.' The same for anything I would bring up. Only the devil could have created a document that let people claim everything is already in it."

## A Farmhouse on the Sais Plain, Outside of Fez, 2008

We had been travelling all day, five of us accompanying a mutual friend involved in a complex divorce. Settled for the night at a relative's farm we talked and ate well past midnight. At one point we somehow got onto the subject of the missionaries who were known to one of our number when he was growing up in Sefrou. A born raconteur who had earlier regaled us with hilarious and insightful stories, he now jumped up on the banquette and began to sing in Arabic 'Jesus loves us every one.' When I asked what impact the missionaries had on him he said they never tried to make him convert, that they taught him many things, but that (as he put it) 'I was really there for the sweets!'[1]

\*\*

---

[1] "As a rule, before [Maud Cary, the missionary in Sefrou known popularly as 'Miss Terri,'] opened her Bible to speak to the women in their homes, she dug into her bag for a few sweet candies for the kids." Evelyn Stenbock, *"Miss Terri!"* (Lincoln, NE: The Good News Broadcasting Assn., 1970), 76. On the trip described, see Lawrence Rosen, *The Culture of Islam* (Chicago: University of Chicago Press, 2001), 3–20.

## Missions to Morocco

Christian missionaries are hardly newcomers to North Africa. The early Christian church flourished in North Africa, even though riven by the factionalism of Arians, Donatists, Pelagians, and Roman Catholics. In the second and third centuries, North Africa was the home of martyrs such as Origen ("the greatest genius the church ever produced") and Cyprian (a Berber and master of Latin style), as well as Tertullian ("the founder of Western theology"), Augustine of Hippo, and Augustine's equally sainted Berber mother, Monica. Indeed, it remains something of a mystery how, after having been one of the new faith's most important communities, Christianity so thoroughly disappeared from the region.[2] Franciscan monks, seeking to reverse the Church's fortunes in the area, explored the religious terrain – and often suffered martyrdom – in the Middle Ages, as did the fourteenth-century mathematician and polymath Ramon Llull, who, after becoming a lay associate of the Franciscan order, was stoned to death in Tunisia.[3]

The modern era of Christian missionizing in Morocco really begins in the late nineteenth century. It is true that, as early as 1834 – and intermittently from the 1840s to the1870s – Western missionaries worked in the country, but at that time they were almost exclusively seeking to convert the Jews.[4] It was in the 1890s that several British and American groups established missions in Morocco. Among them were the London-based North Africa Mission (NAM), the Scottish-based Southern Morocco Mission, and the Gospel Missionary Union (GMU) headquartered in the American Midwest.[5] Like so many of their colleagues the missionaries tended to regard the most

---

[2] See, e.g., C. J. Speel, II, "The Disappearance of Christianity from North Africa in the Wake of the Rise of Islam," *Church History*, 29, 4 (December 1960): 379–97.

[3] See John Tolan, "'Saracen Philosophers Secretly Deride Islam'," *Medieval Encounters*, 8, 2–3 (2002): 184–208, at 200–205 and citations therein.

[4] Jean-Louis Miège, "Les missions protestantes au Maroc (1875–1905)," *Hespéris*, 42, 1–2 (1955): 153–92, at 154.

[5] Further details of missions throughout North Africa may be found at "An Old Missionary," "Missions in North Africa," *The Muslim World*, 25, 4 (1935): 391–95; and Miège, "Les missions protestantes." On the NAM, see Francis Rue Steele, *Not in Vain: The Story of the North Africa Mission* (Pasadena: William Carey Library Pub., 1981).

inhospitable places as potentially the most rewarding: In the words of a missionary to Sefrou, "While the Muslim world is considered among the most difficult to reach for Christ, we must continue to go to Muslims. As in the process of searching for rare jewels, God's finest rewards await those who search in the hardest of places."[6] Although only a handful in number, yet with extraordinary self-confidence, the proselytizers cried out (in the words uttered at his departure in 1894 by Henry Hammer of the GMU), "Lift up your eyes, Morocco, for a gleam of light is coming to you."[7] Whether that light remained forever dim or occasionally illuminating, it did play a small but perhaps not unimportant role in those parts of Morocco to which it was directed.

The focus of much of my own work in Morocco having been just south of Fez in the city of Sefrou and the tribal regions of the Middle Atlas Mountains it is to the work of the NAM and GMU in that area that I will attend most closely. Indeed, missionaries were present in the Sefrou region from the 1890s until the 1960s.[8] Reading reports published in the NAM's journal *North Africa*, the GMU's *The Gospel Message*, and having worked in the latter's unpublished archives, the moments of first contact at the turn of the twentieth century come through quite vividly, particularly since the initial reception given

---

[6] Ila Marie Davis, with Evelyn Stenbock-Ditty, *A Gleam of Light: The Trials and Triumphs of a Century of Missionary Work in Morocco* (Kansas City, MO: Gospel Missionary Union, 1998), 168.

[7] *Ibid.*, passim. The number of missionaries varied over the years: The NAM grew from nine in 1886 to thirty-seven at the end of the century while those from the Southern Morocco Mission remained at nineteen during this period and those of the GMU grew to thirteen in 1900. Miège, "Les missions protestantes," 159. Including several small groups the total in 1900 was eighty-one, plus seventeen aides, in nineteen stations in the country. *Ibid.*, 190.

[8] The first group of GMU missionaries arrived in Tangiers on January 9, 1895, their leader calling Morocco "a land of filth, dirt, and pestilence, a land of 'Darkness, despair and death'," where (he fully expected) some of the missionaries would be martyred. George W. Collins, "Missionaries and Muslims: The Gospel Missionary Union in Morocco, 1895–1912," *Wichita State University Bulletin* 51, 3 (August 1975): 3–17, at 3. For more detail, see Dennis H. Phillips, "The American Missionary in Morocco," *The Muslim World*, 65, 1 (January 1975): 1–20, at 6–8. The GMU mission in Sefrou was established in 1904; missionaries from the NAM, who entered Sefrou in the 1890s, only spent summers there for a few years. For the activities of both missionary groups in Sefrou (including photos) see, Davis, "A Gleam of Light."

the missionaries by the local Moroccans was quite mixed.[9] In fact, the two missionary groups did not always get along, the British at first being critical of their more aggressive American brethren whose open-air preaching and "itinerating" in the rural areas, they feared, might make matters more difficult for everyone.[10] While the missionaries of the GMU certainly preached the gospel at every opportunity, theirs was, however, more the approach Max Weber characterized as exemplary prophecy, which "points out the path to salvation by exemplary living," rather than emissary prophecy, which "addresses its demands to the world in the name of a god."[11] Perhaps that is

---

[9]   "The children in the streets often reviled us and spat at us and threw stones. In the houses women frequently said they'd like to kill us or burn us alive if they dared." Elizabeth Tryon, quoted in Collins, "Missionaries and Muslims," 8–9. By 1909, however, we read: "There is a very remarkable change in the attitude of the Fez people towards Europeans, and even we missionaries have never found them so friendly as now. The cursing and spitting in the streets, which used to be very common when a Christian passed, are now conspicuous by their absence." *North Africa*, New Series, (August-September 1909): 126. The publications of the two main missionary groups are: *North Africa*, a monthly from the North Africa Mission, originally called the Mission to the Kabyles and other Berber Races of North Africa, that first began publication in London in December 1884, and *The Gospel Message* which was published by the GMU beginning in 1892. Many issues of *North Africa* are available online at https://missiology.org.uk/journal_north-africa-01 .php?utm_source=subscribers&utm_campaign=6b9fdc78cb-EMAIL_ CAMPAIGN_2020_05_02_08_05_COPY_01&utm_medium=email&utm_ term=0_6d6c7759d8-6b9fdc78cb-137859257

[10]  Writing about the GMU's activities in 1901, Evelyn Stenbock (*"Miss Terri!,"* 31–32) notes: "[T]he British missionaries who lived across the town [Fez] strongly disagreed with the open methods of witness used by the Americans. They differed so strongly that the excellent fellowship between the two groups was cut off completely." However, "The rift between the Americans and the British was quickly healed" (*Id.*, 33). There was also a certain amount of denominational rivalry, especially between the evangelical Protestants and the French Catholic hierarchy, in the years following the establishment of the Protectorate. Moreover, theories about how to missionize among Muslims varied a good deal. See, e.g., Thomas S. Kidd, *American Christians and Islam: Evangelical Culture and Muslims from the Colonial Period to the Age of Terrorism* (Princeton: Princeton University Press, 2013), 47–53. Many missionary groups advocated translating the Bible into the local languages as a key to gaining converts, but while portions were occasionally translated into Arabic and Berber to the best of my knowledge there was no complete translation into either language by these missionaries.

[11]  Max Weber, *From Max Weber*, Hans Gerth and C. Wright Mills, eds. (Oxford: Oxford University Press, 1946), 284–85.

why, in those early days, the missionaries were largely successful in avoiding problems with the local population. This, in turn, opened the way for them to employ some medical aid and secular education as a vehicle for presenting a life they hoped Moroccans would wish to emulate.[12] Unlike missionary groups operating in many other parts of the world at the turn of the twentieth century, the GMU in particular was not, it must be emphasized, oriented toward social reform or a "civilizing mission."[13]

Throughout their years in Morocco it is important to keep in mind, too, how few in number were the missionaries: The NAM had a total of thirty-seven in 1900, while the GMU went from a high of thirteen in 1898, to nine in 1905, and only six or seven in 1912, half of whom were always women. Spread out at different times in Fez, Meknes, Larache, El Ksar, Sefrou, and Boulmane, the Americans were stretched even thinner by illness and work in the rural areas. Reduced already by 1912 to just Meknes and Sefrou one could hardly expect them to have had a very dramatic impact on Moroccan society. And indeed, if the number of converts were the appropriate measure for any of the missionary groups their effects would approach the null point. But if impact is not to be measured in the number of converts other measures, however inexact, may be more suggestive.

Three issues thus arise when one considers the role of Christian missionaries from the English-speaking world in Morocco: First, were the missionaries valuable chroniclers of what was happening in Morocco, particularly from the late nineteenth century through the early years of the Protectorate? If they were not themselves representatives of a nation seeking to colonize Morocco did this place them in a position to be more "neutral" observers? Indeed, were their reports of use to their

[12] Some of the NAM missionaries had medical training; none of those from the GMU did. See, J. Rutherfurd and Edward H. Glenny, *The Gospel in North Africa* (London: Percy Lund, Humphries & Co., 1900), 198. Nevertheless, those without actual training dispensed medicines quite freely. On the missionaries' medical work, see also Miège "Les missions protestantes," 175–76.

[13] As one missionary later put it, the heathens "needed to be saved, not civilized; That the Missionary's business was to preach the Gospel, not to educate." Collins, "Missionaries and Muslims," 11. That is not to say no educational work was done: In fact, the missionaries did at times separate preaching from secular education, mainly on matters of science. Initially, however, opposition in Fez led to the imprisonment of some parents who had allowed their children to attend such classes. See, *North Africa*, 1894, 28.

own governments and the colonizing forces? Second, were the missionaries in any significant sense agents of change: Were they important in most Moroccans' first contacts with Euro-Americans and were these contacts vital to the local population's introduction to Western medicine, technology, and women's roles? And third, what does the current regime's approach to Christian missionaries tell us about the relation of the government to the religious parties in Morocco and to the monarchy's commitment to religious freedom? We will take up each of these considerations in turn.

### Reliable Witnesses?

To what extent were the missionaries' reports accurate reflections of events and social patterns? Bias may, of course, creep in, however inadvertently, to the comments of any observer, so the question for the missionaries is whether their very objective – to promulgate the Gospel of a foreign religion – is enough to make us suspect their accounts. Perhaps surprisingly, as one reads through the missionaries' records, religious purpose and everyday observation are kept quite separate, as a result of which the missionaries appear as remarkably able and reliable witnesses for the historian and social scientist studying this period. In their letters home, in their personal diaries, and in the communications published by their organizations one can trace both their activities and the information others would have garnered from their presence in places few if any others from the West had penetrated. Historians can, therefore, mine the publications and archives of both the NAM and the GMU to great advantage, especially for the period from the 1890s through the early years of the Protectorate. Consider, for example, the accounts of the events of 1894–1906 and 1911–12.

At first the information sent home by the British missionaries was rather sparse. Early in June 1894, soon after the death of the sultan Moulay el-Hassan I, the missionaries reported that it was "a time of great scarcity, almost amounting to famine, in Fez and the surrounding country," although the new crop was expected to be more abundant than usual.[14] Reports, like those of Miss Emma Herdman

---

[14] *North Africa*, October 1894, 119.

of the NAM, gradually began to contain details about the struggle for succession.[15] In a rare nod toward internal Moroccan politics, several of the American missionaries favored the succession of Moulay Abdelaziz, who they saw as more open to the West – which for them simply meant more open to allowing missionaries to preach the Gospel – than his father or brothers.[16] For the most part, though, at this point the missionaries were mainly concerned about finding places to live and Moroccan assistants (*colporteurs*) upon whom they could rely as intermediaries.[17] True, there were those who saw a connection between their presence and the great powers vying for control of Morocco, but there is no evidence that these missionaries ever served as direct agents of their respective home governments. Yet the information they conveyed was noted by Western representatives. In succeeding years, the missionaries reported on very local matters others may have missed: They noted, for example, that smallpox was so prevalent that "as a result, children are scarce in Moorish homes, and there are very few large families,"[18] or something of the tone of the times as in the story of the "Moorish gentleman" in Sefrou who told them that one good man could get forty of his neighbors into heaven, "but I don't know a man good enough in Sefroo or Fez to be able to do it."[19] As the missionaries of both the NAM and GMU became

---

[15] Albert J. Issacs, *A Biographical Sketch of Emma Herdman* (London: S. W. Partridge, 1900), 62.

[16] For background on Abdelaziz, see *The Gospel Message*, October 1902. On May 20, 1903 Mr. Welliver, commenting on the tribal rebellions in the country, writes from Larache: "As we believe a stable government to be a divinely appointed institution, we must needs pray God to send us such, and to reestablish the throne of Mulai Abd al Aziz, if he be God's chosen minister." *The Gospel Message*, June 1903, 12. Abdelaziz remained sultan until 1908.

[17] In the case of Sefrou, I actually met and interviewed the Berber from the I'awen fraction of the Ait Youssi, Hamou ou Jel, who served as colporteur for the GMU missionaries at the turn of the century. The relationship was mixed: At one point, Clinton Reed reports that while they were away Hamou sold the missionaries' belongings and made off with the proceeds (*The Gospel Message*, March 1909); at another, when his fellow villagers objected to a missionary's presence, Hamou dared anyone to attack his guest, saying "He hasn't taken your sheep or your wives: he just prays. So leave him be." Interview with retired missionary Don Petersen, GMU, Smithville, MO, November 17, 1970.

[18] *North Africa*, January 1898, 5–6, containing a letter from Miss Dennison dated October 13, 1897.

[19] *North Africa*, September 1893, 105–6.

more familiar with the country and more adept at the language their reports dealt increasingly with local political conditions.

The reports are especially good on the local circumstances in the Sefrou area during the turn of the twentieth century when Omar al-Youssi, who was both the pasha of the city and administrator (*qaid*) of the rural Ait Youssi tribe, was in power. Appreciating that Sefrou was "so situated as to be a 'strategic point'," the NAM correspondent detailed the tribal fights occurring throughout the region.[20] Similarly, detailed information was given about the Zaian tribal leader, Moha ou Hamou, tribal succession fights in the Middle Atlas after Qaid Omar al-Youssi was killed in 1904, and the events in 1909 involving such key opponents of the sultan as Bouhamara and Muhammad al-Kittani.[21] Perhaps most striking are the accounts of 1911 and 1912 from Fez and the surrounding region.[22] Missionaries from the GMU were in both Sefrou and Fez at the time and reported on the rebellion of the sultan's troops, the activities of the region's tribes, and the attitudes toward the sultan in the run-up to the French Protectorate. The missionaries' reports are noteworthy for their focus on local events and the effects on Moroccans of various social backgrounds.

Several points, then, become clear from reading the missionaries' accounts. First, the missionaries are highly circumstantial in their description of local events. They are not simply enumerating the frequency of their preaching or the numbers of people to whom they have given medical aid, nor do they simply reaffirm their faith or repeat pious platitudes. It may be true that they expected the readers of their published letters to picture their daily life and make financial contributions to the work accordingly, and certainly, too, the style of writing can feed into the readers' expectation of the heroic missionary in a distant land of unbelief. But these accounts were also available to another readership, namely the politicians and government officials

---

[20] *North Africa*, October 1901, 114. See also reports by the American missionaries for this period, *The Gospel Message*, April 1901, 2 and June 1901, 2.

[21] On Moha ou Hamou, see *North Africa*, January 1905 and March 1905; on the continuing chaos following the death of Qaid Omar al-Youssi, see *The Gospel Message*, June 1907; on Bouhamara and al-Kittani, see *The Gospel Message*, May 1909; for an account claiming the chaos of the countryside in 1909 has been exaggerated, see *North Africa*, August–September 1909.

[22] See, especially, *The Gospel Message* for May through September 1911, and Mr. Reed's account from Fez in *The Gospel Message*, June 1912.

who would have found in them precisely the sort of local detail no other respondent was making available. Indeed, there are indications that, while not directly servicing the officials' needs for intelligence, the missionaries' reports were read and were important to those who had an interest in which European powers were going to control Morocco at this critical time.[23] Thus, in the period 1890–1905, as Miège claims, missionaries undoubtedly played something of a political role: "Their implantation in the heart of the country, their knowledge of the language and customs, their relations with important officials allowed them to be valued sources of information."[24] Though Miège is careful to note that it is difficult to tell how important their information was, it does appear that at times diplomats found the missionaries' information highly useful even when, at other moments, they found their proselytizing ardor potentially disruptive to their own government's relations with the Moroccan state.[25] In a more measured assessment, George W. Collins argues that while the GMU sought assistance in the enforcement of the Anglo-American treaty of 1856 granting foreigners the right to rent or lease housing the missionaries never pressed for American involvement in Morocco: "One may conclude ... that while missionaries elsewhere may have been fundamental forces for American intervention and imperial expansion, that was not the case in Morocco."[26]

Whatever the uses made of their messages home, the missionaries were, then, remarkably unbiased in their reporting. Jeremiads aimed at Islam and its adherents' moral condition were almost always set apart from reporting about on-the-ground events. And because their only real political concerns related to their ability to conduct proselytizing activities they rarely expressed opinions affecting the interests

---

[23] Elsewhere, at certain moments in the Middle East and beyond, American missionaries were effectively used as spies, and their experience did not go unnoticed by those who were in the process of forming the US spy agencies: See Matthew Avery Sutton, *Double Crossed: The Missionaries Who Spied for the United States during the Second World War* (New York: Basic Books, 2019).

[24] Miège, "Les missions protestantes," 182.

[25] *Ibid.* See also the incidents mentioned by Miège, *Ibid.*, 185–86.

[26] For examples of the missionaries using the American consul to press for their right to housing, see also Phillips, "The American Missionary in Morocco," 11. Phillips, *Ibid.*, 20, concludes: "American missionaries to Morocco conceived of themselves as servants of God, not offshoots of an American cultural tradition."

of their home states. In sum, the missionaries' reports are accurate, contain a level of local color not found elsewhere, and are sufficiently separable from their remarks as proselytizers that a high degree of reliability inheres in the accounts they left behind.

## Agents of Change?

For all the merits of their descriptions, the main concern of the missionaries, of course, was converting nonbelievers. While other missionary organizations made social reform programs integral to their calling, this was not true for the British and even less so for the Americans. As Collins notes of the GMU, "in terms of field activities it had little interest in sociological considerations."[27] Although the Americans rejected operating primarily as a medical or educational mission, they did have available Western medicines and techniques that were valuable to communities subject to both endemic and adventitious ailments. The numbers of those vaccinated and otherwise receiving medical attention from all the different missionary groups operating in Morocco in this period are, if accurate, truly astonishing: some 350,000 by 1900, not including home visits and hospitalizations.[28]

Impressive as such numbers are impact is not easily reduced to a single metric. If one were to assess the missionaries' effects, one would have to consider three domains in particular: the demonstration of scientific accomplishment, the impact of personal encounters with a Westerner (perhaps most notably those involving women), and the missionaries' limited but perhaps not wholly insignificant role as suppliers to the outside world of information about the economy of the country.

Many Moroccans learned about Western science and technology well in advance of the colonial period through their encounters with the missionaries. For example, the Muslims took readily to vaccination which "brings great crowds of them, as they are very anxious to have the small-pox 'taken out' of their children."[29] Astronomy appears to have been a subject some Moroccans found especially intriguing. Mission houses demonstrated electricity as soon as it became available and their use of photography also intrigued the Moroccans.

[27] Collins, "Missionaries and Muslims," 11.
[28] Miège, "Les missions protestantes," 176.     [29] North Africa, June 1911, 88.

**Figure 7.1** American missionary ladies in Morocco, c. 1950. Courtesy: Advent Ministries.

Of great significance was the encounter of Moroccan women with the female missionaries (Figure 7.1). It is noteworthy that nearly half of the missionaries of all groups were women, usually single (though a number did marry fellow missionaries in the field). "The women missionaries often dressed in native garb and gained access without difficulty into the feminine confines of Moroccan homes."[30] Thus, without having as their main purpose bringing Morocco into the new world of science and technology or creating programs for change in the position of women, the missionaries did have the effect of demonstrating what another world might look like to many who were seeing its

---

[30] Phillips, "The American Missionary in Morocco," 14. Even after the French established local dispensaries, one NAM missionary writes, "The women generally prefer to come to the missionaries, though they are not qualified doctors, rather than to French officials, as they meet with more sympathy from them." *North Africa*, New Series, May–June 1917, 37.

claims and products for the first time. Their presence, always problematic to Moroccan officials, was, however, to grow no less challenging
in recent years even as their activities were diminishing.

## Current Situation of Christian Missionaries

To a number of Moroccan Muslims, the presence of any Christian
missionaries has been a serious irritant, while to the monarchy it has
had to be balanced against Western opinion and aid. In 1930, when
the French sought to divide the Berbers from the Arabs by placing
them under different legal regimes, many Moroccans feared that this
was the first step in an attempt to convert the former to Christianity.
Protesters demanded an end to missionary activity, transfer to
Muslims of Franciscan orphanages and schools, and termination of
Protectorate support for the Catholic church.[31] In more recent years,
so long as the missionaries were relatively circumspect, the government has let them remain in the country. At particular moments,
however, during even the most recent decade, the Moroccan government, responding in part to the promptings of the religious parties, has
expelled missionaries, closed their charitable facilities, and intimidated
some of the roughly 1,500 Moroccans reported to have converted to
Christianity.[32] Interdenominational problems have also resurfaced: A
2008 report noted:

Archbishop Vincent Landel told Reuters he would not baptize a Moroccan
convert as it is against the law. He said U.S.-funded missionaries had made
life harder for the Roman Catholic church in north Africa. "It upsets everything because all these evangelical converts lack restraint and discretion —
they do any old thing," he said. "And to Muslims there's no difference
between a Catholic, an evangelist or a Protestant, so in their minds the head

[31] See Jonathan Wyrtzen, *Making Morocco: Colonial Intervention and the
    Politics of Identity* (Ithaca: Cornell University Press, 2015), 1–4.
[32] This number of Moroccan Christians is given by Tom Pfeiffer, "Christian
    Missionaries Stir Unease in North Africa," *Reuters World News*, December
    5, 2008. Numbers, however, vary enormously and no exact count can be
    regarded as wholly reliable. Foreign missionaries had been ordered out of
    the country on earlier occasions: In 1967 they were given eight days to leave.
    See, e.g., Dave and Neta Jackson, *Risking the Forbidden Game* (Minneapolis:
    Bethany House Publishers, 2002), 151; Davis, *A Gleam of Light*, 126–28; and
    Stenbock, *"Miss Terri!,"* 139–40.

of all the Christians must be the Catholic Archbishop." Islamic leaders say missionaries exploit people with a weak understanding of their religion, target the poor and the sick and try to win over north Africa's Berbers by telling them Islam was imposed on them by Arabs. "These are unethical methods," said Mohammed Yessef, general secretary of the Superior Council of Ulemas, Morocco's highest religious authority. "Islam is the religion of God. It is neither Arab nor Berber. When people respond positively (to missionaries), it is when they don't have their full freedom," said Yessef. "Once they recover their normal health and situation, they recover their ability to decide.[33]

Other incidents occurred around the same time. In late March 2009, it was reported that Morocco "has expelled five Christian missionaries because they were 'illegally' trying to convert Muslims to Christianity," the four Spaniards and a German woman having been detained after meeting with Moroccan converts in Casablanca.[34] One year later, as *The Economist* reported, a similar action was taken against "Christian missionaries who ran the 'Village of Hope' home for children 80km (50 miles) south of Fez.... The 16 aid-workers had cared for abandoned children for over a decade when, in March, the Moroccan authorities sent inspectors to the orphanage, then gave the workers a few days' notice to leave the country. Witnesses reported distraught farewells between the Moroccan children and the foreigners who had acted as foster parents."[35] The 2010–11 Arab Spring, which led to public protests and a new Moroccan constitution, added to the tensions, with debates over religious freedom unresolved and, in some instances, converts reportedly being detained, beaten, and threatened.[36]

---

[33] Pfeiffer, "Christian Missionaries."

[34] Worthy News Staff, "Morocco Expels Christian Missionaries," *Worthy News*, March 29, 2009. The report continues: "The Cooperative Baptist Fellowship (CBF) of Kentucky works in several Moroccan cities, often with refugees passing through the country from sub-Saharan Africa.... It is not clear if they are still in-country after recent expulsions."

[35] *The Economist*, "Morocco's Evangelical Christians: Stop Preaching or Get Out," *The Economist*, July 29, 2010.

[36] Karen Graves, "Christians in Morocco: A Crisis of Faith," *U.S. News*, September 30, 2015. Graves further notes: "Attempting to convert a Muslim to another religion – also called 'shaking the faith of a Muslim' – is a crime punishable with up to three years imprisonment and a substantial fine, though recently there has been discussion to delete the law." The few converts made at the end of the nineteenth century were treated even worse: See the story of one such convert at Phillips, "The American Missionary in Morocco," 13.

In the early years of the present century, the few remaining mission groups had also reduced their presence, operated clandestinely, or left Morocco altogether. In 2001, the GMU changed its name and overall orientation worldwide. Known now as Avant Ministries, they seek to implant self-sustaining churches in various countries, Morocco not being among them.[37] Assistance from American administrations, who have not prioritized the rights of Christians in northern Africa, has not been forthcoming: The U.S. Commission on International Religious Freedom, for example, does not monitor any of the North African countries.[38] Yet despite the tiny numbers of missionaries and their few converts Western missionization continues to be a point of irritation to the more fundamentalist political parties and a convenient whipping boy in attempts to move the regime farther along their preferred path. As a result, it is very unlikely that, covert missionizing aside, there will be a resurgence of Christian missionizing in any part of North Africa in the foreseeable future.

* * *

The missionaries failed in their central goal – the conversion of Moroccans to Christianity. Exact numbers of converts are not available, but clearly there was only a handful: In Sefrou itself, I know of only two in nearly three-quarters of a century.[39] Self-doubt appears

---

See also Immigration and Refugee Board of Canada, *Morocco: The situation of individuals who abjure Islam (who apostatize), including their treatment by society and by the authorities; the repercussions of a fatwa of the High Council of Ulemas condemning apostates to death, including the reaction of the government (2016-April 2018)*; and Tony Assaf, "Maroc: La conversion de musulmans au christianisme soulève la colère dans le pays," *Aleteia*, March 30, 2015. Fr.aleteia.org.

[37] See https://avantministries.org/history (accessed August 24, 2022).

[38] www.uscirf.gov/all-countries. Indeed, it is unclear how serious the Trump administration was about pursuing the treatment of Christians and others within their broader foreign policy perspective. See Mattathias Schwartz, "The 'Religious Freedom' Agenda," *The Atlantic*, July 16, 2019.

[39] This number was confirmed by one of the missionaries I interviewed at the GMU headquarters in 1970. The names are given in Stenbock, *"Miss Terri!,"* 138, and in Jackson, *Risking the Forbidden Game*, 1 and 150, where they become the subjects of a fictional story. The story of one convert in Sefrou is related by his son in Ed Ksara, *My Life Story* (Springfield, MO: The Ethnic Life Stories Project, 2002). https://thelibrary.org/lochist/els/ksara.pdf. See,

often in the missionaries' reports: Two missionaries who served for
long periods in Morocco are said to have destroyed their diaries, so
disappointed were they in the wasted efforts of a lifetime.[40] The pattern was set early on: In 1909, Clinton Reed wrote, "we cannot recall
a single instance of true conversion, and not more than one of real
awakening."[41] Many factors may have contributed to this overall
failure: the lack of any clear plan by the missionaries, the security
Moroccan Muslims had in their own identity, and the people's long
history of managing contacts with foreigners. And yet, the encounter
of Middle Eastern Muslim and midwestern Evangelical may be seen as
a story of mutual toleration. Alternatively, the encounter may simply
have helped to articulate and reinforce existing patterns rather than
alter or undermine either. But even in that separate reassurance, there
was recognition that a portion of oneself was held – held even in trust –
by others who were true to their faith. The final assessment offered by
Miège is, therefore, a fair one:

les missionaires aient contribué largement à atténuer le préjugé xénophobe
des marocains.... Ils donnaient aussi des européens une autre image que
celle fournie par les négociants uniquement voués à leurs intérêts ou par
les affairistes peu scrupuleux si nombreaux dans les port du pays.... Dans
l'ouverture du Maroc de la fin du xix siècle, dans la conquête pacifique de
ses populations les missions ont joué un rôle non négligeable. [The missionaries contributed substantially to easing the xenophobic bias of the

generally, the assessment by Miège, "Les missions protestantes," 184–85. See
also Stenbock, *"Miss Terri!,"* 56, where, for example, she says there were
no converts in El Ksar ("city of disappointment"), and her statement about
converts at the beginning of her biography of Maud Cary: "No one knows
their number. Some who were baptized were insincere. Some who were
sincere were not baptized." (*Ibid.,* 5) One member of a prominent Fez family
reportedly converted at some time in the 1930s and joined a priestly order.
Wyrtzen, *Making Morocco,* 3, n. 6.

[40] Self-doubt was, however, a trope among missionaries, and it is not easy to
determine when the criticism of oneself and others was genuine or an expected
style of personal assessment. See, e.g., *The Gospel Message,* September 1908,
2. See also Stenbock, *"Miss Terri!,"* 46 for an example involving Maude Cary
("Miss Terri"), the American missionary who spent many years in Sefrou.

[41] *The Gospel Message,* May 1909, 2. Victor Swanson also writes: "What I have
accomplished since coming here may not seem very much, for no soul has
been turned from darkness to light." *The Gospel Message,* November 1909,
2. George Reed, too, writes: "But, alas! We have no evidence that a single soul
has received the sweet story." *The Gospel Message,* December 1908, 2.

Moroccans.... They also gave Europeans an alternative view to that supplied by the businessmen who were devoted solely to their own interests or the speculators who were less scrupulous than numerous others in the country's ports.... In opening Morocco at the end of the 19th c., in the quiet conquest of its people, the missions played a not insignificant role.][42]

On her first day in Morocco in July, 1,892 NAM missionary Emma Herdman tells of going down the street of Tangiers "watching for souls."[43] As the generation of those who had contact with Western missionaries passes from the scene the image, to say nothing of the substance, of the proselytizers' gaze – and the reciprocal gaze of the ever-present Moroccan "souls" – will simply fade away. For all their facility with the local languages and the perceptiveness of their reporting of local events, the missionaries, in their passing acquaintance, never really knew the Moroccans, nor did the latter quite know them. And yet each sensed the authenticity and basic civility of the other. The missionaries' role in the contact Morocco made with the West will, then, remain a source of interest for those who wish to fully understand the nation's history and some of the terms that were set by the encounter of Muslim and Christian, an impact that may continue to reverberate for a number of years after the missionaries themselves have departed the scene.

[42] Miège, "Les missions protestantes," 186.
[43] *North Africa*, July 1892, 77.

# PART IV

# Critical

# 8 | *Clifford Geertz, Observing Islam*

*Clifford Geertz was the foremost anthropologist of his day and one of the most profound students of comparative Islam. His first book, The Religion of Java, not only set the tone for his rare combination of detailed ethnography and trenchant analysis but constituted a clear statement about Indonesian forms of Islam and their relation to Hindu and animistic traditions. He did not, however, write an equivalent work for Morocco, thus leaving some readers feeling that he had not quite turned his full attention to the religion of that country in a truly comparable way.*

*In what follows I will suggest that that appraisal is not accurate. For while his brief comparison of Islam in Indonesia and Morocco formed the basis of his book Islam Observed, it was, in fact, as much in his separate study of the Moroccan marketplace that he set forth how Islam deeply informs the workings of everyday exchange and, by implication, constitutes a vital backdrop to the country's political culture. Just as the title of Islam Observed was intended as something of a pun that many people missed, so, too, it is an incomplete reading of Geertz's approach to the ethnography of Islam and its encounters within and beyond its own bounds to ignore his extraordinarily detailed investigation of the place where religion was so critically enacted. By demonstrating that the home of Islam is not only in the mosque or Quranic school but in the marketplace and the venues of conversation Geertz expanded the world of Western Islamic scholarship to the parameters set by the believers themselves.*

\*

Clifford Geertz always said that context matters, and his own work on Islam proved no exception (Figure 8.1). Geertz's interest in Moroccan Islam came about as he sought a place through which he could pursue his comparison of cultures, a comparison he felt was indispensable

151

**Figure 8.1** Clifford Geertz (1926–2006). Mary Cross, photographer. Courtesy: Karen Blu and the estate of Clifford Geertz.

to understanding both the range of cultural variation and the guiding processes through which the benefits of comparison itself could be grasped. Having worked in Java, Sumatra, and Bali he looked for a place that shared some features with Indonesia but whose contrasts would stimulate ideas about the relation of cultural patterns to local circumstance. He had thought for a while about working in Pakistan, but with his children still quite young he and his wife, fellow anthropologist Hildred Geertz, decided that might prove too difficult. Instead, he went to the other end of the Muslim world, and found in Morocco the congeniality and the challenge of a Muslim culture that also appeared to be profoundly different from that of the Indonesian archipelago. He was still in the early stages of his main fieldwork in Morocco when he was called upon to summarize his approach to Islam, a summary that, as it turned out, was to be his most explicit, but, as we shall see, by no means his only substantial analysis of Moroccan Islam.[1] It was in 1966, just as he turned forty, that Geertz was asked to deliver the Terry Lectures at Yale. In less than a decade of publishing he had already produced many of the essays that were soon to be collected in *The Interpretation of Cultures*, essays that immediately established him as a new and brilliant voice in the social sciences.[2] Having concentrated for the preceding dozen years on Indonesia he had only arrived a few months before to initiate sustained fieldwork in Morocco.[3] Whether it was because he had just made contact with the village and descendants of the Moroccan scholar and holy man, Sidi Lahsen Lyusi, or because the commission prompted him to recall the Indonesian saintly figure Sunan Kalidjaga, the challenge of the Terry Lectures brought together several elements that had clearly been emerging in Geertz's work.

In two essays written in the early 1960s Geertz reminded readers that what is distinctive to our species is that we developed the capacity

[1] One reason why *Islam Observed* may have been his most explicit account of Moroccan Islam relates to the initial plan for the volume co-authored by Clifford Geertz, Hildred Geertz, and Lawrence Rosen, *Meaning and Order in Moroccan Society* (New York: Cambridge University Press, 1979). The volume was to have consisted of eight chapters, two each by Clifford Geertz, Hildred Geertz, Lawrence Rosen, and Paul Rabinow. Clifford Geertz was to write on the market and on political culture, while Rabinow was to write one essay on Moroccan Islam and another on the village of Sidi Lahsen Lyussi. As coordinator of the project it was my task to see to it that each author had copies of the relevant portions of each other's complete fieldnotes. In the event, Rabinow was unable to contribute to the volume. Clifford Geertz's own essay on the suq had also grown to monograph length, and Hildred Geertz had also done an extensive analysis of the census data. As a result it was decided to publish the volume instead as three essays signed by each author. Perhaps because of this history Geertz himself never returned to write a separate sustained essay specifically about Moroccan Islam, a subject that did, however, continue to be addressed by several of his students. It will be argued below, however, that the essay on the market is very much an essay on Islam.
[2] Clifford Geertz, *The Interpretation of Cultures* (New York: Basic Books, 1973).
[3] Geertz had made several trips to Morocco before settling on a fieldsite: He had lived for some months in Rabat and had surveyed a number of towns before choosing the Sefrou area as his main site. For a brief account of his search for a fieldsite in Morocco, see his *After the Fact: Two Countries, Four Decades, One Anthropologist* (Cambridge: Harvard University Press, 1995), 67–70. Perhaps uniquely among third world towns, Sefrou was later to hold a conference and publish a book in honor of his work there: *Sefrou: Mémoire, Territoires et Terroirs – Hommage à Clifford Geertz* (Fez: Commission Culturelle, May 2000). For his work in Indonesia Geertz received that nation's highest civilian award.

for culture – the ability to create the categories of our own experience – before, not after, we achieved our present speciation.[4] Moreover, he emphasized that thought is essentially extrinsic: Rather than lurking in some "secret grotto of the mind," it is worked upon in public, through shared symbols, concepts, acts, and orienting events which, proliferated across multiple domains of life, give the appearance to their adherents of being both commonsensical and real.[5] From this baseline, Geertz was now able to elaborate, in a variety of additional essays, his thinking about religion and social ideologies.

In "Religion as a Cultural System," Geertz formulated a working definition of religion that focused on how people cast up, through the symbols he called "the material vehicles of thought," their associated emotions and the sense of order they bespeak – those orientations and concepts that appear to their adherents to partake of the very nature of reality.[6] In "Ideology as a Cultural System" he articulated the view that, as it becomes part of an ideational structure through which the process of encountering a changing world is grasped, religion takes on challenges to common sense that render problematic its coherence and capacity to guide social life.[7] In each of these essays, Geertz's formulations stood in marked contrast to those accepted by many of his intellectual predecessors. Well into the mid-twentieth century comparison in religious studies had been focused on universals and essentials – mysticism, spiritual experience, "ultimate beliefs." But Geertz's own theoretical orientation, worked out in his comparative studies in Indonesia, had instead led him to concentrate on "family resemblances," where similarities and differences form amalgams that are not reducible to a single circumscribed feature. And, no less importantly, Geertz had been finding his own literary style, a style which

[4] Several passages in the present essay previously appeared in my "Introduction" to the Hebrew translation of *Islam Observed: Ayonim B'Islam*, Noam Rachmilevitch, trans., (Tel Aviv: Resling Publishing, 2007), 7–10. The original book is Clifford Geertz, *Islam Observed* (Chicago: University of Chicago Press, 1971).

[5] Geertz here relies, in part, on Eugene Galanter and Murray Gerstenhaber, "On Thought, the Extrinsic Theory," *Psychological Review*, 63, 4 (1956), 218–27.

[6] Originally published in Michael Banton, ed., *Anthropological Approaches to the Study of Religion* (London: Tavistock, 1966), 1–46; reprinted in *The Interpretation of Cultures*, 87–125.

[7] Originally published in David Apter, ed., *Ideology and Discontent* (New York: Free Press, 1964), 47–76; reprinted in *The Interpretation of Cultures*, 193–233.

(as he was later to say) was as integral to the capacity to convince as it was to suiting the mode of analysis to its point.[8] Having discovered that his favorite form of expression was the extended essay he was now able to marshal substance and style to the task of rethinking religious studies as a form of comparative social inquiry.

In his Indonesian work Geertz had explored the ways in which a Weberian ethos suffuses both the marketplace and the ideologies that inform a wide range of social acts. Approaching Morocco in a similar vein he was struck by the contrasting ways in which Islam was incorporated into the culture of the early post-colonial experience. Where the Indonesians played up the image of the state as a ritual center around which political and religious life acquired shape, the Moroccan experience suggested that the governing ethos included a sense of activated spiritual power and collective moral temper that was at once intensely personal and contestably institutionalized. How, in such contrasting environments, was one to understand the differential role of Islam? Indeed, given this contrast, how was one to describe the experience of ordinary people as the state and the market, the mosque and the home all became venues through which people had to learn *how* to believe in a world in which *what* they believed was becoming increasingly contingent on outside forces?[9]

---

[8] On Geertz's style, see Richard A. Shweder, "Cliff Notes: The Pluralisms of Clifford Geertz," in Richard A. Shweder and Byron Good, eds., *Clifford Geertz by His Colleagues* (Chicago: University of Chicago Press, 2005), 1–9; James A. Boon, "Geertz's Style: A Moral Matter," *Ibid.*, 28–37; and Geertz's response, "Commentary," *Ibid.*, 108–24. The volume also contains a complete bibliography of Geertz's work through 2003. For Geertz's analysis of how writing style relates to inclusion in the anthropological canon, see his *Works and Lives: The Anthropologist as Author* (Stanford: Stanford University Press, 1988).

[9] "On the spiritual level, the big change between the days of [the 18th c. Indonesian kingdom of] Mataram and [the contemporaneous sultan of Morocco] Mulay Ismail and today is that the primary question has shifted from 'What shall I believe?' to 'How shall I believe it?'" Geertz, *Islam Observed*, 61. In his review of *Islam Observed* Raymond Firth [*The Journal of Asian Studies*, 28, 4 (August 1969), 909–10, at 909] phrased it this way: "Increasingly, people hold religious views rather than are held by them; there is a difference between being religious-minded and being religious." One is also reminded of the words of Zayd ibn 'Amr, one of the early followers of monotheism, standing beside the Kabaa before he was driven out of Mecca for criticizing the pagan gods, who broke off his criticism and cried: "Oh Allah! If I knew how you wished to be worshipped, I would so worship you; but I do not know." Quoted from Ibn Ishaq, *Sirat Rasul Allah*, 145 in A. Guillaume, *The Life of Muhammad: A*

Geertz loved a richly textured story, one that cried out for deep
interpretation. He thus found, both stylistically and intellectually, that
it was far wiser to begin by telling a story – whether of a contested
funeral (as in one of his first articles) or a riotous cockfight (as in
his most famous article) – and then to unpack its mysteries and its
implications.[10] So, in the stories of two saintly figures he found the
turning point for his analysis. For not only would each appear out
of place in the other's context – the peripatetic Moroccan looking
as odd in Indonesia as the "still point in a turning world" saint in
Indonesia would appear disconnected in Morocco – but each becomes
the embodiment of just those forces that are at work in their people's
distinctive ways of comprehending everyday experience.

Arguing that "there is no ascent to truth without descent to cases"
he demonstrated one of his enduring talents – the capacity to encap-
sulate an entire ethos in a pregnant phrase. He could say that the
Indonesian pattern "is essentially aesthetic; it portrays its ideal," or
characterize the Moroccan cultural pattern as one of "ecstatic moral
intensity." He could note "the solemn self-deception" of both cultures
or remark that for each "naturalness seems increasingly difficult actually to attain." Whether in pointing out the Moroccan "talent for forcing things together which really do not go together" or the "Koranic
moralism" of the marketplace, the specifically Moroccan approach to
the sacred as "an endowment of particular individuals" or the more
general proposition that "nothing alters like the unalterable," his
characterizations never reduced a culture to some professed essential
but raised each to a level of graspable complexity.[11]

Given this orientation Geertz was reluctant to speak about "Islam"
in the abstract, or (perhaps as much for its infelicitous sound as
for its air of collective essentializing) of Islam*s*. As a result, he was
notably critical of much of the work that had been done by Western

*Translation of Ishaq's Sirat Rasul* Allah (Oxford: Oxford University Press,
1955), as cited in Karen Armstrong, *Muhammad: A Prophet for Our Time*
(New York: HarperCollins, 2006), 44–45.
[10] The former article is "Ritual and Social Change: A Javanese Example,"
*American Anthropologist*, 59 (1957), 32–54, reprinted in *The Interpretation
of Cultures*, 142–69; the latter is "Deep Play: Notes on the Balinese
Cockfight," *Daedalus* (Winter 1971), 1–38, reprinted in *The Interpretation of
Cultures*, 412–53.
[11] The quotations in this paragraph are from *Islam Observed*, 22, 30, 33, 17,
61–62, 76, 42, 44, and 56 respectively.

scholars on the subject. Some of these reservations, together with his broader way of thinking about Islam, come out in the reviews he published of others' work on the topic, as well as in his occasional remarks about the contemporary politics of Islam. A closer look at these remarks may, therefore, help place his overall orientation in context.

In his extensive, two-part essay in *The New York Review of Books* in 2003 (for whose title he chose the caption of a famous *New Yorker* cartoon depicting a driver lost at a desert crossroad, "Which Way to Mecca?"), Geertz reviewed more than a dozen books – chosen, he said, after surveying literally dozens more – and divided Western studies of Islam into four broad categories: the "civilizational" studies that compare "east" and "west"; the contrastive studies that try to pick out "good" Islam from "bad," "authentic" from "inauthentic," and "tolerant" from "terrorist"; the studies that attempt to reconcile the Islamic and the non-Islamic through a shared "Abrahamic" or philosophical base; and those that emphasize the local distinctiveness of Islamic cultures, and to some extent their family resemblance, rather than their unitary identity. With each he found fault. The civilizational approach (most notably represented by Bernard Lewis) is, he argued, simultaneously judgmental and nonspecific; the contrastive approach glosses over differences in a vain attempt to sort matters into self-satisfying categories; the "Abrahamic," which by trying to claim that we are all really the same under the surface, produces anodyne approaches to situations that are vastly more complex; and the localists seldom come to grips with what it is that is varying and in response to what forces. When "Islam" is made the direct concern, most writers, Geertz implied, simply bore the reader with their endless repetition of the pillars of faith, their moralizing tone, their characterization of Muslim societies as static and subject to inevitable forces, and their account of wars, invasions, and fungible dynasties as "a temporal unfolding out of [Islam's] 'primitive,' revelatory moment."[12]

Not surprisingly, Geertz – always delighting in the particular, the *un*-inevitable, the changeable, the contingent – was particularly

---

[12] "Which Way to Mecca?" *The New York Review of Books*, 50, 10 (June 12, 2003), 27. A number of Geertz's essays in *The New York Review of Books* concerning Islam were republished in his *Life among the Anthros* (Princeton: Princeton University Press, 2012).

intrigued by the opinion surveys reported by Riaz Hassan,[13] conclud-
ing that: "Any notion of Islam as a bloc universe, everywhere the same
in content and outlook, can hardly survive such findings. The sense
that everywhere Islam is moving on, if in varying directions, and not
just setting its face against 'modernity,' the West, and internal change,
comes out very strongly."[14] On those rare occasions when he did gen-
eralize Geertz would imply caution with scare quotes, as when he wrote
(following a discussion of architecture in Sefrou, Morocco and education in the Javanese town he studied) that what is occurring "is what
is happening both in those places and elsewhere to 'Islam' as such.
It is losing definition and gaining energy."[15] And when he did speak
about Moroccan or Indonesian Islam it was always in the context of
place, as when he wrote of the former: "Islam in Morocco is sustained
by personages, by a vast, inconstant crowd of severely independent,
grand and middling, middling and petty, religious notables … like the
society generally, an irregular network of irregular figures, constantly
adjusting their plans and allegiances."[16]

Curiously, Geertz did not praise any general work on Islam under
review. But then neither did he mention any of those particularistic
studies he obviously admired, perhaps thinking them too narrow for
the general readership of the *New York Review*. Yet the choice of
what to include and exclude can also be seen as a statement about his
approach to Islamic studies more generally. Three features in particular suggest themselves in this regard: that Islam reveals itself less in
abstract propositions than in its enactment in the rough and tumble
of political, economic, and familial life; that focusing on this emplace-
ment is not only true to the orientation of most Muslims but restrains
the analyst from the very generalizations Geertz found insupportable
in many of the books he critiqued; and that (following the lead of
various pragmatist thinkers) one could indeed compare incomparables
and still resist the allure of essentializing.[17] Each of these propositions
is worth considering in a bit more detail.

[13] Riaz Hassan, *Faithlines: Muslim Conceptions of Islam and Society* (Oxford:
   Oxford University Press, 2002).
[14] "Which Way to Mecca? Part II," *The New York Review of Books*, 50, 11
   (July 3, 2003).
[15] Geertz, *After the Fact*, 165.   [16] *Ibid.*, 58–59.
[17] See Clifford Geertz, "The Pinch of Destiny: Religion as Experience, Meaning,
   Identity, Power," in his *Available Light: Anthropological Reflections on*

Geertz, as we have seen, was always concerned to see the domains in which religion is enacted in everyday life – not in some rarefied domain of spiritual intensity – and for this his favored venue (no doubt following Max Weber's lead) was the marketplace. Whether in *Peddlers and Princes* or in his most extended essay on Morocco, the analysis of the Sefrou suq, Geertz pursued the idea that religion is a system through which people orient their actions in multiple domains of life.[18] It was not that he ignored the emotional or the "experiential." In his William James Lecture in 1998, he had expressed his reservations about James' emphasis on disembodied religiosity and the uselessness of mysticism and spiritualism as categories for comparison. Noting that people nowadays often do not know how they are supposed to feel, Geertz nevertheless concluded that: "'Experience,' pushed out the door as a radically subjective, individualized 'faith state,' returns through the window as the communal sensibility of a religiously assertive social actor."[19] And in the many anecdotes he included in his analytic essays the experiential was certainly an important component of the overall picture he sought to convey.[20] Indeed, bringing matters up to the time of his *Islam Observed* lectures, Geertz could write:

The bulk of our two populations still considers either an inward search for psychic equilibrium or a moral intensification of personal presence the most natural mode of spiritual expression. The problem is that these days naturalness seems increasingly difficult actually to attain ... The transformation of religious symbols from imagistic revelations of the divine, evidences of God, to ideological assertions of the divine's importance, badges of piety,

*Philosophical Topics* (Princeton: Princeton University Press, 2000), 167–86. See also James A. Boon, "Geertz's Style: A Moral Matter," in Shweder and Good, eds., *Clifford Geertz by His Colleagues*, 28–37; and Lawrence Rosen, "Passing Judgment: Interpretation, Morality, and Cultural Assessment in the Work of Clifford Geertz," in *Ibid.*, 10–19.

18 Clifford Geertz, *Peddlers and Princes: Social Development and Economic Change in Two Indonesian Towns* (Chicago: University of Chicago Press, 1963); and his "Suq: The Bazaar Economy in Sefrou," in *Meaning and Order in Moroccan Society*, 123–313. See also the introduction by Daniel Cefai to his translation of Geertz's essay, *Le souk de Sefrou: sur l'économie de bazar* (Saint-Denis: Bouchène, 2003), 7–53.

19 Geertz, *Available Light*, 178.

20 See, e.g., the story of the Jewish merchant in Geertz, *The Interpretation of Cultures*, 7–9, and the story of the Indonesian man being driven crazy by the law in Clifford Geertz, *Local Knowledge* (New York: Basic Books, 1983), 175–81.

has been in each country, though in different ways, the common reaction to this disheartening discovery.[21]

Geertz's aversion to generalizing, whether about Islam or any other social phenomenon, was, as we have noted, displaced by his propensity to think of Islam as a set of variations that bore a "family resemblance" to one another. This analogy was characterized by Geertz himself in the following terms: "[A] very great deal, in my opinion, rests on family resemblances, the oblique similarities that arise as specific histories take form against the background of persisting ideas."[22] Geertz had borrowed this concept from Ludwig Wittgenstein, and had earlier written:

We think we see striking resemblance between different generations of a family but, as Wittgenstein pointed out, we may find that there is no one feature common to them; the resemblances may come from many different features 'overlapping and crisscrossing.' This sort of approach seems more promising than one that sees the history of Islam ... as an extended struggle of a gentle pietism to escape from an arid legalism. A picture of the Islamic venture derived from 'overlaps' and 'crisscrosses' would be less order and less continuous, a matter of oblique connections and glancing contrasts, and general conclusions would be harder to come by.[23]

All this might seem to skirt the question of how comparison is possible were it not that Geertz saw in such family resemblances the impetus for returning to individual cases with greater insight about what features vary in relation to different contexts such that a coherent entity, one to which people can attach meaning, may result. But he was not unmindful of the temptations of such an approach: "The resolution I have taken not to describe either of my cases [Morocco or

---

[21] Geertz, *Islam Observed*, 61–62.

[22] Clifford Geertz, "Conjuring with Islam," *The New York Review of Books*, 29, 9 (May 27, 1982), 25–28. Geertz employed the idea of family resemblance in his essay about the Sefrou suq when he commented that "the great social formations of the Maghreb do bear a family resemblance to one another that the suq, as one of the most formidable and most distinctive of them, can, when properly understood, throw into more exact relief." "Suq: The Bazaar Economy in Sefrou," in *Meaning and Order in Moroccan Society*, 235.

[23] Clifford Geertz, "Mysteries of Islam," *The New York Review of Books*, 22, 20 (December 11, 1975), 18ff. Compare Geertz's use of Wittgenstein's concept of family resemblances with its usage in Rodney Needham, *Belief, Language, and Experience* (Oxford: Blackwell, 1972).

Indonesia] as a reduced version of the other, the bane of a great deal of comparative analysis in the human sciences – Spain lacked Holland's Calvinism; China, Japan's feudality – becomes particularly hard to sustain when you look ... at Islam in North Africa immediately after looking at it in Southeast Asia."[24] And though he followed this by referring to his comparison as "an instructive example of the heuristic uses of belatedly appreciated commotion and muddle," he does not suggest that, as a result, nothing can be said but, quite the contrary, that only in this way can one say something about something, that one can only speak of specific instances and not of "Islam" in so abstract a fashion that it cannot be brought down to cases.[25] One does not, in Geertz's borrowed phrasing, have language but *some* language, and one does not have religion but *some* religion – indeed, some particular, culturally embedded version of that religion.

It is here, too, that Geertz's problems with orientalism also become relevant. In his 1978 book *Orientalism*, Edward Said cited Geertz as one of the few scholars of whose work he greatly approved: "Thus interesting work is most likely to be produced by scholars whose allegiance is to a discipline defined intellectually and not to a 'field' like Orientalism. An excellent recent instance is the anthropology of Clifford Geertz, whose interest in Islam is discrete and concrete enough to be animated by the specific societies and problems he studies and not by the rituals, preconceptions, and doctrines of Orientalism."[26] This opinion took a quick turn, however, when Geertz criticized Said's later book on media coverage of the Middle East, characterizing Said's as "grain of truth arguments" involving a "tone of high panic" that "leave us with a bad taste in the mind, a sense of having been held by the lapels and screamed at by someone reckless to persuade."[27] Thereafter Said spoke of the "standard disciplinary rationalizations and self-congratulatory clichés about hermeneutical circles offered by Clifford Geertz."[28] He wrote of Geertz's "trivial arguments against me,"

24 Geertz, *After the Fact*, 57.
25 The internal quote is from Geertz, *After the Fact*, 63.
26 Edward Said, *Orientalism* (New York: Pantheon Books, 1978), 326.
27 Clifford Geertz, "Conjuring with Islam," reviewing, among other books, Edward Said, *Covering Islam: How the Media and the Experts Determine How We See the World* (New York: Pantheon Books, 1981).
28 Edward W. Said, "Orientalism Reconsidered," *Race & Class*, 27, 2 (1985), 1–15, at 5.

how Geertz thinks of him as "an intemperate left-wing non-Orientalist Christian Palestinian," and stated that, by not also referring to the background of other's whose work he reviewed, Geertz "merely underlines the racist Orientalist habit of reducing the intellectual positions of wogs to their ethnic genealogy."[29]

There were other criticisms of Geertz's work that came from some historians, even ones who were deeply sympathetic to his approach. Geertz has thus been praised and vilified for seeming to pay too much attention to a slice-of-time, synchronistic view of culture, rather than changes that occur over time, and for his concentration on what is shared rather than what is contested by various groupings within a culture. Some, like historian William H. Sewell, Jr., have sought to have the former critique both ways: He characterizes Geertz's work as overly synchronic but then says that "it is more important for a historian to know how to suspend time than to know how to recount its passage."[30] Sewell also notes that Geertz's formulation of cultures as 'models of' and 'models for' tends to gloss over the discrepancies between the two, as analysts make their representations of the world less varied and less susceptible to change than is really the case.[31] Others, emphasizing disagreement *within* a culture, criticized Geertz for ignoring the views of women or other subordinate groupings.[32]

---

[29] Edward W. Said, "Orientalism: An Exchange," *The New York Review of Books*, 29, 13 (August 12, 1982), 44–46. Said goes so far as to falsely say of Geertz's work on the marketplace in Morocco that Geertz gives "no proof that he knows the spoken or written language of that market place." On Geertz's command of colloquial Moroccan Arabic, see below, note 32.

[30] William H. Sewell, Jr., "Geertz, Cultural Systems, and History: From Synchrony to Transformation," *Representations*, 59 (Summer 1997), 35–55, at 41.

[31] *Ibid.*, 47.

[32] Other totally fallacious charges were leveled at Geertz, specifically relating to his fieldwork in Morocco and Indonesia. Thus Daniel Varisco falsely states that Geertz had "no more than a smattering of colloquial Arabic," when in fact he had an excellent command of Moroccan colloquial Arabic (*darija*), something Varisco should at least have had reason to inquiry about given Geertz's clear account in *After the Fact*, 45–46 of his studying the language, an account that was published in 1995, well before Varisco's own book appeared. See Daniel Martin Varisco, *Islam Obscured: The Rhetoric of Anthropological Representation* (New York: Palgrave Macmillan, 2005), 143. Varisco also accuses Geertz of having a thin ethnographic base for his analyses, a statement easily refuted by anyone who wishes to review Geertz's voluminous fieldnotes archived at the University of Chicago's Regenstein

All of this is relevant for an understanding of Geertz's approach to Islam. First, it is clear that few of the critics have read Geertz's entire corpus. Like the blind men surveying the elephant each comes at Geertz's work, as their limited citations reveal, using him for the purposes that most readily suit their own pursuits. Sewell, like many Europeanists, seems never to have read *Agricultural Involution*, the essay on the suq in *Meaning and Order in Moroccan Society*, *The Social History of an Indonesian Town*, or *Peddlers and Princes* – each of which is extremely diachronic in approach.[33] And those who say he ignored "subalterns" never cite *Kinship in Bali*, his afterword in the volume edited by Claire Holt, or various essays in *After the Fact*.[34]

Library. Varisco, who understands neither Geertz's theory of culture nor the nature of such an analytic enterprise, illogically claims that Geertz's views are not supported by reference to natives' own words, thus confusing source material with its explication. Similarly, the Geertz obituary by Lionel Tiger in the *Wall Street Journal* reflects far more on the character of the writer than his subject. See Lionel Tiger, "Fuzz, Fuzz ... It Was Covered in Fuzz," *Wall Street Journal*, November 7, 2006, A.12. And those who think Geertz ignored women need to read such works as *The Religion of Java* (Glencoe: Free Press, 1960) and *Kinship in Bali* [co-authored with Hildred Geertz] (Chicago: University of Chicago Press, 1975). They also need to place their own unfounded claims, as Biddick wrongly asserts, that Geertz engaged in "rhetorical collusion" with dominant males, in the context of his research topics, the division of labor among the members of the Modjokuto (Java) project, developing interests among anthropologists since the 1950s, and the difficulties attendant on a male anthropologist working with women in Muslim societies such as Indonesia and Morocco. See Kathleen Biddick, "Bede's Blush: Postcards from Bali, Bombay, Palo Alto," in John Van Engen, ed., *The Past and Future of Medieval Studies* (Notre Dame: University of Notre Dame, 1994), 16–44. Many of the issues relating to women in the joint fieldwork conducted by Clifford and Hildred Geertz were contained in her publications, including *The Javanese Family: A Study of Kinship and Socialization* (Prospect Heights, IL: Waveland Press, 1989 [1961]), and "The Meaning of Family Ties," in Geertz, Geertz, and Rosen, *Meaning and Order in Moroccan Society*, 315–91.

[33] Clifford Geertz, *Agricultural Involution* (Berkeley: University of California Press, 1963); *Meaning and Order in Moroccan Society*; and *The Social History of an Indonesian Town* (Cambridge: MIT Press, 1965). Geertz's essay on the marketplace from *Meaning and Order in Moroccan Society* has been republished as *Sūq: Geertz on the Market*, edited with an introduction by Lawrence Rosen, (Chicago: HAU/University of Chicago Press, 2022).

[34] Clifford and Hildred Geertz, *Kinship in Bali*; Clifford Geertz, "Afterword: The Politics of Meaning," in Claire Holt, ed., *Culture and Politics in Indonesia* (Ithaca: Cornell University Press, 1972), 319–35; reprinted in Geertz, *The Interpretation of Cultures*, 311–26.

Like Weber, Geertz's individual essays have to be read as chapters of a single, overarching oeuvre, and failure to see that he did not replicate the same data or issues in every separable part of that overall comparativist project is to gravely misread particular parts of it.[35] Second, it is true that the high water period of Geertz's work – the 1960s at Chicago – was one in which the idea of culture as shared symbols was preeminent, but that attention was focused more on the symbols part of the equation than on the extent and modes by which symbols are shared. It is a mistake, however, to think that the issue of internal cultural disagreement was simply ignored. Geertz, like the others at Chicago in those days, did not see in culture the proof of ineluctable forces or reducible patterns of historic necessity, nor did the Chicago scholars fail to consider the highly contested nature of the politics of the developing nations. Reading, for example, the essays in *Old Societies and New States* would show critics that Geertz, the guiding light of that collective volume, viewed culture as something constantly subject to creative alteration rather than mechanical replication even as he focused on how the family resemblance among diverse approaches to a shared set of symbols could hold a society together.[36]

With these points in mind, we can begin to see how central both the shared and the disputed were to Geertz's thinking about Islamic societies. In Javanese culture, for example, Islam was differentially absorbed by the Hinduized *priyayi*, the animistic *abangan*, and the scripturalist *santri*, yet all could, in very significant ways, orient their actions to one another sufficiently so that their shared identity as Muslims could render the formation of a national identity possible. And the intense, even centrifugal, individualism of Moroccans could

[35] Indeed, Geertz's original impetus for the book that became *Meaning and Order in Moroccan Society* was to place great quantities of the data collected by those working with him in and around Sefrou within a single volume so that each would be freer to go about writing shorter, interpretive essays without having to constantly repeat the background data. This idea may have arisen from the critiques by some readers of Geertz's briefer works on Indonesia that he did not supply data to back up his assertions, even though few had read such circumstantial accounts as his *The Religion of Java, The Social History of an Indonesian Town* (Cambridge, MA: MIT Press, 1965), or *Negara: The Theatre State in Nineteenth Century Bali* (Princeton: Princeton University Press, 1980), which laid out such raw information in great detail.

[36] Clifford Geertz, ed., *Old Societies and New States: The Quest for Modernity in Asia and Africa* (New York: Free Press, 1963).

still contribute to a common nation state when the precepts by which alliances are forged were themselves rendered within a shared framework of Islamic legitimization. In each case, internal variation and contestation, as well as the use of diachronic change alongside an assessment of structural forms, was central to Geertz's understanding of Islam's malleable place within each society and time.

Indeed, as Robert A. Segal points out, Geertz's view of meaning in religion always necessitates that action be taken in terms of one's orientations: Neither intent nor attachment to unenacted propositions is sufficient to render a belief system socially and culturally viable.[37] Thus, as Geertz sought to understand the Moroccan and Indonesian experiences of Islam over the forty years he studied them he looked for the places where they were given life, the areas where they were enacted and where they created realities – the marketplace, the political arena, the household, the shared ritual – firmly convinced that one cannot participate in a cultural system without the categories generated by experience receiving some enlivening form. Moreover, just as Aristotle had said that the wise man does not attribute greater specificity to a matter than is appropriate to its nature, Geertz resisted characterizing the events he observed as having a greater precision than seemed to accord with both the actions and the statements he encountered. Just as he argued that Islam did not have some pristine form that occurred at a given moment in Islamic history only to suffer a scattering out, much less diminution, over the course of time, so, too, he stuck to his theory of culture as centered on the publicly worked nature of symbolling behavior that is integral to the highly fluctuating and variable ways people create a common heritage of categories and meanings. From his first major article about an Islamic funeral that went awry in Java because of the different meanings

[37] Segal contrasts Weber and Geertz in the following terms: "For Geertz, the payoff of belief is behaviour. Belief is a guide to behaviour. Culture requires belief so that behaviour will make sense, but culture is behaviour foremost. For Weber, the payoff of behaviour is belief. Behaviour is the justification for belief. Religion prescribes behaviour not merely because adherents need to know how to act but also because their behaviour validates their belief.... Where for Geertz one needs to know what to believe in order to know how to behave, for Weber one needs to know how to behave in order to know what to believe." Robert A. Segal, "Weber and Geertz on the Meaning of Religion," *Religion*, 29 (1999), 61–71, at 70–71.

various Muslim groups attached to their identity, right up to his last iteration of Islam in the introduction he wrote to the Hebrew translation of *Islam Observed*,[38] Geertz sought to point out the poignant, and not necessarily successful, attempts to settle views that, as the acts and utterances of his informants revealed, were by no means static or beyond analytic grasp.

It is here, then, that one can see how the essay on the market in Sefrou was, in no small way, an essay on Islam. For if, to paraphrase Geertz's characterization of the work of Malinowski and Victor Turner, the Balinese rituals are in large part engines of status, so too the Moroccan marketplace is a forum for moral action.[39] This morality is neither abstract nor unlinked to Islam. Quite the contrary, it *is* Islam – its bespoken manifestation in a world where workable relationships among men are central to the retention of a community of believers, its expression of a world in which chaos is to be averted by the regularization of interpersonal engagement, and its enactment in a realm where the idea of what it is to be a Muslim receives one of its most characteristic, if variant, manifestations. In this regard, Geertz attended very carefully to the specifically Islamic institutions of the marketplace – the *ḥabus* (mortmain), the *zawiya* (brotherhood), and the *shari'a* (Islamic law). But he also explored the relation of these institutions and the broader culture of integrative orientations, appreciating that "in a country notorious for a clamorous sort of piety" a good deal of the effect of Islam

is diffuse, a general coloring of style and attitude in commercial relationships that only extended ethnographic description could capture, and then but obliquely. Some of it, also, is only skin deep – Quranic prohibitions against interest taking, gambling, or trafficking in gold that seem to exist mainly to be circumvented. But some of it is precise and powerful, built into specific institutional forms whose impact on commercial life is as readily visible as that of transport, taxation, or the rhythm of the seasons. Among

---

[38] See the Hebrew translation, cited above at note 1, of *Islam Observed*, 11–17.

[39] Speaking of the ritual exchange mechanism described by Malinowski and Turner's of the liminal mukanda ritual of the Ndembu, Geertz says "If kula magic is an engine of action, mukanda is a school for passion." Clifford Geertz, "'To Exist Is to Have Confidence in One's Way of Being': Rituals as Model Systems," in Angela N. H. Creager, Elizabeth Lunbek, and M. Norton Wise, eds., *Science Without Laws: Model Systems, Cases, Exemplary Narratives* (Durham: Duke University Press, 2007), 212–24, at 219.

the world religions, Islam has been notable for its ability to sort its utopian and its pragmatic aspects into distinct and only partially communicating spheres – the former left as ideals to be affirmed, explicated, codified, and taught; the latter cast into ingenious pieces of social machinery regulating the detailed processes of community life.[40]

For Moroccans to say, therefore, that "it is by the Grace of God that contentiousness is put between the buyer and the seller" is only to demonstrate that Islam is what Muslims do and say, and how much it is part of the Arabo-Berber version of Islam that the market should be a key venue for demonstrating that religion and moral action are inseparable.[41]

Three things, then, came together in Geertz's work on Islam: (1) that local meanings, which may once have been more defined by social group attachments, had, in the period of his own observations, increasingly become loosed from those groupings and rendered more capable of being moved, synthesized, rearranged, or ignored by individual personalities acting independently of the places or collectivities within which such meanings had once been implanted; (2) that the capacity to orient one's actions toward others on the basis of knowledge drawn from social origins, kinship, or territorial base had shifted with migration, population growth, patterns of gender employment, and colonial contact, but that the emotional attachment to finding one's footing in these changing circumstances through some rationale that could properly be called Islamic remains very intense; and (3) that the human propulsion to constantly recreate the categories of our experience is just as likely to produce highly localized orientations, rather than simply "globalized" patterns, as has been the case at many other moments in our cultural histories. Thus among the most significant changes, he saw occurring

[40] "Suq: The Bazaar Economy in Sefrou," in *Meaning and Order in Moroccan Society*, 150–51.
[41] "The orthodox impulse is activist; it does not reject intellectualism but subordinates it to the end of moral dynamism. The philosophers' reality is an immobile eternal truth; the orthodoxy's ultimate reality is also eternal truth, but being primarily a moral truth, it must result in moral action. The orthodox conception of truth is therefore not of something which merely is but essentially of something which 'commands'." Fazlur Rahman, *Prophecy in Islam: Philosophy and Orthodoxy* (London: George Allen and Unwin, Ltd., 1958), 110.

in the Muslim world are (1) "the progressive disentanglement ... of the major religions ... from the places, peoples, and social forma- tions, the sites and civilizations, within which and in terms of which they were historically formed" and (2) "the emergence of religious persuasion, inherited or self-ascribed, thinned-out or reinforced, as a broadly negotiable, mobile and fungible, instrument of public identity – a portable persona."[42]

*Islam Observed*, Geertz said, was a pun – in the dual sense of exam- ining Islam and attending to it as a *participant*-observer. In any event, he said, people didn't get the pun. Yet the punning exercise was not without its own value: It underscored that without some *comparative* examination one may assume that things must be the way they appear in any given situation because of some inherent necessity, whereas comparisons show the variability of every cultural feature. Indeed, without some circumstantial involvement, the actual meaning of an enterprise may lack traction altogether. Notwithstanding some criti- cisms that largely missed the point, Geertz's definition of religion, for example, not only holds up well under comparison but continues to re-focus attention on the specifics of culturally distinctive manifesta- tions of Islamic commonalities. His 'definition' of religion thus cre- ates not a rigid dictionary bounding of religion but a proper emphasis on how religion connects with numerous other domains in the life of an adherent.[43]

Indeed, decades on, Geertz's insights continue to be of enormous value to our present understanding of the world. It remains quite true, as he said, that the wider a religion becomes the more precarious it becomes, that we ignore the local at our peril, that turmoil is internal however much it is externally stimulated, and that "scripturalism seems likely to remain in the position of cheering on a modernism whose every advance undermines its own position." As one confronts a world in which the temptation of the universal can seduce even the well-intended

---

[42] The phrase "a portable persona" was used in both Geertz's Frazer Lecture, "Shifting Aims, Moving Targets: On the Anthropology of Religion," *The Journal of the Royal Anthropological Institute*, 11, 1 (March 2005), 1–15, and in his introduction to the Hebrew translation of *Islam Observed*.

[43] See, in regard to Geertz's characterization of religion, the misplaced critique by Varisco discussed above at note 32. For a more balanced appraisal, see Fred Inglis, *Clifford Geertz: Culture, Custom, and* Ethics (Cambridge, UK: Polity Press, 2000).

interventionist into self-deluding acts, Geertz's prescient reminder that people will seek local meanings for their local lives should give pause to those who think that events must unfold in a predetermined way. In the end, Geertz's quest was always for that "social history of the imagination" in which "the real is as imagined as the imaginary." For if the members of the two Muslim cultures to whose comprehension he devoted his lifelong efforts teach us anything, he seems to be saying, their "struggle for the real," their encapsulation of their religious life as "a materialized idea," deeply suffuses the structure of their interpersonal orientations – and with them the ways in which we who share a world with them must also struggle to comprehend their meaning and the trajectory of our entangled lives.

# 9 | *Orientalism Revisited*
## *Edward Said's Unfinished Critique*

*Edward Said was undoubtedly the most well-known and controversial student of the Muslim world during his lifetime (Figure 9.1). His critique of Western scholarship and journalism of that world colors much of our view of what the Orientalist scholars presented and how their writings affected the policies and judgment of Islam and its adherents. The merits and shortcomings of Said's critique have been the subject of decades of discussion and controversy, and the present essay will not seek to extend that discussion as such. Rather, it will suggest that in certain respects Said's critique did not go far enough and in doing so rather missed the mark – that in fact Western Orientalists operated with several assumptions that need to be made more explicit if the appraisal of their work and that of many current commenters on the Muslim scene are to be fully understood. Extending Said's critique is not the same as endorsing or reproving it. Instead, it is to clarify the underlying ideas that have informed certain academic encounters with the cultures of the Middle East and by rendering them explicit to place criticism of their precepts on a less adversarial foundation than was true in Said's own work.*

*

With the 1978 publication of *Orientalism*, Edward Said launched a critique of Western scholarship on the Middle East that still reverberates through academic and public debate. He saw in the Orientalists (to borrow the phrasing of Barnaby Rogerson) "the notion that the West has distorted and romanticized the history of its Eastern opponents as a prelude to weakening and then conquering them."[1] By characterizing Middle Eastern cultures as incapable of adapting to modern

---

[1] Barnaby Rogerson, *In Search of Ancient North Africa* (London: Haus Publishing, 2017), 15.

**Figure 9.1** Edward Said (1935–2003). Credit: Briantrejo, CC BY-SA 3.0, via Wikimedia Commons.

life, the early Orientalists, in Said's view, hid their colonial, and indeed racist, biases. In the process, he suggested, Orientalists fooled themselves – and Westerners generally – into believing that their studies were undertaken with total neutrality. Said particularly attacked Bernard Lewis as the contemporary exemplar of this entrenched view. In a series of exchanges, he argued that such scholarly bias contributed to the failure of the West to recognize Palestinians as a distinct people or to value Middle Eastern nations except for their oil and gas.[2] While Said did not live to see how Lewis' views would influence the policies in Iraq of President George W. Bush's administration, the terms of his critique still divide scholars. Despite decades of controversy, however, neither Said's most recent supporters, such as Juan Cole and Rashid Khalidi, nor his most ardent critics, such as Raphael Patai and Daniel Pipes, have succeeded in subjecting Said's concerns to a serious analysis that might address the central question: Can scholarship on the Middle East ever be freed from its political context?

---

[2] See, e.g., Edward Said, Oleg Grabar, and Bernard Lewis, "Orientalism: An Exchange," *The New York Review of Books*, August 12, 1982.

To address this question, we must return to Said's contentious book. Here, in the final section of *Orientalism* (entitled "The Latest Phase"), the controversy begins. Even someone with only a passing acquaintance with the works that Said attacks may find reason to pause. For it is here, describing the writings of his contemporaries, that Said was most obviously selective, exaggerating, and intemperate, mixing time periods, suggesting that those who actually interview Arabs secretly regard them as "despised heretic[s]," and hinting at covert sexual fantasy just because a scholar notes that the root for the Arabic word for "revolution" refers to a camel "rising up."

Said argued that throughout Western history writers on the Middle East, regardless of the divergent attitudes of their day, reinforced an image of Arabs and Muslims as unvarying, incompetent, and unreflective. But to Said, "the Orient" was a creation of the Western imagination; Orientalism, he said, was "a kind of Western projection onto and will to govern over the Orient." The vision cast up by Orientalists gave authority to attitudes and actions they willingly or unwittingly supported. Following Foucault, Said saw the Orientalists of each era attributing the same features to Arabs – racial inferiority, Islamic fanaticism, unbridled sexuality, craven acquiescence to power – that yielded a caricatured East from which the West has never shaken free. Asserting that "Orientalism has historically been one department … of liberal humanism," he argued more broadly that "the general liberal consensus that 'true' knowledge is fundamentally nonpolitical … obscures the highly if obscurely organized political circumstances obtaining when knowledge is produced." "Representations," he concluded, "have purposes … [they] are formations … deformations."

Robert Irwin is a good example of someone who strongly disagrees with Said. Defending his discipline in *Dangerous Knowledge: Orientalism and Its Discontents*, Irwin pulls no punches in referring to Said's work: "That book seems to me to be a work of malignant charlatanry in which it is hard to distinguish honest mistakes from willful misrepresentations."[3] Irwin, building on misgivings from the last chapter of *Orientalism*, writes that if Said was wrong about the present his account of earlier Orientalists might be equally suspect. Like Said, Irwin takes us through the history of Western writings

---

[3] Robert Irwin, *Dangerous Knowledge: Orientalism and Its Discontents* (Woodstock, NY: Overlook Press, 2006).

on the East, appraising the work of some famous scholars and some so obscure they may be unfamiliar even to specialists. Irwin readily acknowledges these writers' foibles and eccentricities. Thus Guillaume Postel (born 1510), "the first true Orientalist," was "a complete lunatic" who thought everyone needed to return to speaking Hebrew; Abraham Wheelocke (c. 1593–1653), holder of the first chair in Arabic at Cambridge, was interested in sea monsters and mermaids; and Athanasius Kircher (1601–1680), to whom "the torch of mad linguistics passed," "devised a vomiting machine and eavesdropping statues, as well as a kind of piano powered by screeching cats."

But Irwin has a larger story to tell. Those who may fairly be called Orientalists certainly were, in his view, men (and, very rarely, women) of their times, but they were devoted to studying the languages of the region and establishing the relation of Islam and its history to Jewish and Christian sources. They were not overtly political, he says, nor, except in rare and more recent times, even involved in conversation with policymakers. Irwin's characteristic way of dealing with the inveterate racists is simply to read them out of the category of Orientalists. Thus, Ernest Renan's (1823–1892) hostility to Semites suggests he was not a 'real' scholar, and like-minded writers "did not need to have Orientalists invent racism for them." He concludes that "racist attitudes in any period or region are the product of the natural tendency to think in generalities." But this etiology of opinions avoids an essential point – not well expressed by Said either – about consequences: Whatever their origins and purposes, students of the region often set the terms of subsequent discussions. If Orientalists claimed that the East was a linguistically exceptional and theologically undeveloped culture with highly elaborate legal strictures, their ways of framing the issues had repercussions for political no less than common discourse: One does not have to be a policymaker to affect policy.

It is not enough, then, to complain – as Irwin does – about the banality of observing that scholars are not always objective. Indeed, he treats texts as if they had no political effects, as if (in earlier periods) salvation were the preeminent concern and attachment to royalists or mercantilism were incidental, and as if the explication of a text did not in itself imply unstated criteria. In thus evading Said's larger and more difficult question about the political and intellectual effects of scholarly analysis – such as the constant references to the Prophet

Muhammed as lascivious – Irwin retreats to the assumptions that continue to inform so much of Orientalist study.

While Said and his critics disagree about the existence of a hidden, malignant political agenda written into the entire course of Orientalist scholarship, both fail to analyze fully the assumptions that may entail a certain bias toward the peoples and cultures of the region. When Said says that "the core of Orientalist dogma persists" – that it "flourishes today in the forms I have tried to describe" – he fails to consider whether assumptions about language, textual analysis, and social dynamics may be capable of a substantial degree of autonomy or whether, as he uncritically assumes, they necessarily lead to adverse judgments of those studied.

Like other defenders, Irwin thinks that Orientalist approaches can always be divorced from negative views of the region, while Said thinks they are inextricably linked. A more helpful project would be to explore without prior judgment some of the Orientalists' intellectual assumptions and consider whether they can be teased apart from political implications. Sorting those assumptions from their potential bias and latent import will highlight why the analyses offered by both Said and Irwin have serious limitations. Any such list of Orientalists' assumptions, then, would have to include the following:

*Etymology is destiny.* For a very long time, philology was at the heart of the Orientalist enterprise. While some used it as a sort of linguistic astrology – a way of determining humanity's fate through the discovery of root languages or the design of the Biblical voice – the European philologists could simultaneously embrace and distance themselves from actual speakers. Irwin cites Abbé Barthélemy's statement that "one does not learn these languages to speak them" – nor, by implication, to speak with "them."[4] In the twentieth century, philology simply got transmogrified. No self-respecting contemporary Orientalist comments on a text or a word without showing its "original" meaning, commonly implying that, whatever accretions may have

---

[4] This attitude may be found among some scholars to the present day. While serving on the visiting committee of a major Middle East Studies program, the students complained to me and my colleagues that none of the colloquial forms of Arabic was being offered. When our committee raised the issue with the leading professor in the department, we were curtly told that there was no need to speak with people of the region since the only valuable comments they would have to make would be embraced in the written form of the language.

attached themselves over the centuries, the word's true meaning is its earliest meaning. This is the attitude, for example, of Bernard Lewis in *The Political Language of Islam* and almost every entry in *The Encyclopedia of Islam*. Rather than seeing language in its living – to say nothing of psychological – context, it is thought all but sufficient to access its earliest meaning to grasp its timeless essence. This focus has allowed the philological enterprise to be carried along – without the need for interdisciplinary insight – into the ongoing appraisal of texts. Such an approach does not, as Said would have it, necessitate a biased view of the *mentalités* of modern Arabic speakers, but it can certainly perpetuate the assumption that the scholar knows better than the native-speaker the true meaning of his or her expressions.

*Linguistic exceptionalism*. Arabists to this day remark on the extraordinary difficulty of the language – its vast vocabulary, its nuanced meanings, its challenge to the human voice box. When, however, Irwin says that Thomas van Erpe (1584–1625) was accused of magic because he learned Arabic so easily and then makes note of his own difficulties in learning the language, his conceit is doubled: What geniuses some of these Orientalists were to grasp this complex language, and how talented must those, like Irwin himself, be who have finally conquered it! Indeed, one still encounters Orientalists whose enunciation is so hypercorrect that it may be wondered of them, as it was said of David Margoliouth, the sometime Laudian Professor of Arabic at Oxford, that his Arabic was so pure no Arab could understand him.

This linguistic mystification nurtures the idea that the thoughts of speakers of these languages must be quite different from those of other language users, that only those scholars vested with full control of the language can appraise its attendant cultures, and that a very long apprenticeship is required for such mastery. This mystification is carried over into popular works, such as Jonathan Raban's *Arabia Through the Looking Glass* and Karen Armstrong's *Islam*, where Arabic is made to appear vastly complex and elusive. Indeed, the image that Arabic speakers get lost in the fantasy of their linguistic pirouettes ("we will drive them into the sea") reinforces stereotypes with vast political repercussions. Once again, the Orientalists' change in assumptions reinforces key elements of the earlier pattern. If linguistic exceptionalism was once the demonstration of how Middle Eastern languages formed the common denominator for Semitic thought, now the very differences among languages validate the specialists' knowledge and the claim that with linguistic competence no further need exists for interdisciplinary training or extraneous theorizing. The resulting division of knowledge between departments of Middle East studies and various disciplines – more than the biases that Said saw in Westerners' attitude toward the East and that Irwin writes out of the field – may be the single greatest contributor to Orientalism's limitations.

*Change is slow and destabilizing.* To most Orientalists, everything has been downhill for Muslims since the Abbasids (750–1258), or the late medieval period – or indeed since the advent of Islam. Change, in this view, is often equated with instability, and the proper measure of any period or institution is the distance it has strayed from some "original" moment. For example, one reads in work such as Kurt Vikør's *Between God and the Sultan* how Islamic law is now a pale reflection of its formative self, and almost nothing can be learned from its current operation that would be useful in understanding its past.[5] At a recent gathering of Islamic-law scholars, I could not find a single one who had set foot in a present-day Muslim court or who, like the onetime dean of Islamic-law studies in the West, Joseph Schacht, could see the advantage in refining questions for their own periods of study by doing so. Even such fine scholars as Wael Hallaq and Baber Johansen, by their emphasis on texts, perpetuate the unsupported presumption (as Noel Coulson said) that the chair is not only more comfortable but more influential than the bench.[6] Instead of seeing Islamic law as a kind of common-law variant – in which power is significantly dispersed to the local level and changing social concepts are brought up through local practice – even Orientalists with no training in law continue to accept unreflectively that the shariʿa is a legal system well-suited to the analytic categories of European law. Whether in studies of Arab science, literature, or architecture, Orientalists similarly possess a nostalgia that exceeds the sensibility of even the most jaded Levantine. The resultant bias against the value of present thought is

---

[5] Knut S. Vikør, *Between God and Sultan: A History of Islamic Law* (London: Hurst & Co., 2005).

[6] See Noel J. Coulson, *Conflicts and Tensions in Islamic Law* (Chicago: University of Chicago Press, 1969); Baber Johansen, "Casuistry: Between Legal Concept and Social Praxis," *Islamic Law and Society*, 2, 2 (1995), 135–56; and Wael B. Hallaq, *Restating Orientalism* (New York: Columbia University Press, 2018).

not one of hegemonic prejudice in Said's sense but one of intellectual assumptions that have become professional blinders.

*Facts speak for themselves.* This phrasing, which can still be heard in lectures by such influential Orientalists of our day as Michael Cook and Patricia Crone, serves both as a measure of status in the field ("I can recite more 'facts' than you can") and as a bulwark against the intrusion of other disciplines. Orientalists are splitters, not lumpers: They delight in collecting the particular and regard as natural the compartments of knowledge into which they divide their studies. Thus, law and custom are distinct, and a specialist in the shariʿa is unlikely to see important connections for his work in poetry, the logic of mosaic design, or everyday concepts of time and space. As a result, the kinds of popular source material scholars of early modern Europe or the history of India, China, or Japan would regard as no less useful than diplomatic, military, or scholarly writings simply do not form a significant part of the contemporary Orientalists' textual base.

Comparison and theorizing also drop out when the sheer weight of "facts" is accumulated. Irwin, who has little positive to say about current Orientalist scholarship, is characteristic in being tone-deaf to the work of social scientists. Just as the earlier Orientalists saw no merit in talking to "the natives," Irwin ignores the contributions of field-based studies, many of which are deeply respectful of the historical work of Orientalists. Other commenters, such as Zachary Lockman, can cite very few examples to back the claim that Said influenced a line of subsequent Middle Eastern scholarship.[7] Indeed, as a president of the Middle East Studies Association, Lockman (like Irwin) should know that the organization was founded to get away from constant focus on the Arab–Israeli dispute and that for many years only the president of the association, rotated yearly between a pro-Arab and a pro-Israeli scholar (in what was quaintly thought of as "the Lebanese solution"), was licensed to make sustained judgmental comments on the conflict at the meeting's annual banquet. Nevertheless, after initial involvement with the organization, many social scientists dropped out simply because regional interests could not overcome the Orientalists' lack of involvement in discipline-based issues. While Irwin gives welcome attention to Russian and Israeli Orientalists, as well as Muslim critics

---

[7] Zachary Lockman, *Contending Visions of the Middle East: The History and Politics of Orientalism* (Cambridge: Cambridge University Press, 2004).

of Said, neither he nor Said consider how theories always inform the choice of facts, and hence the impossibility of facts ever speaking with utter neutrality for themselves.

*Orientalists as mullahs manqués.* Many of the Orientalists in Irwin's account act as though they know the true reading of Muslim texts better than the believers themselves. If, in their rarefied post-philological studies, they sometimes act like cultural cannibals – endeavoring to express what their subjects purportedly cannot say well for themselves – at other times they act like cultural game wardens – preserving and shepherding the misguided to the correct solutions. Hence, it is still no more necessary than it was for earlier Orientalists to consult with living Arabs, Persians, or Turks, or to see how such contact might lead scholars to new ideas and sources that could inform their own historical interpretations. That Irwin can point to very few Orientalists, even at present, who evince sincere respect for the people of the region is not unrelated to the belief that, since the texts are central and Orientalists know the texts, Orientalists know best.

\*\*\*

The disputes engendered by Said's work may seem an academic spat that should be restricted to seminar rooms and department cocktail parties. But two very important considerations suggest otherwise. First, the Orientalists' expertise, whether situated in the academy or the think tank, has great influence on the terms by which nonspecialists address the region. If Orientalists convince others that Arabic requires either brilliant linguistic skills or decades for mastery, one may end up, as we in the United States have, with only a handful of State Department and FBI employees certified in the language at the highest level. Sir Hamilton Gibbs's assertion in the 1950s that "upon the Arab mind the impact of artistic speech is immediate; the words [pass] through no filter of logic or reflection" is no more ill-informed than Thomas L. Friedman's current assertion that people in the Middle East will not trust your straightforward reporting because, "if you can't explain something with a conspiracy theory then don't try to explain it at all."[8] Thus, secondly, choosing terms that suggest there is

---

[8] Thomas L. Friedman, "In Iraq the Least Bad Option Is the Best We Can Do," *New York Times*, January 15, 2005.

such a thing as "the Arab mind" or that all change in the region has been a form of cultural entropy, can have, even without direct consultation, a dramatic effect on national attitudes and policies.

Sherlock Holmes once said to his companion, "'Pon my word, Watson, you are coming along wonderfully. It is true that you have missed everything of importance, but you have hit upon the method." To this day, Orientalists have confounded Holmes's assertion: They have produced much important information even though their methods are crabbed and antiquated. Edward Said, more Watson than Holmes, got much of the substance wrong, but his method – looking at discourse as an artifact of a writer's context – was basically sound. Before his death in 2003, Said spoke of his attachment to "intransigence, difficulty, and unresolved contradiction." If encounters with the Muslim world are to achieve a balance of insight and respect, it is precisely in embracing such orientations that we can be moved to reconsider whether our assumptions are leading us to conclusions neither facts nor methods can fully support.

# Envoi

There is no ascent to truth without descent to cases.

*Clifford Geertz*

We deserve all our encounters: they are in concert with our destiny and have a significance it behooves us to discover.

*François Mauriac*

The encounters we have described may, in the words of novelist P. D. James, be "not so much two ships passing in the night as two ships sailing together for a time but always bound for different ports." Whether it is the Muslim artist confronted by an imperceptible cosmos he wishes to reduce to the palpable, a tribesman who wants his customary law-ways to be part of his accepted faith, or a youth who hopes her future will be folded within a revised structure of power, every meeting with another ripples out in its systemic effects in ways that are as uncertain as they are capricious. "We could have created you all the same," says the Quran, but by making each nation, each tribe, each person unlike any other the voice of Islam carried from its outset a vision of obligation to know one another and a cosmic order in which difference is the ally, not the foe.

Our encounters may well define our destinies: In that "peculiar aura and soothing tint of contingent encounters," it may even be said of us all that "they were forced together – and found that they preferred it."[1] Such encounters will, of course, be ongoing; the value of having to make the effort to attend to difference will inform Islam

---

[1] The first quote is from Belgian painter and author Erik Pevernagie's "Twilight of Desire"; the latter from novelist Simon Van Booy, *The Illusion of Separateness* (New York: HarperCollins, 2013).

all its days. And while that will, at times, entail conflict, it will also be against the background of appreciating, as the Tradition of the Prophet proclaims, that, in the world as in the marketplace, "contention has been placed between buyer and seller" for a reason – that they may confront their differences and out of their encounters find a realistic path to peace.

# Bibliography

Lahcen Achy, "Moroccan Youth Struggle to Find Employment Opportunities," Al-Monitor, June 30, 2013. al-monitor.com

Afghanistan Study Group, A New Way Forward: Rethinking U.S. Strategy in Afghanistan (2010). www.afghanistanstudygroup.com

Akbar Ahmed, *Postmodernism and Islam* (London: Routledge, 2004).

Samer Akkach, *Cosmology and Architecture in Premodern Islam* (Albany: State University of New York Press, 2005).

Aida Alami, "Morocco's Stability Is Roiled by Monthslong Protests over Fishmonger's Death," *New York Times*, August 26, 2017.

Aida Alamijan, "Morocco Said to Ban Sale of Burqas, Citing Security Concerns," *New York Times*, January 11, 2017.

Salim Al-Hassani, "New Discoveries in the Islamic Complex of Mathematics, Architecture and Art," Muslim Heritage, 2007. www.muslimheritage.com/article/new-discoveries-in-islamic-complex

Abdulmajeed Alshalan, Currupt Practices in Saudi Arabia, S.J.D. Thesis, University of Indiana School of Law, June 2017. www.repository.law.indiana.edu/etd/45

Deborah Amos, Eclipse of the Sunnis (Washington: Public Affairs, 2010).

'An Old Missionary,' "Missions in North Africa," *The Muslim World*, 25, 4 (1935): 391–95.

David Apter, ed., *Ideology and Discontent* (New York: Free Press, 1964).

Tim Arango, "Dozens Killed in Iraq Suicide Attack," *New York Times*, July 18, 2010.

Karen Armstrong, *Muhammad: A Prophet for Our Time* (New York: HarperCollins, 2006).

Thomas Arnold, *Painting in Islam* (Oxford: Clarendon Press, 1928).

Ragui Assaad, Christine Binzel, and May Gadallah, "Transition to Employment and Marriage among Young Men in Egypt," *The Middle East Youth Initiative, Working Paper No. 12* (Washington, DC: Brookings Institution Wolfensohn Center for Development and Dubai School of Government, October 2010).

Tony Assaf, "Maroc: La conversion de musulmans su christianisme soulève la colère dans le pays," *Aleteia*, March 30, 2015. Fr.aleteia.org

Associated Press, "Pakistan Detainees Proud of Role in NYC Bomb Case," *New York Times*, May 22, 2010.

Associated Press, "Israel's Daniel Shechtman Wins Nobel Prize in Chemistry," *The Washington Post*, October 5, 2011.

David Axe, "Social Scientists under Fire," *Miller-McCune*, March/April, 2010: 58–69.

Victor F. Ayoub, "Conflict Resolution and Social Reorganization in a Lebanese Village," *Human Organization*, 2 (1965): 11–17.

Ghulam Murtaza Azad, "Conduct and Qualities of a Qadi," *Islamic Studies*, 24 (1985), 51–61.

Peter Baker, "How Obama Came to Plan for 'Surge' in Afghanistan," *New York Times*, December 6, 2009.

Philip Ball, "Fearful Symmetry: Roger Penrose's Tiling," *Prospect*, September 19, 2013.

Michael Banton, ed., *Anthropological Approaches to the Study of Religion* (London: Tavistock, 1966).

Thomas Barfield, *Afghanistan: A Cultural and Political History* (Princeton: Princeton University Press, 2010).

Julien E. Barnes, "Petraeus: U.S. Lacks Afghan Tribal Knowledge," *The Wall Street Journal*, September 2, 2010.

David Baron, "Medieval Islamic Architecture Presages 20th-Century Mathematics," *Harvard University Gazette*, February 22, 2007.

Fredrik Barth, *Nomads of South Persia: The Basseri Tribe of the Khamseh Confederacy* (Oslo: University of Oslo Publications, 1961).

Michael Baxendall, *Painting and Experience in Fifteenth Century Italy* (Oxford: Clarendon Press, 1972).

Ruth Behar, "The Anthropologist's Son," *The Chronicle of Higher Education*, 55, 14 (2008): B99.

Khalid Bekkaoui and Ricardo René Larémont, "Moroccan Youth Go Sufi," *The Journal of the Middle East and Africa*, 2, 1 (2011), 31–46.

Khalid Bekkaoui, Ricardo René Larémont, and Sadik Rddad, "Survey on Moroccan Youth: Perception and Participation in Sufi Orders," *The Journal of the Middle East and Africa*, 2, 1 (2011), 47–63.

Joseph Berger, "Despite Law, Few Trafficking Arrests," *New York Times*, December 4, 2009.

Kathleen Biddick, "Bede's Blush: Postcards from Bali, Bombay, Palo Alto," in John Van Engen, ed., *The Past and Future of Medieval Studies* (Notre Dame: University of Notre Dame, 1994), 16–44.

Bikya News, "Morocco: Women Battle against Domestic Abuse," *Women Living under Muslim Laws*, May 13, 2013. wluml.org

John Bohannon, "Quasi-Crystal Conundrum Opens a Tiling Can of Worms," *Science* 315 (2007): 10.

James Boon, *Other Tribes, Other Scribes* (Cambridge: Cambridge University Press, 1982).

James A. Boon, "Geertz's Style: A Moral Matter," in Shweder and Good, eds., *Clifford Geertz By His Colleagues* (Chicago: University of Chicago Press, 2005), 28–37.

Simon Van Booy, *The Illusion of Separateness* (New York: HarperCollins, 2013).

Charis Boutieri, *Learning in Morocco: Language Politics and the Abandoned Educational Dream* (Bloomington: Indiana University Press, 2016).

Mark Bowden, "The Professor of War," *Vanity Fair*, May, 2010.

Nathan J. Brown, *The Rule of Law in the Arab World: Courts in Egypt and the Gulf* (Cambridge: Cambridge University Press, 1997).

Gregory Buck, "Algorithms of Boundless Beauty, a Review of Jean-Marc Caséra, 'Arabesques: Decorative Art in Morocco'," *Science* 292, 5516 (2001): 445–46.

David Bukay, "The Religious Foundations of Suicide Bombings." *Middle East Quarterly* 13, 4 (2006): 26–36.

Elizabeth Bumiller, "Unlikely Tutor Giving Military Afghan Advice," *New York Times*, July 17, 2010.

Titus Burckhardt, "The Void in Islamic Art," *Studies in Comparative Religion* 4 (1970): 96–99.

Edmund Burke, III, "Mohand N'Hamoucha: Middle Atlas Berber," in Edmund Burke, II, ed., *Struggle and Survival in the Modern Middle East* (Berkeley: University of California Press, 1993), 100–13.

John F. Burns, "3 Britons Convicted in Plot to Blow Up Airliners," *New York Times*, July 8, 2010.

M. G. Carter, "Infinity and Lies in Medieval Islam," in U. Vermeulen and D. De Smet, eds., *Philosophy and Arts in the Islamic World* (Leuven: Uitgeveru Peeters, 1998), 233–42.

Daniel Cefai, trans., Clifford Geertz, *Le souk de Sefrou: sur l'économie de bazar* (Saint-Denis: Bouchène, 2003).

Pierre Centlivres and Micheline Centlivres-Demont, "The Story of a Picture: Shiite Depictions of Muhammad," *ISIM [International Institute for the Study of Islam in the Modern World (Leiden)] Review* 17 (2006): 18–19.

W. K. Chorbachi, "In the Tower of Babel: Beyond Symmetry in Islamic Design," *Computers and Mathematics with Applications* 17 (1989): 751–89.

Cynthia Chou and Geoffrey Benjamin, eds., *Tribal Communities in the Malay World: Historical, Cultural and Social Perspectives* (Singapore: Institute of Southeast Asian Studies, 2003).

Juan Cole, *The New Arabs: How the Millennial Generation Is Changing the Middle East* (New York: Simon & Schuster, 2014).

George W. Collins, "Missionaries and Muslims: The Gospel Missionary Union in Morocco, 1895–1912," *Wichita State University Bulletin* 51, 3 (1975): 3–17.

Sam Collyns and James Jones, "'America Used to Be Our Enemy No. 1. But Now It's al-Qaida,' Say Former Insurgents," *The Independent* [London], September 29, 2010.

Jules Crétois, "Moroccan Women Face Hardships in Textile Factories," *Al-Monitor*, April 15, 2013. al-monitor.com

Noel Coulson, *A History of Islamic Law* (Edinburgh: Edinburgh University Press, 1965).

Noel J. Coulson, *Conflicts and Tensions in Islamic Law* (Chicago: University of Chicago Press, 1969).

Geoffrey Cupit, *Justice as Fittingness* (Oxford: Clarendon Press, 1996).

Ava Cutler, "Moroccan Mosaics: A Creative Blend of Art, Nature, and Mathematics," *Morocco World News*, April 5, 2020. www.moroccoworldnews.com/2020/04/298478/moroccan-mosaics-a-creative-blend-of-art-nature-and-mathematics/

Loai M. Dabbour, "Geometric Proportions: The Underlying Structure of Design Process for Islamic Geometric Patterns," *Frontiers of Architectural Research*, 1 (2012): 380–91.

Bouzou Daragahi, "Middle East: Against the Law," *Financial Times*, October 31, 2013.

Ila Marie Davis, with Evelyn Stenbock-Ditty, *A Gleam of Light: The Trials and Triumphs of a Century of Missionary Work in Morocco* (Kansas City, MO: Gospel Missionary Union, 1998).

Karka Dieseldorff, "US Court Says Morocco's Justice Is 'Fundamentally Fair'," *Morocco World News*, October 7, 2015.

Maureen Dowd, "The Evil of Lesser Evilism," *New York Times*, May 11, 2010.

Paul Dresch, "Imams and Tribes: The Writing and Acting of History in Upper Yemen," in Philip S. Khoury and Joseph Kostiner, eds., *Tribes and State Formation in the Middle East* (Berkeley: University of California Press, 1991), 252–87.

Baudoin Dupret, ed., *Standing Trial: Law and the Person in the Modern Middle East* (London, I. B. Tauris, 2004).

Baudoin Dupret, Maurits Berger, and Laila al-Zwaini, *Legal Pluralism in the Arab World* (The Hague: Kluwer Law International, 1999).

David B. Edwards, *Heroes of the Age: Moral Fault Lines on the Afghan Frontier* (Berkeley: University of California Press, 1996).

David B. Edwards, *Before Taliban: Genealogies of the Afghan Jihad* (Berkeley: University of California Press, 2002).

Moha Ennaji, "Why Morocco's Burqa Ban Is More Than Just a Security Measure," *U.S. News*, February 1, 2017; reprinted from *The Conversation*,

January 31, 2017. http://theconversation.com/why-moroccos-burqa-ban-is-more-than-just-a-security-measure-72120

Neli Esipova and Julie Ray, "One in Four in North Africa Desired to Migrate before Unrest," *Gallup News*, April 29, 2011. http://news.gallup .com/poll/147344/one-four-north-africa-desired-migrate-unrest.aspx

Richard Ettinghausen, "The Character of Islamic Art," in *The Arab Heritage*, Nabih Amin Faris, ed. (Princeton: Princeton University Press, 1946).

Richard Ettinghausen, "The Early History, Use and Iconography of the Prayer Rug," in *Islamic Art and Archaeology: Collected Papers*, Richard Ettinghausen, ed. (Berlin: Gebr. Mann Verlag, 1984), 282–97.

Richard H. Fallon, Jr., "'The Rule of Law' as a Concept in Constitutional Discourse," *Columbia Law Review*, 97 (1997), 1–56.

Laurie Fendrich, "The Lie of the Portrait," *The Chronicle Review: The Chronicle of Higher Education*, 52 (2005): B10–11.

Dexter Filkins, "Afghan Tribe, Vowing to Fight Taliban, to Get U.S. Aid in Return," *New York Times*, January 28, 2010.

Raymond Firth, review of Clifford Geertz, *Islam Observed, The Journal of Asian Studies*, 28, 4 (1969), 909–10.

Morton Fried, *The Evolution of Political Society* (New York: Random House, 1967).

Thomas L. Friedman, "In Iraq the Least Bad Option Is the Best We Can Do," *New York Times*, January 15, 2005.

David A. Funk, "Traditional Islamic Jurisprudence: Justifying Islamic Law and Government," *Southern University Law Review*, 20 (1993), 213–94.

Eugene Galanter and Murray Gerstenhaber, "On Thought, the Extrinsic Theory," *Psychological Review*, 63, 4 (1956), 218–27.

Jim Garamone, "Afghanistan Now Has Forces, Resources, Petraeus Says," *Armed Forces Press Service*, December 23, 2010. www.defense.gov/news/ newsarticle.aspx?id=60702

Louis Gardet, *Dieu et la destinée de l'homme* (Paris: Librairie Philosophique J. Vrin, 1967).

Clifford Geertz, "Ritual and Social Change: A Javanese Example," *American Anthropologist*, 59 (1957), 32–54.

Clifford Geertz, *The Religion of Java* (Glencoe, IL: Free Press, 1960).

Clifford Geertz, *Agricultural Involution* (Berkeley: University of California Press, 1963).

Clifford Geertz, ed., *Old Societies and New States: The Quest for Modernity in Asia and Africa* (New York: Free Press, 1963).

Clifford Geertz, *Peddlers and Princes: Social Development and Economic Change in Two Indonesian Towns* (Chicago: University of Chicago Press, 1963).

Clifford Geertz, *Social History of an Indonesian Town* (Cambridge: MIT Press, 1965).

Clifford Geertz, *Islam Observed* (New Haven: Yale University Press, 1968).

Clifford Geertz, "Deep Play: Notes on the Balinese Cockfight," *Daedalus* (1971), 1–38.

Clifford Geertz, "Afterword: The Politics of Meaning," in Claire Holt, ed., *Culture and Politics in Indonesia* (Ithaca: Cornell University Press, 1972), 319–35.

Clifford Geertz, "Mysteries of Islam," *The New York Review of Books*, 22, 20 (1975), 18ff.

Clifford Geertz, "Art as a Cultural System," *Modern Language Notes* 91 (1976): 1473–99.

Clifford Geertz, *The Interpretation of Cultures* (New York: Basic Books, 1977).

Clifford Geertz, "Suq: The Bazaar Economy in Sefrou," in Clifford Geertz, Hildred Geertz, and Lawrence Rosen, *Meaning and Order in Moroccan Society* (New York: Cambridge University Press, 1979), pp. 123–313.

Clifford Geertz, *Negara: The Theatre State in Nineteenth Century Bali* (Princeton: Princeton University Press, 1980).

Clifford Geertz, "Conjuring with Islam," *The New York Review of Books*, 29, 9 (1982), 25–28.

Clifford Geertz, *Local Knowledge* (New York: Basic Books, 1983), 175–81.

Clifford Geertz, *Works and Lives: The Anthropologist as Author* (Stanford: Stanford University Press, 1988).

Clifford Geertz, *Available Light: Anthropological Reflections on Philosophical Topics* (Princeton: Princeton University Press, 2000).

Clifford Geertz, "Which Way to Mecca?" *The New York Review of Books*, 50, 10 (2003), 27.

Clifford Geertz, "Which Way to Mecca? Part II," *The New York Review of Books*, 50, 11 (2003).

Clifford Geertz, "Shifting Aims, Moving Targets: On the Anthropology of Religion," *The Journal of the Royal Anthropological Institute*, 11, 1 (2005), 1–15.

Clifford Geertz, "'To Exist Is to Have Confidence in One's Way of Being': Rituals as Model Systems," in Angela N. H. Creager, Elizabeth Lunbek, and M. Norton Wise, eds., *Science without Laws: Model Systems, Cases, Exemplary Narratives* (Durham: Duke University Press, 2007), 212–24.

Clifford Geertz, *Life among the Anthros* (Princeton: Princeton University Press, 2012).

Clifford Geertz, *Sūq: Geertz on the Market*, edited with an introduction by Lawrence Rosen (Chicago: HAU/University of Chicago Press, 2022).

Clifford Geertz and Hildred Geertz, *Kinship in Bali* (Chicago: University of Chicago Press, 1975).

Hildred Geertz, *The Javanese Family: A Study of Kinship and Socialization* (Prospect Heights, IL: Waveland Press, 1989 [1961]).

Andrew Gell, *Art and Agency: An Anthropological Theory* (Oxford: Oxford University Press, 1998).

Gian Gentile, "A Strategy of Tactics: Population-Centric COIN and the Army," *Parameters: US War College Quarterly*, 39 (2009): 5–17.

Katherine. S. Gittes, *Framing the Canterbury Tales: Chaucer and the Medieval Frame Narrative Tradition* (New York: Praeger, 1991).

Cyril Glassé, "Images," in Cyril Glassé, ed., *The New Encyclopedia of Islam*, 4th ed. (Lanham, MD: Rowman & Littlefield, 2013), 213.

Asli Gocer, "A Hypothesis Concerning the Character of Islamic Art," *Journal of the History of Ideas* 60 (1999): 683–92.

Roberto González, *American Counterinsurgency: Human Science and the Human Terrain* (Chicago: Prickly Paradigm Press, 2009).

Roberto González, "Going 'Tribal': Notes on Pacification in the 21$^{st}$ Century," *Anthropology Today* 25, 2 (2009): 15–19.

Erica Goode, "Worrisome Signs of Tension Beset Sunni-Led Awakening Groups in Iraq," *New York Times*, September 22, 2008.

Oleg Grabar, *The Mediation of Ornament* (Princeton: Princeton University Press, 1992).

Oleg Grabar, "Seeing and Believing: The Image of the Prophet in Islam: The Real Story," *The New Republic*, no. 4871 (2009), 433–37.

Karen Graves, "Christians in Morocco: A Crisis of Faith," *U.S. News*, September 30, 2015.

Ernst J. Grube, *The World of Islam* (New York: McGraw-Hill, 1967).

Guillaume, Alfred, *The Life of Muhammad: A Translation of Ishaq's Sirat Rasul Allah* (Oxford: Oxford University Press, 1955).

Mohammed M. Hafez, *Manufacturing Human Bombs: The Making of Palestinian Suicide Bombers* (Washington, DC: United States Institute of Peace Press, 2006).

Wael Hallaq, *A History of Islamic Legal Theories* (Cambridge: Cambridge University Press, 1999).

Wael B. Hallaq, *Restating Orientalism* (New York: Columbia University Press, 2018).

István Harittai, ed., *Fivefold Symmetry* (Singapore: World Scientific Publishing Co., 1992).

David M. Hart, *Qabila: Tribal Profiles and Tribal-State Relations in Morocco and on the Afghanistan-Pakistan Frontier* (Amsterdam, Netherlands: Het Spinhuis, 2001).

Riaz Hassan, *Faithlines: Muslim Conceptions of Islam and Society* (Oxford: Oxford University Press, 2002).

Michael Hastings, "The Runaway General," *Rolling Stone*, June 22, 2010.

Jeff Hecht, "Medieval Islamic Tiling Reveals Mathematical Savvy," *New Scientist*, February 22, 2007.

Steffen Herzog, *Princes, Brokers, and Bureaucrats: Oil and State in Saudi Arabia* (Ithaca: Cornell University Press, 2011).

Marshall G. S. Hodgson, *The Venture of Islam, Vol. I* (Chicago: University of Chicago Press, 1974).

Marshall G. S. Hodgson, *The Venture of Islam, Vol. II* (Chicago: University of Chicago Press, 1974).

Marvine Howe, *Morocco: The Islamist Awakening and Other Challenges* (New York: Oxford University Press, 2005).

Timothy Hsia, "Counterinsurgency – All Things to All Men," *New York Times*, May 21, 2010. Human Terrain Team Handbook. https://publicintelligence .net/human-terrain-team-handbook/2008

Frederick Charles Huxley, *Wasita in Lebanon* (Ann Arbor: Museum of Anthropology, University of Michigan, 1978).

David Ignatius, "A Demographic Shift in the Muslim World," *Washington Post*, February 8, 2013.

Immigration and Refugee Board of Canada, *Morocco: The Situation of Individuals Who Abjure Islam (Who Apostatize), Including Their Treatment by Society and by the Authorities; the Repercussions of a Fatwa of the High Council of Ulemas Condemning Apostates to Death, Including the Reaction of the Government (2016-April 2018)* (Canada: Immigration and Refugee Board of Canada, 2018).

Fred Inglis, *Clifford Geertz: Culture, Custom, and Ethics* (Cambridge, UK: Polity Press, 2000).

Robert Irwin, *Dangerous Knowledge: Orientalism and Its Discontents* (Woodstock, NY: Overlook Press, 2006).

Albert J. Issacs, *A Biographical Sketch of Emma Herdman* (London: S. W. Partridge, 1900).

Dave Jackson and Neta Jackson, *Risking the Forbidden Game* (Minneapolis: Bethany House Publishers, 2002).

Greg Jaffe, "To Understand Sheiks in Iraq, Marines Ask 'Mac'," *The Wall Street Journal*, September 10, 2007.

Baber Johansen, "Sacred and Religious Element in Hanafite Law – Function and Limits of the Absolute Character of Government Authority," in Ernest Gellner, et al., *Islam et Politique au Maghreb* (Paris: Editions du CNRS, 1981), 281–303.

Baber Johansen, "Casuistry: Between Legal Concept and Social Praxis," *Islamic Law and Society*, 2, 2 (1995), 135–56.

Ward Just, *The Weather in Berlin* (New York: Houghton Mifflin Company, 2002).

Art Keller, "Exclusive: al Qaeda Bomb-Factory Video," *Foreign Policy*, May 14, 2010.

Sarah Kershaw, "The Terrorist Mind: An Update," *New York Times*, January 9 2010.

Jason Keyser, "Bin Laden Endorses Failed Attempt to Bomb US Jet," *The Washington Post*, January 24, 2010.

Ruhallah Khapalwak and David Rohde, "A Look at America's New Hope: The Afghan Tribes," *New York Times*, January 29, 2010.

Thomas S. Kidd, *American Christians and Islam: Evangelical Culture and Muslims from the Colonial Period to the Age of Terrorism* (Princeton: Princeton University Press, 2013).

David Kilcullen, *The Accidental Guerrilla* (New York: Oxford University Press, 2009).

David Kilcullen, *Counterinsurgency* (New York: Oxford University Press, 2010).

David D. Kirkpatrick, *Into the Hands of the Soldiers: Freedom and Chaos in Egypt and the Middle East* (New York: Viking, 2018).

Linda Komaroff, *The Gift Tradition in Islamic Art* (New Haven: Yale University Press, 2012).

Takis Konstantopoulos, "Penrose Tilings in Helsinki." http://randomprocessed .blogspot.com/2014/11/penrose-tiling-in-helsinki.html (2014).

Serge Kovaleski, "Obama's Organizing Years, Guiding Others and Finding Himself," *New York Times*, July 7, 2008.

Alan B. Krueger, *What Makes a Terrorist: Economics and the Roots of Terrorism* (Princeton: Princeton University Press, 2008).

Ed Ksara, *My Life Story* (Springfield, MO: The Ethnic Life Stories Project, 2002). https://thelibrary.org/lochist/els/ksara.pdf

Christian Lange, *Paradise and Hell in Islamic Traditions* (Cambridge: Cambridge University Press, 2015).

John Leland, "Iraq's Ills Lead Former Exiles to Flee Again," *New York Times*, November 27, 2010.

Primo Levi, *The Drowned and the Saved* (New York: Vintage, 1989).

Oliver Leaman, *Islamic Aesthetics: An Introduction* (Notre Dame: Notre Dame University Press, 2004).

Herbert J. Liebesny, *The Law of the Near and Middle East* (Albany: State University Press of New York, 1975).

Yvon Linant de Bellefonds, *Des donations en droit musulman* (Cairo: D. Photiadis, 1935).

Yvon Linant de Bellefonds, "Hiba," in Bernard Lewis, et al., eds., *Encyclopedia of Islam*, 2nd ed., Vol. 3 (Leiden, Netherlands: E. J. Brill, 1971), 350–51.

Zachary Lockman, *Contending Visions of the Middle East: The History and Politics of Orientalism* (Cambridge: Cambridge University Press, 2004).

Peter J. Lu and Paul J. Steinhardt, "Decagonal and Quasi-Crystalline Tilings in Medieval Islamic Architecture," *Science* 315 (2007): 1106–10.

George R. Lucas, Jr., *Anthropologists in Arms: The Ethics of Military Anthropology* (Lanham, MD: AltaMira Press, 2009).

Montgomery McFate, "The Military Utility of Understanding Adversary Culture," *Joint Force Quarterly*, 38 (2005): 42–48.

Montgomery McFate and Janice H. Laurence, eds., *Social Science Goes to War: The Human Terrain System in Iraq and Afghanistan* (Oxford: Oxford University Press, 2015).

Timothy S. McWilliams and Kurtis P. Wheeler, eds., *Al-Anbar Awakening: American Perspectives, Vol. I* (Berkshire, UK: Books Express Publishing, 2009).

Laura U. Marks, *Enfoldment and Infinity: An Islamic Genealogy of New Media Art* (Cambridge, MA: The MIT Press, 2010).

Louis Massignon, "Le Temps dans la pensée islamique," *Eranos-Jahrbuch, 1951*, 20 (Zurich: Rhein-Verlag, 1952): 141–48.

Mark Fathi Massoud, *Shariʿa, Inshallah: Finding God in Somali Politics* (Cambridge: Cambridge University Press, 2021).

Matthew Melvin-Koushki, "Powers of One: The Mathematization of the Occult in the High Persianate Tradition," *Intellectual History of the Islamicate World*, 8 (2017): 127–99.

Ariel Merari, *Driven to Death: Psychological and Social Aspects of Suicide Terrorism* (Oxford: Oxford University Press, 2010).

Jean-Louis Miège, "Les missions protestantes au Maroc (1875–1905)," *Hespéris*, 42, 1–2 (1955): 153–92.

Greg Miller, "Man Claims He Aided Times Square Suspect," *The Washington Post*, May 14, 2010.

Joshua Mitchell, *Tocqueville in Arabia: Dilemmas in a Democratic Age* (Chicago: University of Chicago Press, 2013).

Gary W. Montgomery and Timothy S. McWilliams, eds., *Al-Anbar Awakening: American Perspectives, Vol. II* (Berkshire, UK: Books Express Publishing, 2009).

Adrian William Moore, "Infinity and Beyond," *Aeon*, March 8, 2017. https://aeon.co/essays/why-some-infinities-are-bigger-than-others

Omar W. Nasim, "Toward an Islamic Aesthetic Theory," *The American Journal of Islamic Social Sciences* 15 (1998): 71–90.

Gülru Necipoglu, *The Topkapi Scroll* (Santa Monica: Getty Center, 1995).

Rodney Needham, *Belief, Language, and Experience* (Oxford: Blackwell, 1972).

David R. Nelson, "Quasicrystals," *Scientific American* 225 (1986): 42–51.

Network of Concerned Anthropologists, *The Counter-Counterinsurgency Manual* (Chicago: Prickly Paradigm Press, 2009).

Barack Obama, "Text: Obama's Address on the War in Afghanistan," *New York Times*, December 2, 2009.

Barack Obama, "Remarks by the President at the Acceptance of the Nobel Peace Prize," Washington: The White House, Office of the Press Secretary, December 10, 2009.

Barack Obama, "Text: Obama's Nobel Remarks," *New York Times*, December 11, 2009.

George Packer, "Knowing the Enemy: Can Social Scientists Redefine the 'War on Terror'?" *The New Yorker* (2006): 58–69.

Stephania Pandolfo, *Impasse of the Angels: Scenes from a Moroccan Space of Memory* (Chicago: University of Chicago Press, 1998).

Alexandre Papadopoulo, *Islam and Muslim Art* (London: Thames and Hudson, 1979).

Robert A. Pape and James K. Feldman, *Cutting the Fuse: The Explosion of Global Suicide Terrorism and How to Stop It* (Chicago: University of Chicago Press, 2010).

Rudolph Peters, *Crime and Punishment in Islamic Law* (Cambridge: Cambridge University Press, 2005).

"Petraeus: Afghan Tribes Could Fight Militants," *Military Times*, November 6, 2008.

Tom Pfeiffer, "Christian Missionaries Stir Unease in North Africa," *Reuters World News*, December 5, 2008.

Dennis H. Phillips, "The American Missionary in Morocco," *The Muslim World*, 65, 1 (1975): 1–20.

Micky Piller, *Escher Meets Islamic Art* (Bussum, Netherlands: Uitgeverij Thoth, 2013).

Jerrold M. Post, *The Mind of the Terrorist: The Psychology of Terrorism from the IRA to al-Qaeda* (New York: Palgrave Macmillan, 2007).

David Powers, *Law, Society, and Culture in the Maghrib, 1300–1500* (Cambridge: Cambridge University Press, 2002), 95–140.

Sebastian R. Prange, "The Tiles of Infinity," *Aramco World* (September–October 2009): 24–31.

Fazlur Rahman, *Prophecy in Islam: Philosophy and Orthodoxy* (London: George Allen and Unwin, Ltd., 1958).

Youssef Rapoport, "Matrimonial Gifts in Early Islamic Egypt," *Islamic Law and Society*, 7, 1 (2000), 1–36.

William K. Rashbaum and Karen Zraick, "Government Says Al Qaeda Ordered N.Y. Plot," *New York Times*, April 23, 2010.

Frank Rich, "Freedom's Just Another Word," *New York Times*, September 5, 2010, WK5.

Barnaby Rogerson, *In Search of Ancient North Africa* (London: Haus Publishing, 2017).

Nir Rosen, *Aftermath: Following the Bloodshed of America's Wars in the Muslim World* (New York: Nation, 2010).

Nir Rosen, "Something from Nothing: U.S. Strategy in Afghanistan," *Boston Review*, January/February 2010.

Lawrence Rosen, *Bargaining for Reality: The Construction of Social Relations in a Muslim Community* (Chicago: University of Chicago Press, 1984).

Lawrence Rosen, *The Anthropology of Justice: Law as Culture in Islamic Society* (Cambridge: Cambridge University Press, 1989).

Lawrence Rosen, *The Justice of Islam: Comparative Perspectives on Islamic Law and Society* (Oxford: Oxford University Press, 2000).

Lawrence Rosen, *The Culture of Islam: Changing Aspects of Contemporary Muslim Life* (Chicago: University of Chicago Press, 2002).

Lawrence Rosen, "Passing Judgment: Interpretation, Morality, and Cultural Assessment in the Work of Clifford Geertz," in Richard A. Shweder and Byron Good, eds., *Clifford Geertz by His Colleagues* (Chicago: University of Chicago Press, 2005), 10–19.

Lawrence Rosen, *Varieties of Muslim Experience: Encounters with Arab Cultural and Political Life* (Chicago: University of Chicago Press, 2008).

Franz Rosenthal, *A History of Muslim Historiography* (Leiden: Brill, 1952).

Franz Rosenthal, "Gifts and Bribes," *Proceedings of the American Philosophical Society*, 108 (1964), 135–44.

Franz Rosenthal, "Hiba," in Bernard Lewis, et al., eds., *Encyclopedia of Islam*, 2d ed., Vol. 3 (Leiden, Netherlands: E. J. Brill, 1971), 342–50.

Olivier Roy, *Globalised Islam: The Search for a New Ummah* (London: Hurst, 2004).

J. Rutherfurd and Edward H. Glenny, *The Gospel in North Africa* (London: Percy Lund, Humphries & Co., 1900).

Malise Ruthven, *Islam in the World*, 2nd ed. (New York: Penguin, 1984).

Abdulaziz Sachedina, *Islamic Biomedical Ethics* (Oxford: Oxford University Press, 2009).

Marshall Sahlins, *Tribesmen* (Englewood Cliffs, NJ: Prentice-Hall, 1968).

Edward Said, *Orientalism* (New York: Pantheon Books, 1978).

Edward Said, *Covering Islam: How the Media and the Experts Determine How We See the World* (New York: Pantheon Books, 1981).

Edward Said, Oleg Grabar, and Bernard Lewis, "Orientalism: An Exchange," *The New York Review of Books*, August 12, 1982.

Edward W. Said, "Orientalism: An Exchange," *The New York Review of Books*, 29, 13 (1982), 44–46.

Edward W. Said, "Orientalism Reconsidered," *Race & Class*, 27, 2 (1985), 1–15.

Noor Liza Mohamed Said, et al., "Revocation of Gift (Hibah) According to Islamic Law and Its Practice under Syria Civil Law 1949," *International Business Management*, 7, 1 (2013), 1–7.

Marc Sageman, *Understanding Terror Networks* (Philadelphia: University of Pennsylvania Press, 2004).

Marc Sageman, "Testimony to Senate Intelligence Committee" 2009. www.fpri.org/transcripts/20091007.Sageman.ConfrontingalQaeda.pdf

David E. Sanger, "U.S. Pressure Helps Militants Overseas Focus Efforts," *New York Times*, May 7, 2010.

Charlie Savage, "Holder Backs a Miranda Limit for Terror Suspects," *New York Times*, May 9, 2010.

Mattathias Schwartz, "The 'Religious Freedom' Agenda," *The Atlantic*, July 16, 2019.

James C. Scott, *The Art of Not Being Governed: An Anarchist History of Upland South-East Asia* (New Haven: Yale University Press, 2010).

Robert A. Segal, "Weber and Geertz on the Meaning of Religion," *Religion*, 29 (1999), 61–71.

"Self-Immolation Attempts Shock Morocco," *The National*, January 21, 2012, www.thenational.ae/world/africa/self-immolation-attempts-shock-morocco-1.390292

Kalev Sepp, "Best Practices in Counterinsurgency," *Military Review*, May–June, 2005: 8–12.

William H. Sewell, Jr., "Geertz, Cultural Systems, and History: From Synchrony to Transformation," *Representations*, 59 (Summer 1997), 35–55.

Ido Shahar, "Legal Pluralism and the Study of Shari'a Courts," *Islamic Law and Society*, 15, 1 (2008): 112–41.

Scott Shane and Eric Schmidt, "Norway Announces Three Arrests in Terrorist Plot," *New York Times*, July 8, 2010.

Ian Shapiro, ed., *The Rule of Law: Nomos XXXVI* (New York: New York University Press, 1994).

Adam Shatz, "The Hypnotic Clamor of Morocco," *New York Review of Books*, March 30, 2016.

Richard A. Shweder, "Cliff Notes: The Pluralisms of Clifford Geertz," in Richard A. Shweder and Byron Good, eds., *Clifford Geertz by His Colleagues* (Chicago: University of Chicago Press, 2005), 1–9.

Ilana F. Silber, "Bourdieu's Gift to Gift Theory: An Unacknowledged Trajectory," *Sociological Theory*, 27, 2 (2009), 173–190.

Steven W. Silliman, "The 'Old West' in the Middle East: U.S. Military Metaphors in Real and Imagined Indian Country," *American Anthropologist*, 110, 2 (2008): 237–47.

Steven Simon, "The Price of the Surge: How US Strategy Is Hastening Iraq's Demise," *Foreign Affairs*, 87 (2008): 57–76.

Diane Singerman, "The Economic Imperatives of Marriage: Emerging Practices and Identities among Youth in the Middle East," *Middle East Youth Initiative Working Paper Number 6* (Washington, DC: Brookings Institution Wolfensohn Center for Development and Dubai School of Government, 2007).

Michael Slackman, "Stifled, Egypt's Young Turn to Islamic Fervor," *New York Times*, February 17, 2008.

Priscilla P. Soucek, "The Life of the Prophet: Illustrated Versions," in *Content and Context of Visual Arts in the Islamic World*, Priscilla P. Soucek, ed. (University Park, PA: Pennsylvania State University Press, 1988), 193–218.

Armando Spataro, "Why Do People Become Terrorists? A Prosecutor's Experiences," *Journal of International Criminal Justice*, 6, 3 (2008): 507–24.

Francis Rue Steele, *Not in Vain: The Story of the North Africa Mission* (Pasadena: William Carey Library Pub., 1981).

Paul J. Steinhardt, "Medieval Islamic Mosaics and Modern Maths," *Islamic Arts and Architecture*, March 25, 2011. http://islamic-arts.org/2011/medieval-islamic-mosaics-and-modern-maths/

Paul J. Steinhardt, "Quasicrystals: A Brief History of the Impossible," *Rendiconti Fisiche Accademia Lincei*, 2012. wwwphy.princeton.edu/~steinh/Steinhardt_Rendiconti%20Lincei%202012.pdf

Paul J. Steinhardt, *The Second Kind of Impossible: The Extraordinary Quest for a New Kind of Matter* (New York: Simon & Schuster, 2019).

Sebastian Smith, "US Accuses Top Al-Qaeda Leaders in NY Bomb Plot," *New York Times*, July 7, 2010.

C. J. Speel, II, "The Disappearance of Christianity from North Africa in the Wake of the Rise of Islam," *Church History*, 29, 4 (1960): 379–97.

Avi Max Spiegel, *Young Islam: The New Politics of Religion in Morocco and the Arab World* (Princeton: Princeton University Press, 2015).

Evelyn Stenbock, *"Miss Terri!"* (Lincoln, NE: The Good News Broadcasting Assn., 1970).

Jessica Stern, "5 Myths about Who Becomes a Terrorist," *The Washington Post*, January 10, 2010, B4.

Marilyn Strathern, *The Gender of the Gift: Problems with Women and Problems with Society in Melanesian Anthropology* (Berkeley: University of California Press, 1986).

Matthew Avery Sutton, *Double Crossed: The Missionaries Who Spied for the United States During the Second World War* (New York: Basic Books, 2019).

Soraya Syed, "Unity and Diversity: Lessons from Sacred Islamic Art," *Q-News: The Muslim Magazine*, 337 (2001): 37.

The Economist, "Iraq's Tribes May Hold the Balance of Power." *The Economist*, May 22, 2010.

The Economist, "Morocco's Evangelical Christians: Stop Preaching or Get Out," *The Economist*, July 29, 2010.

Lionel Tiger, "Fuzz, Fuzz ... It Was Covered in Fuzz," *Wall Street Journal*, November 7, 2006, A.12.

John Tolan, "'Saracen Philosophers Secretly Deride Islam'," *Medieval Encounters*, 8, 2–3 (2002): 184–208.

Trading Economics, "Morocco Unemployment Rate." https://tradingeconomics.com/morocco/unemployment-rate

University of Cambridge, "The Myth of the Arab Spring," October 18, 2011, www.cam.ac.uk/research/news/the-myth-of-the-arab-spring

U.S. Army, "My Cousin's Enemy Is My Friend: A Study of Pashtun Tribes in Afghanistan," Afghanistan Research Reachback Center White Paper, TRADOC G2 Human Terrain System (Fort Leavenworth, KS, September 2009) (unclassified).

Paul Valéry, *The Collected Works of Paul Valéry: The Art of Poetry* (New York: Vintage Books, 1961).

Daniel Martin Varisco, *Islam Obscured: The Rhetoric of Anthropological Representation* (New York: Palgrave Macmillan, 2005).

Stephen Vernoit, "Artistic Expressions of Muslim Societies," in *The Cambridge Illustrated History of the Islamic World*, ed. Francis Robinson (Cambridge: Cambridge University Press, 1996), 250–90.

Knut S. Vikør, *Between God and Sultan: A History of Islamic Law* (London: Hurst & Co., 2005).

Frédéric Volpi, "Pseudo-Democracy in the Muslim World," *Third World Quarterly*, 25 (2004): 1061–78.

John Waterbury, "Legitimacy without Coercion," *Government and Opposition* 5, 2 (1970): 253–60.

Max Weber, *From Max Weber*, Hans Gerth and C. Wright Mills, eds. (Oxford: Oxford University Press, 1946).

Steven Weinberg, "Symmetry: A 'Key to Nature's Secrets'," *The New York Review of Books*, October 27, 2011.

Edward Alexander Westermarck, *Ritual and Belief in Morocco, Vol. 1* (Hyde Park, NY: University Books, 1968 [1926].

Brannon Wheeler, "Gift of the Body in Islam: The Prophet Muhammad's Camel Sacrifice and Distribution of Hair and Nails at His Farewell Pilgrimage," *Numen*, 57 (2010), 341–88.

Heather Whipps, "Medieval Islamic Mosaics Used Modern Math," *Live Science*, February 22, 2007. www.livescience.com/4402-medieval-islamic-mosaics-modern-math.html

Brian Whitaker, *What Really Went Wrong* (London: Saqi Books, 2010).

Alfred North Whitehead, *Dialogues of Alfred North Whitehead* (New York: Mentor Books, 1956).

Craig Whitlock, "Facing Afghan Mistrust, al-Qaeda Fighters Take Limited Role in Insurgency," *Washington Post*, August 23, 2010, A01.

John Noble Wilford, "In Medieval Architecture, Signs of Advanced Math," *New York Times*, February 27, 2007.

Timothy Williams and Duraid Adnan, "Sunnis in Iraq Allied with U.S. Quitting to Rejoin Rebels," *New York Times*, October 16, 2010.

Bob Woodward, *Obama's War* (New York: Simon & Schuster, 2010).

Robert Worth, *A Rage for Order: The Middle East in Turmoil, from Tahrir Square to Isis* (New York: Farrar, Strauss and Giroux, 2016).

Worthy News Staff, "Morocco Expels Christian Missionaries," *Worthy News*, March 29, 2009.

Jonathan Wyrtzen, *Making Morocco: Colonial Intervention and the Politics of Identity* (Ithaca: Cornell University Press, 2015).

Farid Zakaria, "In Iraq, an Opening for Successful Diplomacy," *The Washington Post*, December 21, 2009, A19.

# Index